# Futureshock

From AI ethics and cybersecurity to augmented realities, virtual interfaces, and much more, *Futureshock* provides an accessible introduction to the leading-edge topics of today. This collection of writings by experts in their respective fields invites the reader to explore new worlds that race towards us. This book serves as a map that shows the reader vantage points of understanding from which the new digital ecosystem may be seen with clarity. It does not presume any in-depth knowledge on behalf of the reader. Topics are covered from a conceptual angle, with the relevant conceptual architecture introduced without any need for a strong background in abstract mathematics.

The common thread of the topics of this book is the new technologies, their environments and the user engagement and experience with them. There is broad coverage of topics pertaining to learning, design, education, metaverse, engineering, cybersecurity, and AI and ethics. It is organized independently and written purposively to enhance the reader's conceptual literacy so that they may engage with future events in the field critically. By providing a view on the now and next across a broad range of areas, *Futureshock* is positioned as a spring-board for discussion on these and related topics. An important topic on AI and ethics shares about developing and deploying AI systems for social good and considering the diverse and complex ethical challenges that arise.

This book serves the professionals working in their fields as they gain further insight into the new digital ecosystem. It would be of interest to a general audience that is keen to learn about the state of play in the technology space. It can also be used as a supplementary text for students in a course that looks at the current and future issues in computer science.

**Sebastian Sequoiah-Grayson** is a senior lecturer in epistemics at the School of Computer Science and Engineering at the University of New South Wales. His research spans across many areas of human information processing, including substructural epistemic logics, dynamic theories of negative information, data sonification, psychological theories of free will, ethics of computer science and information, and philosophy of mathematics.

# Futureshock
## Happenings in Computer Science

Edited by Sebastian Sequoiah-Grayson

CRC Press
Taylor & Francis Group
Boca Raton London New York

CRC Press is an imprint of the
Taylor & Francis Group, an **Informa** business

Front cover image:grandeduc/iStock

First edition published 2026
by CRC Press
2385 NW Executive Center Drive, Suite 320, Boca Raton FL 33431

and by CRC Press
4 Park Square, Milton Park, Abingdon, Oxon, OX14 4RN

*CRC Press is an imprint of Taylor & Francis Group, LLC*

© 2026 selection and editorial matter, Sebastian Sequoiah-Grayson; individual chapters, the contributors

ISBN: 978-1-032-70274-2 (hbk)
ISBN: 978-1-032-70273-5 (pbk)
ISBN: 978-1-032-70279-7 (ebk)

DOI: 10.1201/9781032702797

Typeset in CMR10 font
by KnowledgeWorks Global Ltd.

*For all members of*
*the School of Computer Science and Engineering,*
*past, present, and future,*
*at the University of New South Wales*

# Contents

**Chapter 3**    The Future of Education Technology ........................................... 36

*Jake Renzella*

**Chapter 4**    Exploring the Integration of Design Thinking into the
                 Engineering Discipline ................................................................. 59

*Alexandra Vassar*

**Chapter 5** How the Metaverse and Brain Computer Interfaces can
Revolutionise the Education Industry.........................................76

*Ali Darejeh and Sara Mashayekh*

**Chapter 6** UX Design Guided by Cognitive Load Theory .............................99

*Nadine Marcus and Alexandra Vassar*

**Chapter 7**    Ripple Down Rules and Classification ...................................... 118

*Eric Martin*

**Chapter 8**    Counterfeits and Kill Switches: How Hardware Security can
                 Impact You.................................................................. 154

*Hammond Pearce*

# Foreword

Merriam Webster dictionary defines future shock as the physical and psychological distress suffered by one who is unable to cope with the rapidity of social and technological changes [1]. The term was first used was in 1965, and subsequently achieved instant name recognition through the book written by Alvin Toffler, co-authored with Heidi Toffler (even though she was not so credited) in 1970 [2]. Of their many true and not-so-true predictions, that of the 'electronic frontier' inspired Steve Case, who went on to start what eventually became AOL [3].

Computing today is unrecognisable from the field that it was in 1970 even to its many protogonists. From its inception as a department within the School of Electrical Engineering in the 1970s, the School of Computer Science and Engineering at UNSW today grapples with many of the frontiers of computer science and their societal impact, some of which contribute to even more future shocks. This volume showcases the prowess of CSE's academic and research community and its efforts at tackling these frontiers and abating the future shocks. The topics are wide ranging, from AI and ethics, educational technology, design thinking and engineering education, the future of computer interface design and cognitive load management and logico-mathematical modelling to ensuring computer hardware security.

My congratulations to the editor Dr Sebastian Sequoiah-Grayson who has brought this volume together, and sincere thanks to all contributors for sharing their perspectives on significant happenings within the computing field at this point in time. I hope the reader finds this volume to be a useful guide in a fast changing landscape.

Prof Arcot Sowmya
*Head, School of Computer Science and Engineering*
*Sydney, 18 December, 2024*

1. https://www.merriam-webster.com/dictionary/future
2. Toffler, Alvin, Future Shock, Bantam Books, New York, 1970
3. https://www.fastcompany.com/1695307/future-shock-40-what-tofflers-got-right-and-wrong, Fast Company. 15 October 2010.

# Preface

When George Knott (then of CRC Press at Taylor and Francis) and I first met to discuss the idea that would turn, eventually, into the book that you are now reading, little did we realise the leap into popular consciousness that computer science was about to make.

It was the tail end of the Covid 19 outbreak, university campuses were still largely deserted, and ChatGPT4 was yet to unleash Turing-test level generative artificial intelligence upon the world.

As George and I sat over tea and coffee at The Lounge, the University of New South Wales' cafe and restaurant perched atop UNSW's Library Tower, we knew that we did not want a book on coding or programming *per se*. There are plenty of books on such things already, and most of this sort of content is disseminated over video these days anyhow.

What we *did want* on the other hand, was something that shared the inside story of computer science as a practised academic discipline today – or share at least those parts of it that are most often hidden from view. We also wanted to share some of the magic that is the School of Computer Science and Engineering at UNSW.

The School of Computer Science and Engineering - abbreviated in the familiar fashion to 'CSE', but referred to by its members as simply "The School" – has been my academic home for the last three years. I have never been happier. The School is vast. There are close to 100 full time academic staff, 7000 undergraduates (this is not a typo), thousands of masters students, and goodness knows how many PhD students and postdocs. The latter are difficult to count, and I am writing this preface only a day or so before the manuscript deadline.

Given the sheer scale of things, the School burns more brightly than the sun. No less importantly however, it is by far and away the best school of computer science in Australia, and one of the best in the world. The rate of growth is incredible to behold. The dedication and goodwill of the academic and professional staff, along with that of those who comprise the student body, make it what it is. As always, it is the people who make the thing the thing that it is. This is unlikely to stop being true any time soon.

I owe many a thank you. Thank you to George Knott himself, for reaching out and for inviting me to publish with CRC in the first place.

Thank you to Aaron Quigley, the Head of School at the time and now Science Director and Deputy Director of CSIRO's Data61. I was new to the School at the time, and due to COVID 19 restrictions was yet to meet many of the School's members in person. Aaron was a sage guide in the early days, and the debt that I owe him is not insubstantial.

This thank you is perhaps the most important of all. It was not long before George Knott departed Taylor and Francis for new adventures, and was replaced by the intrepid Gerald Bok as Commissioning Editor for Computer Science and Statistics at

Chapman and Hall for CRC Press at Taylor and Francis. I have neither the words, the time, nor the space available to convey adequately the extent to which Gerald has demonstrated the very best of human virtues throughout this project, with patience foremost amongst these. Gerald, if you are reading this, I shall never be able to thank you enough.

A very important thank you is to my friend and colleague at CSE, Paul Hunter. Paul's selfless goodwill whilst untangling the more entangled parts of a large LATEX project was singular in getting things over the line. Paul – without whom not. Gerald again, if you are reading this, know that Paul is one of the real reasons for why it is that you were not waiting longer.

To everyone at Taylor and Francis - Gerald Bok, Kasturi Ghosh, George Knott, Chelsea Low, and Katie Peace - thank you for everything.

To all of the contributors to this book – Ali Darejeh, Nadine Marcus, Eric Martin, Sara Mashayekh, Hammond Pearce, Jake Renzella, Alexandra Vassar, and Toby Walsh, I extend to all of you my most sincere thanks for your generosity across time and thought for your contributions.

Very sincerely, I would like to thank our Head of School, Arcot Sowmya. Sowmya's wise counsel and unwavering fairness is the stuff of legend, and rightly so at that. Head of School is a hard job when the School is small. When it is larger than are many universities – as is the case here at CSE – the job is next to unfathomable. Neither this book nor much else would have been possible were it not for Sowmya's leadership over the last several years.

Lastly, but by no means least, I owe my partner Lex absolutely everything. As those of us who have written or edited books know only too well, it is very often a second job on top of the first one. Lex has been by my side every step of the way, navigating somehow an important career and equally important studies of her own. Thank you Lex!

Sebastian Sequoiah-Grayson
*School of Computer Science and Engineering*
*University of New South Wales*
*December 2024*

# List of Contributors

**Ali Darejeh**
School of Computer Science and
    Engineering
University of New South Wales

**Nadine Marcus**
School of Computer Science and
    Engineering
University of New South Wales

**Eric Martin**
School of Computer Science and
    Engineering
University of New South Wales

**Sara Mashayekh**
School of Education
University of New South Wales

**Hammond Pearce**
School of Computer Science and
    Engineering
University of New South Wales

**Jake Renzella**
School of Computer Science and
    Engineering
University of New South Wales

**Sebastian Sequoiah-Grayson**
School of Computer Science and
    Engineering
University of New South Wales

**Alexandra Vassar**
School of Computer Science and
    Engineering
University of New South Wales

**Toby Walsh**
School of Computer Science and
    Engineering
University of New South Wales

# 1 Introduction

*Sebastian Sequoiah-Grayson*
School of Computer Science and Engineering, UNSW Sydney
Kensington, Australia

## 1.1 INTRODUCTION TO VOLUME

"Well that escalated quickly" is the well-known phrase lurking amongst the meme-scapes of the online world. As far as phrases go, it is a useful one for the most part. Things do, perhaps now more than ever before, escalate quickly. In few places has this been more true than in computer science itself.

In the very living memory of even young members of the discipline, computer science was the academic intrigue of the fascinated few. Things have changed. Digital technologies now affect nearly every aspect of our lives – both personally and professionally. Computer science, the discipline of the digital *par excellence*, finds itself now in the center of the academic, political, geopolitical, and popular worlds. From finance to space travel, from medicine to the military, from farming to education, computer science is there in the middle of all of it.

Data is the new gold, and digital information processing is the method of its extraction and refinement. The age of artificial intelligence is upon us, and we are face-to-face with the dawn of quantum computing. Here, amongst cryptocurrencies, cyber warfare, deepfakes, generative artificial intelligence, and more, a genuine conceptual literacy of digital ecosystems is the mark of the modern person.

The purpose of this book is to afford the reader with an opportunity – more than one, it is hoped – to pursue such a literacy directly. The topics have been chosen because they are both important and, by and large, off the radar of much of the general public (if not off the radar of some of the more distant locales of academia).

The one exception to this is the chapter with which the book begins. In *AI and Ethics*, Sebastian Sequoiah-Grayson and Toby Walsh introduce the reader to a topic that is now front and center in many debates on artificial intelligence. Artificial intelligence is an area where the technological capabilities are evolving at warp speed. As such, the authors have worked hard to provide the reader with a grounding in the issues that will withstand such accelerations. To this end, the chapter is organized around a series of exercises of thought and invitations to careful, purposive explorations of foundational issues in ethics and artificial intelligence.

In *The Future of Education Technology*, Jake Renzella explores the potential – both existent and speculative – of computer science technology to affect positive outcomes in higher eduction. Enticingly, there is more afoot here than transactional,

DOI: 10.1201/9781032702797-1

quantitative measures. A passionate pedagogical pioneer, Renzella lays out how it is exactly that computer science technology can bring out the best in both students and teachers alike – in both computer science itself and beyond.

In *Exploring the Integration of Design Thinking into the Engineering Discipline*, Alexandra Vassar has written a powerful anecdotal history of her own exposure to design thinking in the early day of her computer science engineering education, how this affected her intellectual and academic growth, and how it is that she has integrated this into her training the next generations of computer scientists and engineers. With considerable attention paid to the potential of campus-based makerspaces, Vassar reveals the role of creativity in digital technologies, and the potential for its refinement.

In *How the Metaverse and Brain Computer Interfaces can Revolutionise the Education Industry*, Ali Darejeh and Sara Mashayekh explore how virtual and augmented reality technologies – known collectively as *immersive technologies* – affect knowledge acquisition. With the recent advent of affordable brain-computer interfaces, Darejeh and Mashayekh explore the future of interface design and the possibilities that such design affords.

In *UX Design Guided by Cognitive Load Theory*, Nadine Marcus and Alexandra Vassar explore the relationships between user experience and cognitive psychology. From the iPhone to ChatGPT, the psychosocial purchase of digital technologies depend upon an ongoing symbiosis with the ways in which humans navigate their world. Marcus and Vassar take the reader through a careful exploration of the topography of mental structures upon which the success of digital technologies depend.

In *Ripple Down Rules and Classification*, Eric Martin takes theories of knowledge acquisition and learning into the realm of logico-mathematical modelling. Martin explores three subfields of artificial intelligence – *knowledge acquisition, knowledge representation*, and *formal learning theory*, and subsumes them within a single framework of *ripple down rules*. Some mathematical sophistication is required for Martin's chapter, but nothing beyond that which is available in any good introductory book on logic and mathematical reasoning. It is well worth the time taken by the reader to do this, as such a mathematical literacy is the key to unlocking many of the abstract wonders that populate the rich world of theoretical computer science.

In *Counterfeits and Kill Switches: How Hardware Security can Impact You*, Hammond Pearce takes us back to the physical world of *hardware security*. An increasingly vital part of cyber security, *hardware attacks* involve the fatal compromise of "upstream" manufacturing and supply lines. Such compromise can occur via brute physical intercept, or via remote sabotage. Devilishly hard to detect, and easy to scale, hardware attacks present cyber security in particular and computer science and society in general with one of the most exciting, and frightening, challenges today. Pierce presents several promising lines of defence for the ecosystems that will only continue to populate the digital futures that we share.

# 2 AI and Ethics

*Sebastian Sequoiah-Grayson*
School of Computer Science and Engineering, UNSW Sydney
Kensington, Australia

*Toby Walsh*
School of Computer Science and Engineering, UNSW Sydney
Kensington, Australia

## 2.1 AI AND ETHICS

As artificial intelligence (AI) starts to leave the laboratory and enter many aspects of our lives, we need to start worrying about the impact it has. This is especially important when AI is being applied to issues of social good. The target groups we might be trying to help can often be some of the poorest and most disadvantaged in our communities. We might be trying to help homeless people, people with disabilities, racial or other minorities. We might be concerned with the impact of climate change, protecting ecosystems under threat from human actions, or groups in the developing world that are particularly vulnerable. It is therefore essential to consider whether we are doing the right thing. This then requires us to consider a range of ethical questions around the best course of action and around the systems we are building.

## 2.2 ETHICS

Ethics is a branch of philosophy that considers which behaviours are right and wrong. Philosophers have considered these questions for thousands of years and have proposed many different answers. Normative ethics, for example, asks how we might best make *moral judgements*. Moral judgements are claims about the moral or ethical status of some act or other. (In what follows, we will understand 'moral' and 'ethical' to be synonymous.) Examples of moral judgements are statements such as *Lying is wrong, Giving to charity is good, The Beatles' music is depraved, The Manson Family were a bit dodgy*, and so on.

Moral judgements often appear in transparently *prescriptive* form. Indeed, normative ethics is often referred to as 'prescriptive ethics' for just this reason. For example, we might reformulate the four moral judgements above as *One should not lie, One must not listen to The Beatles, One should not mix with members of the Manson Family*, and so on. The Ten Commandments are one of the most well-known bodies of moral judgements in prescriptive form. There are others.

The common-sense, canonical view is that moral judgements can be either true or false, just as with judgements about other matters. The problem waiting for us at this

DOI: 10.1201/9781032702797-2

juncture is largely *epistemic* in nature. Granting the position that moral judgements may be either true or false, how can we *know*, for some moral judgement in particular, that it is in fact a true and correct judgement?

A well-worn and traditional way of responding to such epistemic concerns is through *argument*. An argument consists of one judgement, called the *conclusion*, and some other judgements, called the *premises*. The idea is that a good argument is one by which the premises give us good *reasons* or *justifications* for asserting or believing the conclusion. We often separate the premises from the conclusion with the word 'therefore'. For example – *All humans are mortal*, and *Socrates is human*; therefore, *Socrates is mortal*.

This looks like a good argument. If the premises are true, then they give us good reason to believe the conclusion. The wonderful thing here with this argument is that firstly the premises *are* true, and that secondly their truth is relatively uncontroversial. Other arguments are not so straightforward.

A *moral argument* is one whose conclusion is a moral judgement. But what of its premises? What sort of judgements might give us good reasons to believe a moral judgement? As you will have noticed, moral judgements are very often a point of contention. Consider discussions concerning capital punishment, animal experimentation, sexuality, criminal justice, artificial intelligence, and so on.

A *good* moral argument should make moral judgements *less* contentious by giving us good reasons to accept or reject the moral judgement that is the moral argument's conclusion. How might we go about making such arguments? There are three main answers – *utilitarianism*, *Kantian ethics*, and *virtue ethics*. We will look at all three, starting with *utilitarianism*.

### 2.2.1  UTILITARIANISM

Utilitarianism [22] is a form of *consequentialism*. For consequentialists, *actions* do not have any *intrinsic* moral value. Instead, the only things that *do* have intrinsic moral value are *consequences* or *states of affairs*. Put simply, an act that brings about consequences that are, *overall*, morally good consequences is a morally good act. Similarly, an act that brings about consequences that are, again *overall*, morally bad consequences, is a morally bad act.

Which consequences count as good and bad will depend on the type of consequentialism under consideration. For utilitarians, the only metric that matters is happiness. Specifically, the morally right action will be the one that results in a *maximisation* of happiness over unhappiness (hence 'overall' being emphasised in the paragraph above). As a toy example, suppose that we are considering which of two actions, $A1$ and $A2$ we should perform. Suppose that $A1$ will bring about 10 units of happiness and 5 units of unhappiness or suffering. Suppose also that $A2$ will bring about 10 units of happiness and 11 units of suffering. A *utility measurement U* is the net balance of happiness $H$ over suffering $S$: $H - S = U$. Given this, $A1$ is $10 - 5 = 5$ units of utility, and $A2$ is $10 - 11 = -1$ units of utility. From a utilitarian perspective, $A1$ is the right thing to do.

This is simplified, and contemporary utilitarians will calculate *expected utility* – which is the measure of happiness that *could* be brought about multiplied by the likelihood that it *will* come about – but the motivating idea remains the same. This idea, again, is that it is net amounts of happiness that matter, and only these, when it comes to deciding which of several actions is the right one to do with regard to some given situation. Utilitarianism gives us a clear methodology by which we might arbitrate between competing moral judgements. Its response to the epistemic problem outlined above is clear.

A major attraction of utilitarianism is its epistemic stance towards moral judgements allows for easy compatibility with naturalistic scruples. *Naturalism* deserves a chapter all of its own, but put simply it can be thought of as the rejection of *supernaturalism*. All that exists, according to the naturalist, is the natural world. There is nothing outside of the natural order, so all things must be explained in terms of things within it if they are to be explained properly at all. Since happiness is a state of humans being in the world, measures of utility lend themselves to moral judgements being subsumable by empirical, scientific methodology. Utilitarians reject any claims about immutable, transcendent moral truths.

### 2.2.1.1 Problems and responses

Utilitarianism motivates many modern moral concerns, not least those close to discussions concerning AI. The by now infamous *trolly problem* concerns what it is that we should do in the following scenario. A runaway train car is heading towards a group of people along Track 1, and you are able to switch the track so that the train car is moved onto Track 2, thereby saving the people on Track 1. Is switching the train car to Track 2 the right thing to do? Well, that depends on the situation on Track 2. Is it free of people, unlike Track 1, or does it have people on it too? A crude utilitarianism will say that the right thing to do is to ensure that the train car continues along the track with the fewer number of people. But is this right? What if one track has fewer people, but they are those who are close and dear to us? Utilitarianism appears blind to such considerations. Some utilitarians might insist that we are right to be.

### 2.2.2 KANTIAN ETHICS

Utilitarianism does not locate any intrinsic moral value in actions. All and any moral value to be found in an action are a function of the *consequences* of that action. Deontological or Kantian ethics [17] rejects this view. For Kant, actions *themselves* are the things with primary moral value. Consequences are not a consideration. A misgiving that many have felt with regard to utilitarianism is that it might count any action at all as being morally good if it resulted in a sufficient amount of net happiness. It can justify lying, torture, or slavery, supposing that only a small group of people were treated appallingly, and this resulted in overall net happiness.

Kant, however, thinks that some things are absolutely right and wrong, come what may. Very importantly, according to Kant, we can work out what the correct moral judgements are *simply by thinking about things carefully*. This too is in contrast to utilitarianism, for which empirical evidence plays a central role. For Kant it plays none. Instead, Kantians affirm that moral principles can be discerned through acts of pure reasoning. This is achieved via the *categorical imperative*:

> Act only according to that maxim whereby you can, at the same time, will that it should become a universal law

This is wordy, but what it means is the following. One should only act according to a moral rule if one could want that same rule to be a universal law. The 'could' here is important. It is meant to tie directly to rational conceivability – willing for an inappropriate moral 'law' to be universal is supposed to lead to a position that is inconceivable. It is this inconceivability that functions as a litmus test for moral judgements.

An example helps to understand Kant's categorical imperative. Consider lying and the moral judgement that *one should never lie*. Now suppose that you think it permissible to lie. Via the categorical imperative, consider that the permission to lie was universal. This means that everyone is permitted to lie. If everyone is permitted to lie, then there will be a lot of permissible lying going on. And if there is a lot of permissible lying going on, then there would not be much trust. In fact, there would be so little trust that basic social contracts would be unable to form. If basic social contracts had not formed, then we would not have advanced societies with intellectual institutions. Indeed, we might not have societies at all. But then we would not be here, contemplating the categorical imperative. But this is inconsistent with where we find ourselves and is hence 'inconceivable'. Therefore, it cannot be the case that one is permitted to lie, and hence *do not lie* is a moral law revealed to us via our faculties of pure reason.

Pure reason, or more specifically our ability to think rationally and to act on the basis of our rational deliberations, is for Kant, the mark of a person as opposed to a mere animal. It is also the centre of gravity for Kant's larger ethical enterprise. Unlike animals, we have the capacity to act freely. We are acting freely when we are acting in accordance with our rational will. Although we are not always doing so – sometimes we are acting from instinct or impulse or our emotions – acting on the basis of our rational will means that we are, when doing so, acting freely, or *autonomously*, according to Kant.

We have a duty to not violate or undermine this potential freedom of ourselves and others. This is because to do so would be to undermine one's or another's very personhood. It is this concern that motivates Kant to issue his dictum that we should always treat another person as an end in themselves only and never as a means to an end. If we were treating someone as a means to an end, then we would be treating them as a mere *resource* and not as a *person*. Understandably, Kantian ethicists take a dim view of advertising and marketing, as they depend essentially on manipulation and deceit.

### 2.2.2.1 Problems and responses

A Kantian ethics avoids some of the pitfalls presented by utilitarianism – namely, that otherwise horrific acts such as slavery and torture would count as morally good if they resulted in a sufficient degree of net happiness. However, whereas utilitarianism encounters criticism for deferring too far in the direction of contextual sensitivity, Kantian ethics encounters criticism for refusing any deference to context whatsoever. Infamously, the *come-what-may* condition on Kantian ethics is extreme and allows for no flexibility at all. If a gang of psychopathic murderers turns up at your door looking for their victim – an innocent child who is hiding under your bed, say – then deceiving the murderers by lying to them in order to save the child's life remains the wrong thing to do. An unblinking Kantian response is that the murderers' actions are on them, and them alone. You have an obligation to tell them the truth.

## 2.2.3 VIRTUE ETHICS

We have seen some reasons to be dissatisfied with both utilitarianism and Kantian ethics. What might said of both theories, is that they are *myopic*. The former attempts to reduce morality to the pursuit of utility maximisation, and the latter attempts to reduce morality to the pursuit of maximised rationality. To be sure, pursuing happiness over suffering, and pursuing rationally persuasive justifications of our actions should play a *role* in our moral judgements, but should either be *exhaustive*?

Virtue ethicists [9] do not think so. Uniquely, they locate a distinctive role for *emotions* in moral judgement. Although alien to moral judgements from the perspective of utilitarian and Kantian ethics, a role for the emotions in moral judgements is not without some motivation. By way of example, consider a child gleefully burning ants with a magnifying glass. From a utilitarian point of view, there is no suffering at hand. Indeed, there is quite the opposite, given the resulting happiness of our sunbeam wielding child. Similarly, from a Kantian perspective, it is not obvious that any categorical imperative is being violated. If children were to burn ants one by one at will, then what of it?

According to the virtue ethicist, however, surely we must think that the child is doing *something wrong*, and morally wrong at that. There is something disturbing about the child's emotional reaction, something that betrays a deeper potential problem with their moral *character*. One's character is composed of one's dispositions to act in certain ways in certain circumstances reliably. A *virtue* is a morally *good* disposition, whilst a *vice* is a morally *bad* disposition. But where are the virtues *situated* in relation to the vices, and how might we *know* that a disposition is a virtue rather than a vice? Aristotle's *doctrine of the mean* and *rationality of the passions* are answers to both of these questions, respectively.

The doctrine of the mean is the idea that a virtue is always the average of a pair of vices. As an example, take the virtue of *courage*. Courage, according to Aristotle, lies in between the vices of *cowardice* and *recklessness*. The answer to the epistemic question – to how it is that we might know that a disposition such as courage is in fact a virtue and not a vice – reveals the unique role played by the emotions for virtue ethicists. The emotions, or *passions*, have a central role to play in our rationally discerning the virtues from the vices. How so? Well, just as we use our faculties of visual perception in order to perceive colours, and our faculties of auditory perception in order to perceive sounds, so we use our faculties of *emotional perception* in order to perceive the virtues. Using the example of courage again, it is the emotion of *fear* by which we can perceive courage. But to do this, we must have the emotion in the right amount, or to the right degree. Too much fear will make me a coward, and too little will make me reckless.

Having the right emotion to the right degree in the right situation is not something that we can learn overnight. Instead, it is a skill that we continue to refine throughout our lives. Having other virtues, such as honesty, modesty, benevolence, and so on, is a requirement for having any of them, since they cannot be had in *isolation*. One virtue cannot be had at the expense of another, as a *balance* between the virtues is a virtue in and of itself. Hence the guiding, or *meta-virtue* of *phronesis*, is the most important virtue of them all. Translated often as *practical wisdom*, *phronesis* is the virtue that a truly virtuous person has to have in order to adjudicate between the various virtues for a given situation in the right way.

As distinct from both utilitarianism and Kantian ethics, in virtue ethics one's motive matters greatly to the moral status of one's action. A moral judgement is the right one for utilitarians if action upon it would result in the right consequences. A moral judgement is the right one for Kantians if it is arrived at via the right principles of pure reason. For the virtue ethicist, a moral judgement is the right one if acting upon it exemplifies a *virtuous character*. Merely imitating a virtuous person will not do. One must be moved by the same concerns and emotions, and in the same way, as would be the virtuous person, in order for one to be truly virtuous, and hence truly good.

### 2.2.3.1   Problems and responses

Aristotle, along with many virtue ethicists, holds the view that there is a right function for persons in general, just like there is for axes in general. The unique function of a person (in contrast to other objects and entities) is that they are *rational*. Recalling Aristotle's views on the rationality of the emotions, we are good persons when we are living a good life, and a good life is one led by the pursuit of refined rationality. This position has, unsurprisingly, encouraged accusations that virtue ethics is *elitist*. On this point the virtue ethicist might plead guilty as charged.

A more pointed criticism is that virtue ethics is a *messy* moral theory. One that does not give neat answers to moral questions in anything like the way accomplished by utilitarianism and Kantian ethics. Virtue ethics does not respond neatly to the epistemic question with which we started this discussion – namely how can we *know*, for some moral judgement in particular, that it is in fact a true and correct judgement? Here too the virtue ethicist might plead guilty as charged, and respond that utilitarianism and Kantian ethics are, although impressive intellectually, dangerously simplistic. Morality is many things, the virtue ethicist may say, but neat it is not.

With frameworks of normative ethics now familiar to us, we may turn our attention to applications in artificial intelligence.

## 2.2.4 ETHICAL FRAMEWORKS: FURTHER READING AND AN EXERCISE

For a detailed exploration of the ethical requirements imposed by AI via autonomous vehicles – one that is especially relevant to the exercise below, see [3].

Hooker and Kim [15] develop a systematic deontological approach to the ethics of AI. They take the rule-based nature of deontological ethics to be uniquely suited to machine applications, and they present their theory formally via quantified modal logic.

Shannon Vallor [24] articulates and defends a carefully argued position for virtue ethics within the philosophy of technology and the ethics of AI. Vallor's analysis includes a nuanced exposition of virtue ethics itself and covers social media, privacy concerns, armed military robots, *transhumanism* (the augmentation of human minds and bodies by technology into the 'posthuman' realm), and more.

---

**Exercise 1:**

Recall the 'trolley problem' from the problems and responses section for utilitarianism above. The trolley problem soon becomes elaborate. For example, what if there are two people on the first track and one person on the second? Should you intervene in this case? Again, a crude utilitarianism would say that you should, as all things being equal, it is better to act in order to ensure that only one person is killed rather than two. More elaborately, what if there is one young person on the first track, with their entire life ahead of them, and on the second track there are five people, all of whom are old and very near the end of their lives? More elaborately still, what if the choice is between ten people on one track who are cruel and sadistic and one person on the other who has dedicated their life to benevolent medical research? Does the track on which either person or persons are on make a difference, morally speaking, to our actions?

Here is your exercise. Imagine that you are responsible for designing the collision-avoidance protocols for driverless cars/autonomous vehicles. Given that the avoidance measures taken by such vehicles will be programmed in from the outset, the decisions that one thinks should be made with regard to the nature of such protocols map very closely to the decisions that one thinks should be made with regard to various elaborations of the trolley problem.

Consider and reflect upon the following. What do you think that the avoidance-protocols should be from utilitarian, Kantian, and virtue ethics perspectives? Which of these, if any, do you think would guide you best when it comes to deciding on such protocols? If people's identities and 'social standing' could be detected by the vehicles (by mobile devices or facial recognition say), then should this be a relevant factor? Should all vehicles be programmed with the

---

same protocols, or should they be permitted to vary – from private vehicles to those of the emergency services, perhaps? Should drivers be able to choose from different 'protocol packages' when purchasing or upgrading a vehicle? Should such protocols be adjustable from within a vehicle, much like cruise control? Are the vehicles aware of the protocols under which other vehicles in their environment are operating? All answers here will be important; none of them will be easy.

## 2.3   ETHICAL PRINCIPLES FOR AI

Ethical frameworks like utilitarianism provide a mechanism to argue for the right course of action. They can be applied to human decision-making just as well as machine decision-making. Indeed, they were all initially devised to understand human and not machine decision-making. We next consider how we might specialise such arguments to AI. In particular, we ask how we might instantiate such moral judgements to deal with the particular challenges thrown up by artificial intelligence?

It turns out that there are many different answers to this question. Many governments, corporations, and NGOs have proposed somewhat different sets of ethical principles to govern the responsible deployment of AI. For example, in June 2018, Google announced a set of principles to guide its use of AI.

**Google's AI principles:**
We believe that AI should

1. Be socially beneficial.
2. Avoid creating or reinforcing unfair bias.
3. Be built and tested for safety.
4. Be accountable to people.
5. Incorporate privacy design principles.
6. Uphold high standards of scientific excellence.
7. Be made available for uses that accord with these principles.

In addition to the above principles, Google also promised not to 'design or deploy AI in the following application areas':

1. Technologies that cause or are likely to cause overall harm.
2. Weapons or other technologies whose principal purpose or implementation is to cause or directly facilitate injury to people.
3. Technologies that gather or use information for surveillance violating internationally accepted norms.
4. Technologies whose purpose contravenes widely accepted principles of international law and human rights.

One of these principles seems unnecessary. Contravening international law is already prohibited, by law. Others are not really concerned with ethics. For example, upholding standards of scientific excellence is good to ensure scientific progress, replicability, etc. It is not particularly concerned with any moral judgements. You might compare Google's principles with the ethical principles for the use of AI put forward by the US Department of Defence in February 2020.

---

**The US Department of Defence's ethical principles for the use of AI:**

1. Responsible. Department of Defence personnel will exercise appropriate levels of judgement and care, while remaining responsible for the development, deployment, and use of AI capabilities.
2. Equitable. The Department will take deliberate steps to minimise unintended bias in AI capabilities.
3. Traceable. The Department's AI capabilities will be developed and deployed such that relevant personnel possess an appropriate understanding of the technology, development processes, and operational methods applicable to AI capabilities, including with transparent and auditable methodologies, data sources, and design procedure and documentation.
4. Reliable. The Department's AI capabilities will have explicit, well-defined uses, and the safety, security, and effectiveness of such capabilities will be subject to testing and assurance within those defined uses across their entire life-cycles.
5. Governable. The Department will design and engineer AI capabilities to fulfil their intended functions while possessing the ability to detect and avoid unintended consequences, and the ability to disengage or deactivate deployed systems that demonstrate unintended behaviour.

---

You can find many similar principles in the dozens of ethical frameworks proposed to govern AI in the last half a dozen years. How do you make sense of this diversity of views? One reason for such diversity is that some of these principles are in conflict. For instance, transparency can make a system less robust, as bad actors can now manipulate its behaviours. As a second example, we might place different emphasis on collective good versus individual harms. Different frameworks may make different decisions about such trade-offs.

We can also learn from other (older) technologies. After all, artificial intelligence isn't the first technology to touch our lives, and every other technology we have invented has introduced ethical challenges.

One field where we have worried greatly about the impact of new technologies on people's lives is medicine. It's not surprising that ethics has been a major concern in medicine, as doctors are often dealing with life-or-death situations. As a result, medicine has some very well-developed ethical principles to guide how technology touches our lives. Indeed, if we put to one side the thorny issue of machine autonomy, medicine appears to provide an adequate set of ethical principles to guide the development of artificial intelligence. There are four core ethical principles that have been developed over the last two millennia and that are used to steer medical practice.

The first two principles commonly considered in medical ethics are *beneficence* and *non-maleficence*. These are closely related. Beneficence means 'do good', while non-maleficence means 'do no harm'. Beneficence involves balancing the benefits of a treatment against the risks and costs it will bring. A medical intervention that has a net benefit is considered ethical. Non-maleficence, on the other hand, means avoiding harm. Of course, harm may not be totally avoidable, but any potential harms should be proportionate to the potential benefits.

Many of the AI principles put forward in Google's or the US DoD principles follow, in fact, from ensuring beneficence and non-maleficence. For instance, being built and tested for safety is needed to ensure AI doesn't do unnecessary harms. Invasion of privacy is a common harm that AI may enable. And insisting that AI systems should be socially beneficial follows from beneficence.

The third principle commonly considered in medical ethics is *autonomy*. It requires medical practitioners to respect the right of people to make informed decisions about their own medical care. Consent from a patient is essential before any medical treatment. And patients need to understand all the risks and benefits and to be free from coercion as they make decisions. Again, some of the AI principles put forward by Google follow from valuing the autonomy of humans as they interact with an AI system. Human accountability, for example, follows from a respect for human autonomy. Other ethical principles like transparency enable autonomy to be achieved. And respect for human autonomy explains why deceptive AI is to be avoided.

The fourth and final principle commonly considered in medical ethics is the somewhat fuzzy principle of *justice*. This obliges us to distribute fairly benefits, risks, costs and resources. In particular, the principle of justice requires both the burdens and the benefits of new medical treatments to be distributed equally across all groups in society. As before, many proposed AI principles follow from seeking justice. Justice requires that AI systems should avoid creating or reinforcing unfair bias. AI systems should also be transparent and provide explanations so that justice can be seen to have been achieved.

Of course, AI is not medicine. The four ethical principles commonly used in medicine are a very good start, but by far not the end of what we need for AI. Unlike medicine, artificial intelligence does not have the common aims and fiduciary duties found in medicine. AI also lacks the long and rich professional history and norms found in medicine, which ensure that these ethical standards are upheld. In addition, AI lacks the robust legal and professional structures found in medicine to ensure accountability.

---

**Four central principles of medical ethics.**

**Beneficence:** do net good.
**Non-maleficence:** do no harm.
**Autonomy:** respect human autonomy.
**Justice:** distribute fairly benefits, risks, costs and resources.

---

### 2.3.1 ETHICAL PRINCIPLES FOR AI: FURTHER READING AND AN EXERCISE

For a detailed survey and attempt to unify the many different ethical principles proposed for AI see [11]. For a discussion of ethical factors essential for projects focused on AI for social good see [12].

---

**Exercise 2:**

Recall again the trolley problem (exercise 1).

Consider and reflect upon the following. What do you think that the avoidance-protocols for a driverless car/autonomous vehicle should be, based on Google's AI principles? Would the US DoD's ethical principles suggest any different protocols or implementation decisions? If people's identities and 'social standing' could be detected by the vehicles (by mobile devices of facial recognition say), then based on Google's AI principles, should this be a relevant factor? According to Google's AI principles, should all vehicles be programmed with the same protocols, or should they be permitted to vary – from private vehicles to those of the emergency services say? Should drivers be able to choose from different 'protocol packages' when purchasing or upgrading a vehicle from Google? Should such protocols be adjustable from within a vehicle, much like cruise control? Are the vehicles aware of the protocols under which other vehicles in their environment are operating?

---

## 2.4 DECIDING TO USE AI

Perhaps the most important ethical question that is often not asked is whether we should actually use AI. Once we have made the decision to use AI, we can use principles like beneficence, non-maleficence, autonomy and justice to guide its responsible deployment. But there remains the fundamental questions of whether we should have used AI in the first place. Consider the following.

**Case study (Physiognomy).**
In 2018, Michal Kosinski and Yilun Wang made headlines by publishing controversial research claiming that computer vision algorithms could predict a person's sexuality from a single image of their face. In 2021, Kosinski doubled down by publishing follow-up work claiming that computer vision algorithms could also predict a person's political orientation, again from just a single image of their face. These are both examples of technologies that are chilling if they work and chilling if they don't.

Suppose, for a moment, you could predict someone's sexuality from a single image. There are a number of countries where homosexuality remains illegal. In Afghanistan, Brunei, Iran, Mauritania, Nigeria, Saudi Arabia, Somalia and the UAE, homosexuals can even be sentenced to death. There are several other countries where homosexuals face persecution and violence. You have to ask, then, why Wang and Kosinski did their work in the first place. What possible good can come from software that can detect a person's sexuality from an image of their face? It's not hard to imagine such software being put to some awful uses.
Wang and Kosinski argued in response:

*"You might wonder if such findings should be made public lest they inspire the very application that we are warning against. We share this concern. However, as governments and companies seem to be already deploying face-based classifiers aimed at detecting intimate traits, there is an urgent need for making policymakers, the general public, and gay communities aware of the risks that they might be facing already. Delaying or abandoning the publication of these findings could deprive individuals of the chance to take preventive measures and policymakers the ability to introduce legislation to protect people."*

But what preventative measures could individuals possibly take in one of those countries where homosexuality is illegal? Facial surgery or fleeing the country would seem to be the only possible actions an individual has to avoid harm. And what prevents policymakers in places like Saudi Arabia and UAE from useing these technologies not to protect but to prosecute homosexual people?

It is becoming common to see 'redlines' being identified where AI should not be used, or used with strong oversight. For instance, the proposed EU AI act identifies a number of high risk applications of AI that will be subject to stringent regulation. These include predictive policing and sentencing tools in law enforcement, welfare payment systems and student assessment tools. In addition, the act also identifies a number of prohibited applications of AI, including subliminal marketing tools, 'real-time' remote biometric identification systems except in very specific situations like an imminent terrorist attack, and 'social scoring' tools that we see being used in China.

There are other applications of AI where the risks and benefits are less clear-cut. One challenge is to have a good understanding of the societies on which one is trying to have social impact. What are the existing injustices that might be amplified by these systems? Do the benefits justify any harms? Are the harms concentrated on a particular minority? These are often difficult questions to answer, as they concern the sort of society we want to construct. How do we share limited resources across society? How do we resolve conflicts between your freedom of speech and my rights to a civil reception? And how do we balance short-term growth against long-term sustainability?

### 2.4.1   DECIDING TO USE AI: FURTHER READING AND AN EXERCISE

There is very little literature on deciding when to use (or not use) AI for a project. We encourage our readers, therefore, to refelct upon and share their experiences. One exception is [27] which focuses on agent-based approaches to AI but is somewhat dated. For a specific domain like medicine, articles can be found that explore the unintended and unfortunate effects of using AI (e.g. [4]).

---

**Exercise 3:**

Recall again driverless cars/autonomous vehicles.

Reflect upon and consider the following questions. What are the benefits of in-troducing autonomous vehicles? What are the potential harms? Which groups will benefit? Which groups might be harmed? How might we mitigate the harms? How safe do autonomous vehicles need to be before they are permitted on public roads? What sort of errors are acceptable? And what are unacceptable? If autonomous vehicles are safer than human driven vehicles, should humans be banned from driving? How do we safely introduce driverless cars into a world currently full of human driven vehicles?

---

## 2.5   FAIRNESS CONCERNS

One area where AI systems have raised significant and challenging issues is around fairness. This is not because fairness is a new issue. We have worried about issues of fairness, justice and equity for thousands of years. Such concerns play an important role, for instance, in the teachings of many religions, from Christianity through Bud-dhism to Islam. AI does, however, put some of these issues on steroids. We break down the teachings of this section into seven simple lessons.

## LESSON 1: DATA IS HISTORICAL AND THEREFORE INHERENTLY BIASED

Suppose you are building a machine learning system to predict where poachers poach based on past poaching data. By its very nature, historical data reflects the biases of the system in which it was captured. Perhaps patrols focused on particular watering holes and so caught more poachers near to these? There might have been significant poaching at other places, but you never found out about this. If you are not careful, you will bake into your AI systems these historical biases.

---

**Case study (Google Translate):**
In 2017, the media organisation Quartz uncovered significant gender biases in Google Translate. In Finnish, for example, there is only one pronoun, 'hän' that covers the third person singular. In English, on the other hand, there are two such pronouns, 'he' and 'she'. So when Google Translate goes from Finnish to English, it has to choose whether 'hän' means 'he' or 'she'. Despite significant work on this issue since 2017, the results remain disappointing.

| Finnish | English |
|---|---|
| Hän tekee työn. | He does the work. |
| Hän huolehtii lapsista. | She takes care of the children. |
| Hän tekee rahaa. | He makes money. |
| Hän tekee kotityöt. | She does the housework. |
| Hän on pääministeri. | He is the prime minister. |
| Hän on vaalea. | She is blond. |
| Hän juo olutta. | He drinks beer. |
| Hän hakee avioeroa. | She is filing for divorce. |

In fact, Finland is the only developed country in the world where fathers spend more time daily with their school-aged children than mothers. Finland also recently had a female leader, the world's youngest serving prime minister, and all five parties in the then coalition government were led by women.

Tools like Google Translate are trained on large corpa, and this gender bias can be found in such English (and perhaps Finnish) texts. Despite knowing about this, it is proving difficult to remove such biases from the translations even for companies with the resources and expertise of Google.

---

## LESSON 2: YOU OFTEN DON'T HAVE THE STATISTIC YOU'RE PREDICTING

Suppose you are building a machine learning tool to predict to which people to offer loans. The problem is that you don't have a statistic for how likely someone is to pay back a loan. You might therefore use a proxy such as a credit score. But there may be individuals with a poor credit score who were never lent money in the past but would pay back a loan. Using a proxy is creating a feedback loop that will reinforce this bias.

As a second example, suppose you are trying to increase engagement on your social media platform. The problem is that you can't easily measure how engaged people are with the site. Of course, you can run carefully designed studies where you monitor and question people about their engagement. But it is much easier to use simple proxies like the time users spend on the platform and the number of links on which they click. And as Facebook has demonstrated over many years now, this proxy encourages extreme content and polarisation of users, rather than positive and constructive engagement.

---

**Case study (patient care):**

Powers *et al.* studied a widely used tool to identify patients for 'high-risk care management' programs [20]. Such programs provide additional resources for complex and chronic conditions to help ensure that patient care is well coordinated. In the US and elsewhere, such interventions are widely considered to be highly effective at improving outcomes and satisfaction while reducing costs. Unfortunately, their analysis uncovered a significant racial bias in the tool. This bias more than halved the number of Black patients identified for extra care. The bias occurs because there's no simple measure for the 'health need' of a patient so the algorithm used past health costs as a proxy for a patient's health needs. However, less money has historically been spent on Black patients for a variety of medical, sociological and political reasons. The tool thus falsely presumes that Black patients are healthier than equally sick White patients.

---

## LESSON 3: BIAS OFTEN CANNOT BE ELIMINATED

A natural response to the identification of unwanted bias in AI tools is to look to eliminate such bias. While methods exist to reduce bias (e.g. pre-processing methods to modify the data before modelling to make it more representative, in-processing methods to address discrimination during training, and post-processing methods such as adjusting thresholds to trade accuracy for fairness), it is worth noting that not all bias can be eliminated. Inductive bias is an important feature of machine learning algorithms – how do they choose between different possible outputs given new input data not seen in training? Algorithms need to work on unseen inputs and so need an appropriate inductive bias.

Consider a setting like selecting people to short list and interview for a job, or deciding on a patient from a long waiting list to receive a donated organ. You are choosing one or more candidates from a possibly large set. There is no unbiased answer. It should be biased towards the most capable at the job, or the most deserving of a transplant. It should hopefully not be biased on grounds that society finds unfair such as race or gender. This may, however, throw up challenging problems. What if there is a greater prevalence of kidney disease in a particular minority community?

How do we compare a transplant for an old person who is very sick with a young person who is less sick? And how do we decide exactly who to short list for an interview? Is it not fair simply to select those with the best qualifications. Perhaps they come from privileged groups with better access to education. An algorithm will, however, require you to be precise about such issues.

## LESSON 4: FAIRNESS MEANS MANY THINGS – WE NEED TO CHOOSE ONE

This brings us to a fundamental question. What precisely does fairness mean? This is not an easy question to answer as fairness means many different things and is applied in different ways in a number of different contexts. For example, in classification, fairness might mean we treat different groups identically, while in resource allocation, fairness might mean that no individual envies another's allocation. Deploying AI systems requires us to be much more exact about what fairness means. In the past, we could leave it up to human judgement and accountability. However, we now need to code it precisely.

Let us return to the problem of classification. What does it mean to classify fairly? There have been at least 21 different mathematical definitions of fairness studied by machine learning researchers [25]. Here are just a few of the most popular to give you an idea:

**Demographic or statistical parity:** people within different groups have the same chance of a positive classification. For instance, the same fraction of Asian and Caucasian people should be offered a loan. Note that this ignores that Asians and Caucasians might have a different likelihood of successfully paying off a loan.

**Equal opportunity:** eligible people with the different groups have the same chance of a positive classification. More precisely, the true positive rate for different groups should be identical. For instance, the same fraction of Asian people who would successfully repay a loan are actually offered a loan as Caucasian people. Note that this ignores how (in)accurately we classify those people, Asian or otherwise, who would not successfully repay the loan.

**Equal precision:** in the different groups, the same fraction of those classified positively are correctly classified. For instance, the same fraction of people in each group offered a loan will successfully repay the loan. Note that this ignores the accuracy of those classified ineligible for a loan.

**Casual non-discrimination:** changing the protected feature does not change the outcome. For instance, changing the input race from Asian to Caucasian does not change if someone gets offered a loan.

**Fairness through unawareness:** A protected feature should not be used in the classification. For example, race should not be an input in deciding who gets a loan. Often this is not enough as ML systems are very good at identifying correlations, and there can be correlated features (e.g. ZIP or postal code might be closely correlated with race and so the system might learn to discriminate on ZIP code).

The fundamental challenge is that these different fairness measures are typically incompatible except in three degenerate circumstances: (1) the classifier is 100%

accurate; (2) the classifier is 0% accurate; (3) the different groups are actually identical in every way. We therefore typically face a trade-off problem since optimising one fairness measure may make another worse. The question then becomes what sort of trade-off are we prepared to accept?

---

**Case study (COMPAS):**

No discussion of fairness is complete without mention of this controversial case. The Correctional Offender Management Profiling for Alternative Sanctions (COMPAS) is a decision support tool developed by Northpointe and used by US courts in at least 20 different states to assess the likelihood of a defendant reoffending.

Investigations have revealed significant racial biases in its predictions [10]. In particular, the tool has been shown to fail to provide equality of opportunity. Many more Black people who will not go on to reoffend are predicted by the tool to reoffend than White people. On the other hand, Northpointe has vigorously defended the tool as it is optimised to ensure equality of precision. Black people who are predicted by the tool to reoffend will actually go on to reoffend at a similar rate to White people.

This is a classic example of how we cannot optimise multiple measures of fairness simultaneously and must choose which we prefer. Is it better to avoid locking up people who won't reoffend? Or should we care more that no racial group is disproportionately locked up incorrectly?

---

## LESSON 5: FAIRNESS GOES TO THE CORE OF A JUST SOCIETY

The identification of these sorts of trade-offs brings us back to some fundamental issues about what it is for society to be just and fair. Do we, for instance, adopt a utilitarian perspective where we maximise the total utility and worry about the net good to society as a whole? Or do we adopt a more egalitarian perspective where we minimise any individual harms and worry about just the worst off? AI tools may let us create new market places that can force us to make such difficult choices.

Consider, for example, a health insurance company that data mines the UK Biobank containing genotypical and phenotypical information for half a million people. Suppose this identifies a new genetic test for bowel cancer. Through no fault of their own, people who fail this test might now have increased health insurance rates. Is this fair or should the burden of treating these people continue to be shared across society? As a second example, consider a machine learning tool used by a supermarket to analyse sales data and increase profits. What if this tool suggests offering discounts on sugary drinks to customers with children? Or to increase the cost of vegetarian meals despite the calls by climate activists for less meat in our diets?

## LESSON 6: DIVERSITY IN TEAMS HELPS

Building AI systems responsibly is complex and difficult. There are plenty of traps awaiting the unwary and little in the way of standard procedures to avoid them. To compound matters, AI is a field lacking diversity. The percentage of women has stubbornly remained around 20%, and many groups (racial, queer, etc.) remain underrepresented. Diversity in the teams building AI is an important goal to strive for in order to help ensure tools are built that deploy AI fairly and responsibly. Businesses report that more diverse teams are better at spotting bias, better at creative thinking, and better at scaling solutions across the enterprise.

## LESSON 7. COMPUTERS CAN NEVERTHELESS MAKE BETTER DECISIONS THAN HUMANS

Despite all these reservations, humans are terrible at making good decisions, and it is not hard to do better. Behavioural economics is a catalogue of examples of human decision-making that are far from optimal. Let us list a few of our cognitive biases: anchoring, belief bias, confirmation bias, distinction bias, the endowment effect, the framing effect, the gambler's fallacy, hindsight bias, information bias, loss aversion, normalcy bias, omission bias, present bias, the recency illusion, systematic bias, risk aversion, selection bias, time-saving bias, unit bias, and zero-sum bias. Our poor decision-making runs the gauntlet from A to Z.

Economists consider *homo economicus* a perfect rational and optimal decision maker. The reality is that humans are neither rational nor optimal. Loss aversion is one such example. Suppose you toss a fair coin where if the coin lands on heads you win $1001, but on tails you lose $1000. This is a certain win for *homo economicus*. Play the game ten times and *homo economicus* expects to be $10 ahead. But most people will avoid tossing the coin even once since our psychological response to losses is greater than that to gains. Another example is risk aversion. Suppose you toss another fair coin, but this time if the coin lands on heads, you win $20, but on tails, you lose $10. Can I pay you $9 to let me play the game in your place? Play the game, and you win on average $10 more than they lose. But most people prefer certainty over risk and take the $9 even though it is less. This is not the choice that rational *homo economicus* makes.

Algorithms offer the promise of defeating all of these cognitive biases, of making perfectly rational, fair and evidence-based decisions. Indeed, they even offer the promise to make decisions in settings either where humans are incompetent, such as decisions that require calculating precise conditional probabilities, or where humans are incapable, such as decisions based on data sets of a scale beyond human comprehension. Unfortunately the reality is that algorithms have done depressing little of this superior decision making yet. It is hard to find examples where algorithms had not simply replaced human decision making but improved upon its fairness.

The one major exception is the National Resident Matching Program. This is a non-profit organisation in the United States created in 1952 that matches medical students with training programs in teaching hospitals. Algorithms here have made the process of matching students to hospitals fairer for the students. In 1995, concern arose within the medical community that the algorithm that had been in use for many years to do the matching of medical students to hospitals favoured the hospitals over the students. The way to fix this bias was simple: switch the inputs to the algorithm around so it favoured the students over the hospitals.

The impact of switching to this 'fairer' algorithm was in fact somewhat more theoretical than practical. The output of the two algorithms are almost identical in practice: Fewer than 1 in 1000 applicants receive a different match. On the plus side, most (but not all) of the few applicants who are matched to different positions by the new algorithm do better. Nevertheless, the change was very important to restore the trust of the medical community in the matching system.

### 2.5.1   FAIRNESS: FURTHER READING AND AN EXERCISE

See [19] for a recent survey on bias and fairness within machine learning. Twenty-one different definitions of fairness are described in [25]. Fairness is a complex idea and means many different things depending on the area and discipline. For instance, see [5] for a short summary of fairness within social choice.

---

**Exercise 4:**

Recall again driverless cars/autonomous vehicles.

Suppose you worked for a company building an autonomous taxi service. This includes a number of AI systems to perceive the environment (e.g. computer vision and LIDAR systems), to reason and act (e.g. path finding algorithms that find the shortest route, algorithms to allocate taxis to waiting customers), and to learn (e.g. traffic and ride prediction methods).

Discuss the following questions in the context of building such a taxi service. What historical biases might be in the data used for training that could create problems? What statistics might we be wanting to predict that are not actually available or easy to collect? What proxies might we collect instead? And what problems might such proxies create? Are there different types of fairness to consider here? How would they impact the design and performance of our taxi service? How can this service make society better, and how might it make it worse?

---

## 2.6   CONCERNS ABOUT AUTONOMY

New technologies can introduce new ethical challenges. Autonomy is arguably the one and perhaps only new ethical challenge that AI introduces. Most of the other challenges that AI introduces like bias are challenges that we have faced before. For example, we have been trying to tackle racial bias for decades. AI may have put the problem on steroids. But it is an old problem. Autonomy, on the other hand, is an entirely novel problem.

We have never had machines before that could make decisions independent of their human masters. Previously machines only did what we decided they should do. In some sense, machines in the past have only ever been our servants. But we'll soon have machines that make many of their own decisions. Indeed, anyone who owns a Tesla car already has one such machine. Such autonomy introduces some very challenging and new ethical questions. Who is accountable for the actions of an autonomous AI? What limits should be placed on an autonomous AI? And what happens if an autonomous AI harms or kills a person, purposefully or accidentally?

The development of self-driving cars is one place where we have seen some of the most detailed and novel discussion around AI and ethics. This is unsurprising. A self-driving car is, in fact, a robot. And we don't build many other robots that can travel autonomously at over 100 miles per hour. Much of this discussion has centred on the 'trolley problems' discussed above. Recall that this is a moral dilemma that was dreamt up by the English philosopher Philippa Foot in 1967. People seem to forget that it is designed to be a *dilemma*, and that like all dilemmas, you are required to choose between two outcomes, both of which are undesirable.

### 2.6.1   AUTONOMY IN WARFARE

Self-driving cars are not designed to kill. In fact, they are designed to do the opposite, to save lives. But when things go wrong, they may accidentally kill people. There are, however, other autonomous machines entering our lives which are designed expressly to kill: lethal autonomous weapons or, as the media like to call them, 'killer robots'. The world faces a very critical choice about this application of autonomy in the battlefield. The technology to build autonomous weapons is ready to cross out of the research lab, and to be developed and sold by arms manufacturers around the world. Ongoing discussions at the UN have so far focused on retaining meaningful human control over lethal autonomous weapons.

First and foremost, there is a strong moral argument against killer robots. We give up an essential part of our humanity if we hand over the decision of whether someone should live to a machine. Machines have no emotions, compassion or empathy. How then can machines be fit to decide who lives and who dies? Beyond the moral arguments, there are many technical and legal reasons to be concerned about whether we can build robots that able to follow the rules of war.

War might appear from the outside to be a rather lawless activity. A lot of people get killed in war. And killing people is generally not permitted in peace time. But there are internationally agreed rules for fighting war. And these rules apply to robots as much as to people. The rules of war distinguish between *jus ad bellum*, literally the right conduct to go to war, and *jus in bello*, literally the right conduct in war. To put it in plainer language, the rules of war distinguish between the conditions under which states may resort to war and, once states are legally at war, the conditions in which warfare is conducted. The two sets of rules are deliberately independent of each other.

*Jus ad bellum* requires, for example, that war must be fought for a just cause, such as to save life or protect human rights. It also requires that war must be defensive and not aggressive, and that it must be declared by a competent authority such as a government. For the present, it is unlikely that machines are going to be declaring war by themselves. It is perhaps reasonable to suppose therefore that humans are still going to be the ones taking us to war.

Let us focus instead on *jus in bello*. The rules governing the conduct of war seek to minimise suffering, and protect all victims of armed conflict especially non-combatants. The rules apply to both sides, irrespective of the reasons for the conflict or the justness of the causes for which they are fighting. If it were otherwise, the laws would be pretty useless as each party would no doubt claim to be a victim of aggression.

There are four main principles to jus in bello, the conduct of war. The first is the principle of humanity, which also goes under the name of the Martens clause. This was introduced in the preamble to the 1899 Hague Convention by Friedrich Martens, the Russian delegate to the convention. It requires war to be fought according to the laws of humanity, and the dictates of the public conscience. The Martens clause is a rather vague principle, a catch all that outlaws behaviours and weapons that the public might find repugnant. How, for instance, do we determine precisely public conscience? The Martens clause is often interpreted to prefer, for example, capturing an enemy over wounding them, wounding over killing, and the prohibitions of weapons that cause excessive injury or pain.

The second principle of jus in bello is that of distinction. You must distinguish between the civilian population and combatants, and between civilian objects and military objectives. The only legitimate target is a military objective. It requires defenders to avoid placing military personnel or materiel in or near civilian objects, and attackers to use those only methods of attack that are discriminate in effect.

The third principle of jus in bello is that of proportionality. This prohibits attacks against military objectives which are expected to kill or injure civilians, or to damage civilian objects which would be excessive compared to the expected military advantage. This principle requires attackers to take precautions to minimise collateral damage, and to choose where possible objectives expected to cause the least danger to civilians and civilian objects.

The fourth and final principle of jus in bello is that of military necessity. This limits armed force to those actions that have legitimate military objectives. This means avoiding inflicting gratuitous injury on the enemy. The principle of necessity overlaps in part with the Martens clauses. Both take account of humanitarian concerns around the wounding of soldiers. And both prohibit weapons that cause unnecessary suffering.

---

**The rules of war:**

**Jus ad bello:** conditions under which states may resort to war.
**Jus in bello:** conditions in which warfare is conducted once states are legally
   at war:

1. principle of humanity (Martens clause);
2. principle of distinction;
3. principle of proportionality;
4. principle of necessity.

---

## 2.6.2   THE MORALITY OF KILLER ROBOTS

Can we build AI systems with significant autonomy that uphold the four principles
of jus in bello, the conduct of war? Consider, for example, the Martens clause. The
majority of the public are against the idea of lethal autonomous weapons. Indeed, as
the UN Secretary General has clearly said, many of us find them morally repugnant.
It seems therefore that lethal autonomous weapons conflict directly with the Martens
clause.

The other three principles are also violated by lethal autonomous weapons. For
instance, we don't know how to build weapons that can adequately distinguish between combatant and civilian. The Kargu drone deployed on the Turkish-Syrian bor-
der uses face recognition to identify targets. And yet we know that, in the wild, such
face recognition software can be incredibly inaccurate. It is hard then to imagine how
the Kargu drone upholds the principle of distinction.

We also cannot build autonomous systems that respect the principles of proportionality and necessity. We can build autonomous systems like self-driving cars that
perceive the world well enough not to cause an accident. But we cannot build systems that make subtle judgements about the expected damage inflicted by a particular
weapon. Or the humanitarian trade-offs between a variety of different targets.

Some of the principles of jus in bello like the principle of distinction may be
achieved by AI systems at some point in the future. In a couple of decades, for
example, machines may be able to distinguish adequately between combatants and
civilians. Indeed, there are arguments that machines may one day be better at upholding the principle of distinction than humans. After all, machines can have more
sensors, faster sensors, sensors that work on wavelengths of light humans cannot
see, even active sensors like radar and LIDAR which work in conditions which de-
feat passive sensors like our eyes and ears. It is plausible then that the killer robots
will one day perceive the world better than humans can.

However, there are other principle such as Martens clause that it is hard to imagine machines will ever be able to uphold. How will a machine understand repug-
nance? How can a machine determine the public conscience? Similar concerns arise

around the principles of proportionality and necessity. Could a machine ever adequately understand the humanitarian concerns that a military commander considered when some insurgents were hiding near a hospital? Till we have acceptable answers to such questions, we must continue to insist on meaningful human control of lethal autonomous systems.

## 2.7 CONCERNS ABOUT TRANSPARENCY

One response to many ethical concerns is that AI systems need to be made more transparent. IBM, for instance, has made transparency a central part of its mission. Indeed, it is one of just three ethical principles that guide IBM's use of AI. But it's not only IBM that has elevated transparency to a position of great importance. It plays a central role in many of the ethical frameworks for AI proposed by governments, corporations and NGOs around the world.

Transparency is certainly a useful tool in building AI systems, especially those with significant autonomy. But at best, it is a means to an end. It is not the end in itself. Indeed, there are situations where transparency is undesirable. For example, many companies use trade secrecy to protect valuable intellectual property. Google rightly does not share the secret sauce to its search algorithm. Not only is this the only way to protect the billions of dollars it invests into improving search, but it also helps prevent bad actors from manipulating search results. Transparency here would be a bad thing.

There are also settings where transparency might not be possible. We have limited transparency into how human vision works. And it is not at all clear that we will ever have significantly greater transparency into human vision. It might be impossible to demand that computer vision systems are magically more transparent than human ones. And would it be right to continue to have millions of road deaths each year around the world in accidents that computer vision could have avoided provided we did not demand transparency?

## 2.8 ENVIRONMENTAL CONCERNS

Arguably the biggest moral problem facing humanity this century is the climate emergency. It's imperative today that we consider how AI may contribute to this ethical challenge. On the one hand, how can AI help tackle the climate emergency? On the other hand, how might AI exacerbate the climate emergency?

In the last few years, it's become fashionable to worry about the terrible amount of energy used by AI algorithms. A widely reported study from 2015 predicted that data centres could be consuming half of global energy by 2030 and would be responsible for a quarter of all greenhouse gases pumped out into the atmosphere. However, reality seems to be shaping up quite differently.

Data centres have been getting more efficient faster than they have been increasing in size, and mostly they've been switching to green renewable energy. Their carbon footprint hasn't therefore increased as predicted back in 2015. Indeed, if anything, the footprint of data centres might have decreased slightly. It would help, of course, if the data centre industry was more transparent about its green future. But even if we discount their still-to-be-delivered promises, the sector is doing a relatively good job.

Another perspective comes not from the total footprint of AI but from the individual. How much energy is used, and carbon dioxide produced, by a single AI model? This is not an easy question to answer. Machine-learning models, for example, come in many different sizes. In May 2020, OpenAI announced GPT-3: at that time, this was the largest AI model ever built with an impressive 175 billion parameters. Infamously, GPT in particular and generative AI in general have come further since then of course.

Training this enormous model is estimated to have produced 85 tonnes of $CO_2$. To put this in perspective, this is the same amount produced by four people flying a round trip from London to Sydney in business class.

This figure of 85 tonnes of $CO_2$ supposes that the energy produced to train the GPT-3 model comes from conventional power sources. In practice, many data centres run on renewable energy. The three big cloud computing providers are Google Cloud, Microsoft Azure and Amazon Web Services. Google Cloud claims to have 'zero net carbon emissions'. Microsoft Azure runs its cloud on 60 per cent renewable energy and has offset the rest since 2014. Indeed, by 2030, the whole of Microsoft plans to be carbon negative. Amazon Web Services, which is the largest provider with well over one-third of the market, is less green. It has, however, promised to be net zero by 2040. Today, Amazon uses around 50 per cent renewable energy when offsets are factored into consideration.

A distinction also needs to be made between training and prediction. It costs a lot more to train a model than to use it to make a prediction. Training can take days or even months on thousands or tens of thousands of processors. Prediction, on the other hand, takes milliseconds, often on a single core. The amount of $CO_2$ produced to make a prediction using even a very large AI model can thus be measured in grams. Generating an image with generative AI is roughly equivalent in carbon footprint to charging one's phone. We should therefore divide the amount of $CO_2$ produced training a model by the number of times the model is actually used to make predictions, or ouputs.

The carbon footprint of AI is thus real but perhaps not the greatest ethical challenge thrown up by AI. We should probably be much more focused on uses of AI that, for example, perpetuate biases of the past. On the other hand, AI does offer the promise to help tackle a number of wicked environmental problems, for reducing the carbon emissions to deliver goods to our homes, to tackling poachers, and managing other threats to biodiversity.

### 2.8.1   ENVIRONMENTAL CONCERNS: FURTHER READING AND AN EXERCISE

Kate Crawford examines in detail the environmental costs of AI [8]. Her analysis goes beyond carbon emissions to include resources such as lithium and rare earth metals used in the hardware as well as the human resources to prepare and label datasets.

---

**Exercise 5:**

Recall again driverless cars/autonomous vehicles.

Suppose you worked for a company building autonomous self-driving pods. Reflect upon and consider the following questions. From an environmental perspective, how many people should each such pod carry? Could such pods actually increases $CO_2$ emissions? You should consider issues like occupancy, distances travelled, parking and utilisation. In most cities today, the average car carries between one and two occupants. Is it possible that occupancy could dip below one person per vehicle if cars were autonomous? You might discuss different scenarios to explore different possible futures.

---

## 2.9 REGULATION AND STANDARDS

In terms of deploying AI responsibly, ethics does not provide a complete solution. Not every person or every organisation will invest the same energy and care in thinking ethically about their application of AI. Ethical judgements can also be highly personal and cultural. In addition, ethical judgements may permit behaviours that, whilst they are not morally wrong, may nevertheless harm society. For example, ethics has little to say about how unsophisticated investors can or should invest their retirement funds. But many countries regulate such investments to protect the unwary. There is therefore also an important role for regulation and standards to support the responsible deployment of AI.

### 2.9.1 AI REGULATION

Artificial intelligence is a generic technology. With other generic technologies such as electricity, we mostly regulate their application to specific tasks. Similarly, the regulation of AI may often be best focused on specific applications (e.g. the use of facial recognition software in law enforcement or the micro-targeting of adverts in social media). We must also be careful that regulation does not stifle innovation.

There is an ongoing project within the European Union to regulate AI as a general purpose technology. The EU Artificial Intelligence Act is risk based. It identifies a list of high-risk applications where there are clear requirements such as safety assessment and risk mitigation before the AI system is put into service or placed on the market. It also identifies applications which are unacceptable to Europe, such as social scoring by governments. Other AI systems of limited risk will nevertheless carry transparency obligations. For example, users of chatbots should be made aware that they are interacting with a machine so they can take an informed decision to continue or step back.

To complement the EU AI Act, the EU also imposes regulation to address liability issues related to new technologies such as AI systems, as well as to revise specific safety legislation such as the General Product Safety Directive to take into account issues raised by AI. Given the impact of existing European legislation such as GDPR (the data privacy laws) and of emerging regulation such as the Digital Markets and Digital Service Acts, the EU AI Act could set a strong precedent for the rest of the planet.

Regulation is also starting to be developed for specific applications of AI. For example, in many countries, specific regulation is being created to manage the responsible deployment of autonomous vehicles. The California Department of Motor Vehicles (DMV) established the Autonomous Vehicle Tester (AVT) Driverless Program in 2018. Under this program, manufacturers can test autonomous vehicles without a human driver. At the end of 2021, seven companies held permits to do such testing.

### 2.9.2  AI STANDARDS

Alongside regulation, there have been significant efforts to define standards for AI systems. The responsible deployment of AI cannot be reduced to simple check lists. There are often complex and subtle issues that need to be considered. Nevertheless, standards can provide a useful starting point.

The Institute of Electrical and Electronics Engineers (IEEE) is the world's largest technical professional organisation dedicated to advancing technology for the benefit of humanity. The IEEE Standards Association is developing a suite of standards for deploying AI systems responsibly. For example, IEEE 7001-2021 is a recently published IEEE Standard for Transparency of Autonomous Systems. It concerns systems that have the capacity to directly cause either physical, psychological, societal, economic or environmental, or reputational harm. Such harm can be indirect, such as unauthorised persons gaining access to confidential data or 'victimless crime' that affect no-one in particular yet have an impact upon society or the environment. The standard aims to provide a framework for developers both to review and, if needed, design features into those systems to make them more transparent.

The International Organisation for Standardisation (ISO) is also engaged in developing standards for AI. For instance, ISO recently published the ISO/IEC TR 24027:2021 standard to address bias in AI systems, especially where AI aids humans in decision making. The standard provides methods for assessing and measuring bias across the AI development lifecycle. The overall aim of the standard is to enable developers to understand and treat bias in AI systems.

### 2.10  EMERGING THEMES

The field of AI and ethics is moving at a rapid pace. In this section we will examine three emerging themes. *Ethics washing* – the simulation of ethical action via the co-option of ethical language and broader pseudo-moral gestures. *Extractivism* – the process of extracting resources such as natural physical resources, as well as labour, data, and social resources such as identity, cultural tropes, and more, by AI for profit. Then as we will see, proper consideration of the issues surrounding ethics washing and extractivism lead quickly to an urgent need to acknowledge and confront the ethics of the relationship between AI and *power*.

### 2.10.1 ETHICS WASHING

*Ethics washing* is the simulation of ethical action via the co-option of ethical language and broader pseudo-moral gestures [26]. The allegation, not without some warrant, is that the dominant approach to AI ethics from within the tech-sector is largely a hollow exercise in marketing and public relations [28].

As just one of a multitude of examples, consider IBM's [16] statement that 'ethics must be embedded in the design and development process of AI creation from the very beginning'. Here 'ethics', and more broadly terms such as 'trustworthy AI', 'ethics by design', and so on, appear as mere buzzwords. Their purpose, and the purpose of ethics washing more widely, is to distract from the need for, and to delay, meaningful regulation in the largely unregulated sphere of AI and machine learning [6], [29].

Ethics washing involves the *instrumentalisation* of ethical language. This presents a twofold challenge. Not only does such instrumentalisation enable the very ethics washing described above, it threatens to conflate such ethics washing with genuine moral philosophy. This conflation risks precipitating *ethics bashing*. As argued forcefully by Elettra Bietti [2], bashing or ridiculing of washed 'ethics' occurs for two main reasons. Firstly, there exists a real tendency to conflate instrumentalised ethics washing with genuine moral philosophy, hence justifiable grievances with the former are extrapolated to the latter. Secondly, there exists either an ignorance of – or an outright hostility to – the possibilities afforded by genuine moral philosophy itself. Genuine moral philosophy, rather than aiding in the production of obscurantist pseudo-ethical slogans, is a mode of inquiry – underpinned by moral argument – that will enable the reasoned and warranted critical analysis of the grounds for the 'ethical' claims produced by the tech-sector's moral laundromat.

Such claims appear often as though they were 'plucked out of thin air' [28], with little if any indication of the normative ethical reasoning, if indeed there was any, out of which they emerged [28]. Moreover, such methodological opacity marginalises our ability to recognise and resolve conflicts that might occur between presumed moral norms on the one hand, and between those norms and the world on the other. One of the benefits of genuine moral philosophy is the mitigation of such marginalisation.

Concerns about ethics washing have extended to wider concerns with *transparency washing*. Transparency washing is a trend that Zalnieriute [29] traces to a 'procedural fetishism' for compliance with micro-issues (such as onboarding modules and 'ethics training' workshops). Such compliance allows for a transparent presentation of itself, at the expense of any meaningful change of practice with regard to moral behaviour. Transparency washing is not the exclusive province of the tech-sector. Rather, it is a cultural artefact that has emerged from a creeping corporate culture of responsibility-avoidance [29]. Transparency can cease to be a means to an end – of reforming practice in light of ethical failings – to become an end in itself.

Of special concern with regard to AI is *participation washing* – the 'exploitative and extractive means of community involvement in the name of participatory design' [1]. Participation washing is box-ticking, masquerading as genuine consultation. It is to treat people and communities as mere resources for reputational management, rather than as genuine partners in a process of moral growth. For example, having persons of colour in an advisory body is an empty gesture if one's AI system continues to misidentify innocent person's of colour as wanted felons, or 'gorillas' [13]. Similarly, consulting members of the queer community is meritless if one's AI is tasked with detecting sexual orientation from physiological features. Recalling the physiognomy case study in this chapter above, organisations such as Queer in AI warn, not without some plausibility, that the weaponisation of such technology – irrespective of its reliability – is horrifying to contemplate [1].

Such ethical concerns take us beyond ethics washing and into considerations of *extractivism* and *power*. We now deal with each of these in turn.

### 2.10.2 EXTRACTIVISM

Extractivism is the process of extracting a resource for profit. Traditionally, the focus has been on the extraction of natural physical resources. Although this remains a focus for the ethics of AI, recent discussions of the ethical cost of extraction have expanded to include the extraction of labour, data, and social resources such as identity, cultural tropes, and more.

The visual tropes used to market AI are clean, disembodied, hyper-realised high-res motifs, smoother than CGI world-scapes that point beyond the concrete and the flesh, promising transcendence. Would that AI be so ethereal.

In reality, AI has emerged from and depends upon not only the space of pure reason and abstract ideas, but also a vast system of extraction of our planet's natural resources. As discussed in this chapter above, Kate Crawford [8], Crawford explores in detail how it is that the lithium mines of Nevada are crucial for contemporary computation. Lithium is the main component of the rechargeable lithium-ion batteries on which all of our mobile devices depend, as do the backup systems of the data centres underpinning machine learning and AI. The manufacturing of such devices imposes a huge carbon footprint. The Bayan Obo mines of Mongolia contain approximately 70% of Earth's rare minerals, and the nearby artificial lake in Baotuo is black with over 180 million tonnes of toxic waste. The need for latex to insulate electrical cables has led to the destruction of the jungles of Malaysia and Singapore. The raw energy consumption of data centres and their cooling costs, from Amazon and Google to the NSA, as discussed above, are real. All of this reveals an infrastructure of AI with ethical imperatives that reach far beyond those suggested by the sci-fi aesthetic with which we are most familiar.

The natural resources of our planet are one dimension of the common. Extractivism affects others – those within the wide category of 'social production and social life' [14]. Cases such as the ImageNet saga highlight the way in which personal details – in this case selfie images – have been harvested and extracted for the sake of training AI. Many millions of personal images were scraped from the internet, without the consent of their owners or subjects. The object and facial recognition systems built from ImageNet's database have played a foundational role in the construction of training datasets for machine learning.

ImageNet's training datasets were not made by ImageNet's AI. Necessarily they must predate it since they were used to train it in the first instance. Instead, the labour was undertaken by outsourcing it to a distributed workforce via Amazon's Mechanical Turk service. This huge-scale labelling task was performed by human workers on piecemeal rates. Here too, this labour-extractivism performed by ImageNet reveals an infrastructure of AI with ethical imperatives that reach far beyond those suggested by any sci-fi aesthetic. Moreover, the labels used for the classification of images were far from ethically benign. Included in the taxonomy were 'hooker', 'ape-man', and worse. Two things are vital here. Firstly, training datasets are never accumulated neutrally [21]. Secondly, and a discussion of this will be forestalled until the following section, acts of classification are acts of *power*.

Our medical histories are categorised and extracted by insurance companies and decisions are made (via the generation of statistical models) by their AI in order to mitigate risks to their revenues that affect our lives. Records of our online behaviour are taxonomised and extracted in order create categories of persons for the sake of prediction algorithms.

Organisations such as Queer in AI have begun to warn against the extraction of marginalised communities by virtue of their exploitation in practices of participation washing as noted in the section above. Projects such as The Feminist Dataset [23], are attempts to accumulate datasets that are, although not morally neutral, aggregated in such a way as to mitigate some of the existent practices outlined so far. However, the massive amount of data required for AI training/machine learning renders projects such as The Feminist Dataset as proofs of concept only [7]. The resources required to implement such a dataset in practice, of such a size as to facilitate real concrete AI training, are simply not within the remit of such projects as they stand. Here again, we can see how an examination of extractivism as it relates to the ethics of AI and machine learning leads quickly to the need for a discussion of *power*.

### 2.10.3 POWER

We have seen above how the infrastructure of artificial intelligence can leverage access to, exploit, and extract resources from across the natural and social domains – from rare Earth minerals and water, to power consumption, labour, social capital, and identity. Such extractivism is both a demonstration and consolidation of great power.

The earlier observation – that training datasets are never accumulated neutrally – is if anything conservative. Crawford [8] goes further, observing that the broader practice of data-scraping, tagging, and using data for systems training is fundamentally a *political* act. The act of tagging, or classification, is one with potentially life-altering consequences.

For example, the Australian government's 'Robodebt' scheme (the automated Employment Income Confirmation System) saw a faulty algorithm *incorrectly and unlawfully* classify hundreds of thousands of Australians as owing the government roughly three billion dollars in repayments for overpaid social security benefits. Quite literally, this was the result of an elementary averaging error. In response to a Federal Court Class Action brought be Gordon Legal, the Australian government has cancelled hundreds of thousands of incorrect debts, and committed to repaying nearly *one billion dollars* in incorrectly and illegally recouped funds to all affected, and over one hundred million dollars in compensation. The scandal stopped the country, and caused incalculable psychological and social harm to nearly half a million social security recipients – those members of society least likely to have the political capital at their disposal required to defend themselves. At the time of writing, a royal commission appears likely.

Where to from here? Crawford [8] quotes philosopher Achille Mbembé [18]:

[AI] is about extraction, capture, the cult of data, the commodification of human capacity for thought and the dismissal of critical reason in favour of programming. Now more than ever before what we need is a new critique of technology, of the experience of technical life.

Before we automate decision making, we might ask what reasons we have for doing so. For example, before succumbing to the fervour for autonomous vehicles, we might interrogate the vendors with some care. How will the vehicles' avoidance systems be guided, and more dramatically, how secure is the software on which they are to run?

Such a critique is not a call to reject artificial intelligence itself. However, in line with the suggestions made in [1], the distance between AI developers and AI users needs to be minimised as a precondition to any dialogue, and dialogue is a precondition to progress. Here our obligations are manifold.

We have an obligation to investigate and communicate the nuances of the ethics of AI, with all of the opportunities and risks that AI affords. Similarly, our obligations with regard to educating ourselves and others, and to facilitate civic discussion of the issues, are very real. Information is power, so we might begin there.

## 2.11 CONCLUSIONS

When developing and deploying AI systems for social good, it is vital to consider the diverse and complex ethical challenges that arise. Checklists cannot be provided to address the many subtle issues that need to be considered. However, this brief introduction will hopefully help you start to ask some of the right questions.

We leave the interested reader with the following for consideration. Many of the issues above have been motivated by concerns surrounding accuracy, bias, and fairness. And rightly so at that. Let us suppose – for the sake of argument – that such concerns have been allayed. Does this imply that ethical concerns have been allayed also? Not obviously.

Consider the situation where a COMPAS-type system has been optimised in such a way as to mitigate the concerns raised above. Suppose also that the accuracy of such a system when it comes to the prediction of recidivism far exceeds that of any human assessor. In this case, the problem of accuracy is, if not mitigated entirely, alleviated somewhat. Would this alleviate ethical worries in turn? This is doubtful. This predictive accuracy would emerge most likely from the sort of computational complexity that would 'black-box' the internal computational mechanisms that led to the recidivism prediction output. In such a scenario, it would not be possible for the presiding magistrate to give *reasons* for their decision, above and beyond a meek testimony along the line is 'Well this is what the program has said, and it is rarely wrong'. This has more that a glimmer of dystopia about it.

In case this scenario comes across as overly speculative, note that academics are facing a real concrete analogue at the time of writing. The cases in question are these where an academic is investigating a student illicit use of generative artificial intelligence in an assessment. The algorithms that check for and give a score on the use of generative artificial intelligence are black-boxed, proprietary applications. Such applications are themselves based upon artificial intelligence, and comprise many millions (or more) of calculations. In these cases, the academic is not able to give the student under suspicion any *reasons* of the sort that we would recognise as reasons *per se*. If the student is to ask for an explanation of why it is that the detection algorithm outputted the prediction that it outputted, what is the academic to say?

Artificial intelligence – generative or otherwise – delivers already on promises of efficiency. We should mind however that efficiency is but one property amongst many. A practice may be inefficient, but of value nonetheless for the practitioner. Examples are many, and include law firm juniors preparing legal briefs, junior academics marking huge numbers of scripts, and more. In these cases and others like them, although the tasks might well be carried out by artificial intelligence in a manner more efficient, to pursue this would be to miss the point entirely. It is through such tasks that we form our character as members of a certain profession. Through them, we learn to put others ahead of ourselves and to distinguish crude material outputs from the acquisition of the moral virtues by which we conduct ourselves as moral agents. How it is that our use of artificial intelligence will contribute to the refinement of human character is a genuinely open question. Our moral duty is to answer it.

## REFERENCES

1. William Agnew, Juan Pajaro, Arjun Subramonian, et al. Rebuilding trust: Queer in AI approach to artificial intelligence risk management. *arXiv preprint arXiv:2110.09271*, 2021.

2. Elettra Bietti. From ethics washing to ethics bashing: A view on tech ethics from within moral philosophy. In *Proceedings of the 2020 Conference on Fairness, Accountability, and Transparency*, pages 210–219, 2020.

3. Jean-Francois Bonnefon, Azim Shariff, and Iyad Rahwan. The social dilemma of autonomous vehicles. *Science*, 352(6293):1573–1576, 2016.

4. Federico Cabitza, Raffaele Rasoini, and Gian Franco Gensini. Unintended consequences of machine learning in medicine. *Journal of the American Medical Association*, 318(6):517–518, 2017.

5. Yann Chevaleyre, Ulle Endriss, Jérôme Lang, and editor= Maudet, Nicolas.

6. Giovanni Comandé. Unfolding the legal component of trustworthy ai: A must to avoid ethics washing. *Version Accepted for Annuario di Diritto Comparato e di Studi Legislativi, Forthcoming*, 2020.

7. Yan Cong and Kristen Zheng. Building a feminist dataset: Confronting algorithmic bias through the practice of thoughtful data collection.

8. Kate Crawford. The atlas of AI. In *The Atlas of AI*. Yale University Press, 2021.

9. Roger Crisp. *Aristotle: Nicomachean Ethics*. Cambridge University Press, 2014.

10. J. Dressel and H. Farid. The accuracy, fairness, and limits of predicting recidivism. *Science Advances*, 4(1), 2018.

11. Luciano Floridi and Josh Cowls. A unified framework of five principles for AI in society. *Harvard Data Science Review*, 1(1), 7 2019.

12. Luciano Floridi, Josh Cowls, Thomas C. King, and Mariarosaria Taddeo. How to design AI for social good: Seven essential factors. *Science and Engineering Ethics*, 26(3):1771–1796, 2020.

13. Jessica Guynn. Google photos labeled black people 'gorillas'. *USA Today*, 1, 2015.

14. Michael Hardt and Antonio Negri. *Assembly*. Oxford University Press, 2017.

15. John N Hooker and Tae Wan N Kim. Toward non-intuition-based machine and artificial intelligence ethics: A deontological approach based on modal logic. In *Proceedings of the 2018 AAAI/ACM Conference on AI, Ethics, and Society*, pages 130–136, 2018.

16. IBM. Every day ethics for artificial intelligence. *https://www.ibm.com/watson/assets/duo/pdf/everydayethics.pdf*.

17. Christine M Korsgaard. *Kant: Groundwork of the metaphysics of morals*. Cambridge University Press, 2012.

18. Achille Mbembe. Thoughts on the planetary: An interview with achille mbembe. In *Decolonising the Neoliberal University*, pages 122–136. Birkbeck Law Press, 2021.

19. Ninareh Mehrabi, Fred Morstatter, Nripsuta Saxena, Kristina Lerman, and Aram Galstyan. A survey on bias and fairness in machine learning. *ACM Computing Survey*, 54(6), jul 2021.

20. Ziad Obermeyer, Brian Powers, Christine Vogeli, and Sendhil Mullainathan. Dissecting racial bias in an algorithm used to manage the health of populations. *Science*, 366(6464):447–453, 2019.

21. Matteo Pasquinelli and Vladan Joler. The nooscope manifested: AI as instrument of knowledge extractivism. *AI & Society*, pages 1–18, 2020.

22. George Sher. *The Utilitarianism*. Hackett Publishing Company, 2001.

23. Caroline Sinders. Feminist data set. *Clinic for Open Source Arts. https://carolinesinders. com/wp-content/uploads/2020/05/Feminist-Data-Set-Final-Draft-2020-0517.pdf*, 2020.
24. Shannon Vallor. *Technology and the virtues: A philosophical guide to a future worth wanting*. Oxford University Press, 2016.
25. Sahil Verma and Julia Rubin. Fairness definitions explained. In *Proceedings of the International Workshop on Software Fairness*, FairWare '18, page 1–7, New York, NY, USA, 2018. Association for Computing Machinery.
26. Ben Wagner. Ethics as an escape from regulation. From "ethics-washing" to ethics-shopping? 2018.
27. Michael J. Wooldridge and Nicholas R. Jennings. Software engineering with agents: Pitfalls and pratfalls. *IEEE Internet Computing*, 3(3):20–27, May 1999.
28. Karen Yeung, Andrew Howes, and Ganna Pogrebna. AI governance by human rights-centred design, deliberation and oversight: An end to ethics washing. *The Oxford Handbook of AI Ethics*, Oxford University Press, 2019.
29. Monika Zalnieriute. "transparency-washing" in the digital age: A corporate agenda of procedural fetishism. *The digital age: a corporate agenda of procedural fetishism*, pages 21–33, 2021.

# 3 The Future of Education Technology

*Jake Renzella*
School of Computer Science and Engineering, UNSW Sydney
Kensington, Australia

## 3.1 THE FUTURE OF EDUCATION TECHNOLOGY

Technology's impact on higher education has fundamentally changed the teaching, learning and assessment environment. Modern institutions have prioritised adopting educational technology to support the scalability and cost reduction towards the massification of higher education. While this has meant increased accessibility of university education, it has also contributed to a modern academic environment associated with degrading student-tutor relationships, student distrust, and regular breaches of academic integrity. Large-Language-Models (LLMs) such as ChatGPT and Gemini are already here, threatening the very fabric of the modern massified higher education environment.

But technology can do more than increase the number of students enrolled in a course. In this chapter, we look forward and explore how educational technology can, has, and will unlock educators' potential to change students' lives. Artificial Intelligence may challenge modern assessment approaches, but alternative applications can provide dynamic, individualised learning pathways which can help tailor experiences to each student. Gamification can improve extrinsic motivation and help students achieve what they did not think possible. Machine learning techniques such as speaker verification can strengthen academic integrity in a student-friendly manner. Advances in extended reality (XR) will change how students interact with learning environments, introducing learning opportunities that were not previously possible, such as transporting students to rich, 3D-modelled worlds where they can interact and practice authentic activities to prepare them for the workforce.

While it is true that technology can introduce friction between the student and educator, with thoughtful and collaborative applications, we have on the horizon the potential to unlock amazing educational experiences which can improve learning outcomes, strengthen academic integrity, and improve student–educator relationships – but it is up to us to build them.

DOI: 10.1201/9781032702797-3

## 3.2   AUSTRALIA'S TECHNOLOGICAL PATH TO MASSIFICATION

Before we explore the future of education and technology, it's important to take a step back in time to understand how technology has aided the education industry to become the behemoth that it is.

Higher education is one of Australia's largest exports. Millions of students come to Australia to attend universities, and by doing so they inject 36.5 billion into the economy per year.

We didn't get here overnight. Figure 3.1 plots enrolments in Australian universities over time since 1949. The dataset used is comprised from two sources: Department of Education from 1949 to 2019, and uCube – Higher Education Statistics for 2001 – 2019 [12].

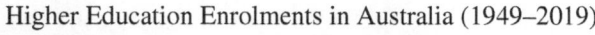

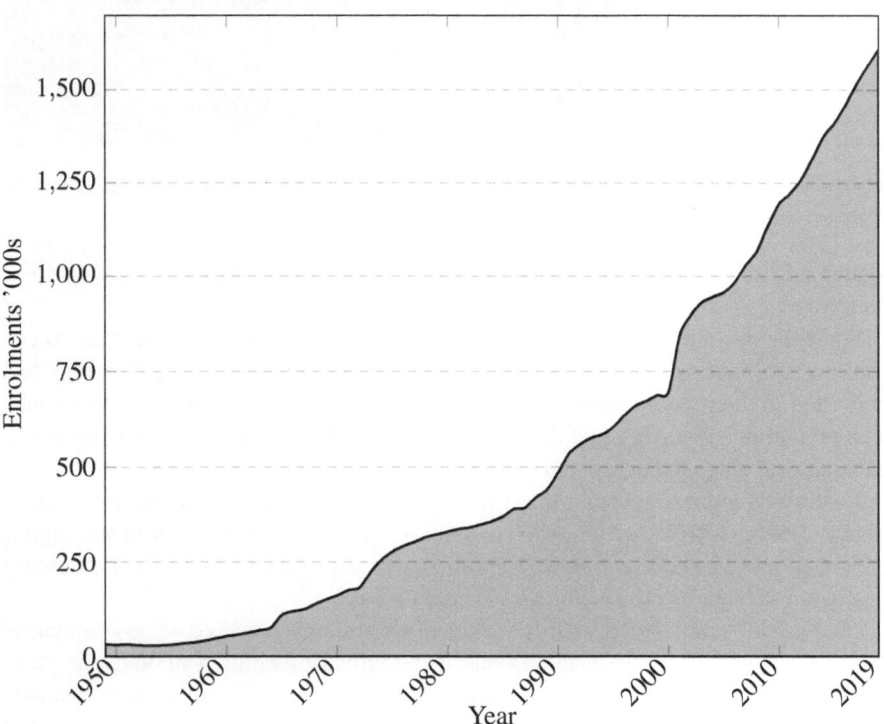

**Figure 3.1**   Growth in Higher Education Enrolments in Australia from 1949 to 2019. 1949 to 2000 sourced from Department of Education. 2001 – 2019 sourced from uCube – Higher Education Statistics

Other than a jump in the early 2000's (commonly attributed to a change in data collection methodology), the climb has been slow and steady. Australia has

**Figure 3.2** A Deakin University academic producing a cassette tape of learning materials, attributed to Deakin University Blog

positioned itself as a major contributor to the global education landscape with clear intention.

Since the dawn of the industry itself, universities have strategically embraced educational technology. Not just as a tool to improve student learning, technology has facilitated in the massification of higher education. This technological adoption has been pivotal in supporting scalability and cost reduction, fundamentally altering the teaching, learning, and assessment environment.

Australia's journey towards becoming an education export powerhouse is inextricably linked with its adoption of technology. Online learning platforms, digital resources, and virtual classrooms have dismantled geographical barriers, allowing Australian universities to reach a global student base.

Deakin University was at the forefront of technology-powered access to education. As early as 1978, the Geelong-based (a regional institution of Victoria, Australia) university utilised the most cutting-edge technology of its time: cassette tapes. Academics recorded educational material such as lectures and discussion prompts onto cassette tapes, which they mailed out to regional students across the country (Figure 3.2) [11].

As early as 1978, we see technology and the "regional university" creating opportunities for pupils which until then, would just not have been possible.

*Off-campus studies suited people from all walks of life but were especially popular with country women, many mature-aged working with families from rural regions. 'The housewife from Wycheproof' was the archetype for which units were written. –* Deakin University Archives

**Figure 3.3** Regional, mature-age students would often congregate in small groups to engage with learning material. – Deakin University Archives

Since 1978, technological infrastructure has only continued to facilitate a sustained increase in student numbers, both domestic and international, and this trend has not faltered. In the 1980's, personal computers started entering classrooms, and the first educational software became available. In the 1990's, CD-ROMS modernised data preservation, and the first Learning Management Systems became available on the early internet. In the 2000's, we see interactive whiteboards and mobile technology improve accessibility and ease of use. In the 2010's, we see the Massive Open Online Courses (MOOCs) boom, with thousands of learners signing up for MOOCs such as Stanford University's Machine Learning course delivered by Andrew Ng, having received 3,739,475 enrolments [4].

So educational technology is nothing new, and while technology has undoubtedly increased the accessibility of university education on a global scale, it has also contributed to a modern academic environment fraught with challenges. Degrading student-tutor ratios and relationships, increased student distrust, and a concerning rise in breaches of academic integrity can be attributed to massification.

Today, large language models (LLMs) such as OpenAI's ChatGPT and Google's Gemini cast a familiar shadow over educational landscapes, threatening to further disrupt the fabric of what it is that educators seek to achieve. These sophisticated AI tools challenge traditional notions of assessment and authorship, adding another layer of complexity to an already strained system.

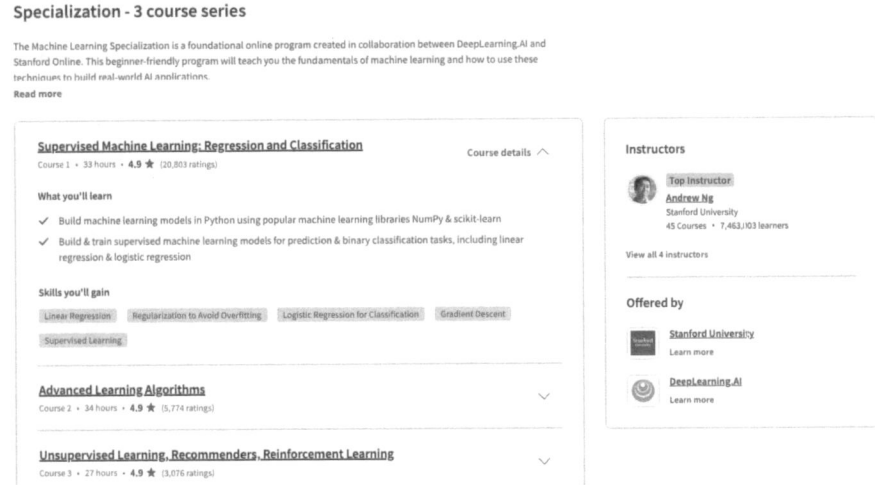

**Figure 3.4**    Andrew Ng's Stanford MOOC on Machine Learning

Yet, as we stand at this technological crossroads, it's crucial to recognise that the same forces that have driven massification also hold the key to addressing its challenges. The potential of educational technology extends far beyond increasing enrolment numbers. With thoughtful and collaborative applications, we have the opportunity to harness technology to unlock previously impossible educational experiences, strengthen academic integrity, and rebuild student–educator relationships.

As we look to the future, the question before us is not whether to embrace technology in education, but how to do so in a way that enhances rather than diminishes the quality of learning. The path forward lies in exploring innovative applications of technology. In this chapter, we will explore key technological forces, and explore the double-edged swords they sheath. In particular, we will explore AI, gamification, machine learning, and extended reality – not as replacements for human educators, but as tools to augment their ability to change students' lives.

The massification of higher education through technology has brought us to where we are today. Now, it's up to us to shape where technology will take us tomorrow.

## 3.3    GENERATIVE AI

Put simply, generative AI refers to artificial intelligence systems based on transformer architectures which are capable of creating new content, such as text, images, or music. Most will be aware of generative AI via the announcement of OpenAI's ChatGPT[1], which shocked academics and everyday users alike when it demonstrated

---

[1]https://openai.com/chatgpt/

a large leap in text generation capabilities. One morning in November of 2023, the world awoke to a tool which could write essays in the voice of Shakespeare, write correct computer programmes, and, of course, most relevant to educators, write complete, passable essays for students.

These capabilities have profound implications for education and society more broadly. Some notable AI figures, including Elon Musk, alongside other prominent tech leaders and researchers, signed an open letter in March 2023, urging a six-month moratorium on training powerful AI systems like GPT-4 [1]. The letter, organised by the Future of Life Institute, expressed concerns about the potential risks and ethical implications of rapidly advancing AI technologies, highlighting the need for shared safety protocols and thorough oversight.

Putting aside the ethical and societal concerns, it is clear generative AI capabilities, notably LLMs will play a significant role in the future of education.

This section explores how generative AI can be utilised in education in three broad categories: student-led use, tool-led use, and a forward look at the promised Personal AI Tutor.

### 3.3.1 STUDENT-LED GENERATIVE AI

Student-led use of generative AI encompasses a variety of pedagogical use of large language model tools such as ChatGPT. Students can leverage these tools directly to brainstorm ideas, generate outlines, and even receive feedback on their writing skills. Already, educators have begun to encourage or incorporate the use of LLMs in learning activities such as tasking students to revise LLM prompts to produce higher quality responses

Generative AI can also assist students in content creation beyond traditional essays. For instance, students might use AI-powered tools to create visual aids for presentations, generate code for computer science projects, or even compose music for creative arts assignments. These approaches not only teach useful, AI literacy skills, but broadens possibilities of learning tasks.

Generative AI tools can also be particularly beneficial for students with diverse learning needs. For example, LLMs are adept at providing real-time language translation, enabling non-native speakers to better understand course materials or engage with their educators. Similarly, text-to-speech and speech-to-text capabilities can assist students with visual or auditory impairments, promoting a more inclusive educational environment.

### 3.3.2 TOOL-LED GENERATIVE AI

Tool-led use of generative AI refers to the integration of AI technologies into existing educational tools and systems, often without direct student interaction with the AI itself.

One potential application of tool-led generative AI are systems integrated into learning management systems (LMS). For example, AI chatbots integrated into LMS

platforms can provide instant responses to common student queries about course lo-
gistics, deadlines, or basic content clarifications. Having a tool which can provide
accurate, and instant responses to frequently asked questions reduces the administra-
tive burden on teaching staff, and ensures students can focus their time on learning
activities.

Assessment is another area where tool-led generative AI could provide significant
value. AI-powered systems can assist educators in quickly generating diverse and
personalised assessment items, reducing the time required for test preparation. Furthermore, these tools can potentially automate the grading process for certain types
of assignments, freeing up valuable teacher time for more high-impact instructional
activities.

Generative AI is also being utilised in the creation of educational content itself.
AI tools can assist in generating textbook supplements, interactive simulations, and
costly graphics which can supplement coursework. This has the potential to dramatically reduce the cost and time associated with developing educational materials,
making high-quality resources more accessible to a wider range of institutions and
learners.

### 3.3.3   LOOKING FORWARD: PERSONALISED AI TUTORS

One of the holy grails of generative AI is that of the personal, AI tutor. The application of LLMs and other generative models to compose an AI study companions or
tutor has been spouted as one of the "game changers" of modern AI.

A 24/7, personal tutor which can motivate, teach, test and otherwise support students along their learning pathway would clearly be a valuable tool, but how far are
we away from this promise becoming a reality?

Firstly, the issue of factual accuracy and reliability is paramount. LLMs are
trained on vast amounts of data, but they are prone to producing incorrect or non-
sensical output. This phenomenon, referred to as 'hallucinations', are one of LLM's
greatest challenges [24], with many efforts seeking to reduce the frequency of the behaviour [23]. In an educational context, where the accuracy of information is crucial,
this presents a significant hurdle. Current AI models lack the ability to consistently
distinguish between factual information and erroneous information, which could potentially mislead students or reinforce misconceptions.

Secondly, while AI models can engage in dialogue with students, they currently
lack the deep understanding of individual student needs, and emotional states that human tutors possess. They are text-based models, which cannot read body language
or social cues. The ability to adapt teaching methods in real-time based on subtle
cues from the student, or to provide motivational support during challenging periods, remains a complex challenge for AI systems where humans will likely remain
superior.

Despite these challenges, progress in this area is rapid and promising. Recent advancements in multi-modal AI models, which can process and generate text, images,
and even speech, are bringing us closer to AI tutoring experiences. These models

could potentially provide visual explanations, respond to verbal questions, and even analyse student handwriting or sketches.

Furthermore, ongoing research in areas such as reinforcement learning and few-shot learning is improving the adaptability and personalisation capabilities of AI models. This could lead to AI tutors that can more effectively tailor their approach to individual students' needs and learning trajectories.

It's also worth noting that the implementation of AI tutors need not be an all-or-nothing proposition. We are likely to see a gradual integration of AI tutoring capabilities into existing educational technologies and practices. For instance, AI-powered homework helpers, interactive textbooks, and personalised quiz generators are already making their way into classrooms and homes.

### 3.3.3.1 Case Study: DCC Help

The Debugging C Compiler (DCC) Help project [20] has been developed by academics at the University of New South Wales (UNSW) to integrate generative AI features into compilers. Compilers, the tools which all programmers use to convert source code into programs that can run on computers, are well known for being hard to use and especially hard to understand when things go wrong. When there are problems with a particular program (for example, a mistyped character or erroneous logic), compilers produce programming error messages which are designed to convey to the programmer what went wrong, and where.

Improving compiler error message quality has been a pursuit as old as the tools themselves, but efforts are aimed at supporting error messages designed to help professional developers quickly find and fix bugs. To improve the code debugging training and support of novice programmers, DCC Help [21] integrated a large language model directly into the compiler. The integration provides accurate, novice-friendly programming error explanations. The family of AI tools has been used over 400,000 times by UNSW Computing students to get back on their feet after a programming error, and is an example of a tool-integrated application of generative AI in education.

Critically, most of the tool's use occurs outside of business hours, demonstrating the role AI-driven tools can play in supporting student learning when the teaching team is not available, as well as reducing strain on limited resources.

By designing custom integration of LLM-powered tools, educators can ensure pedagogical guardrails are enforced. For example, DCC Help limits the frequency in which students can use the tool, providing a gentle reminder that AI help features will not be available in the final exam.

## 3.4 PERSONALISED LEARNING

One of the most promising applications of AI in education is the creation of adaptive or personalised learning systems. These systems use machine learning algorithms to analyse student performance and adjust the learning path in real-time.

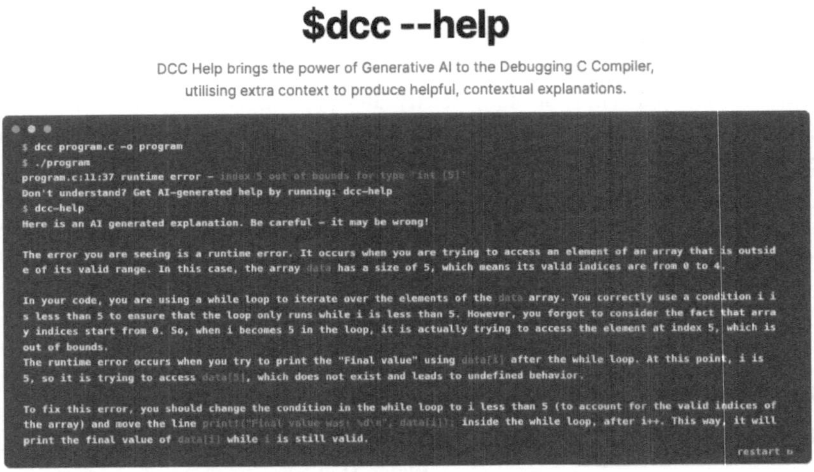

# $dcc --help

DCC Help brings the power of Generative AI to the Debugging C Compiler,
utilising extra context to produce helpful, contextual explanations.

```
$ dcc program.c -o program
$ ./program
program.c:11:37 runtime error - index 5 out of bounds for type 'int [5]'
Don't understand? Get AI-generated help by running: dcc-help
$ dcc-help
Here is an AI generated explanation. Be careful - it may be wrong!

The error you are seeing is a runtime error. It occurs when you are trying to access an element of an array that is outsid
e of its valid range. In this case, the array data has a size of 5, which means its valid indices are from 0 to 4.

In your code, you are using a while loop to iterate over the elements of the data array. You correctly use a condition i i
s less than 5 to ensure that the loop only runs while i is less than 5. However, you forgot to consider the fact that arra
y indices start from 0. So, when i becomes 5 in the loop, it is actually trying to access the element at index 5, which is
out of bounds.
The runtime error occurs when you try to print the "Final value" using data[i] after the while loop. At this point, i is
5, so it is trying to access data[5], which does not exist and leads to undefined behavior.

To fix this error, you should change the condition in the while loop to i less than 5 (to account for the valid indices of
the array) and move the line printf("Final value was: %d\n", data[i]); inside the while loop, after i++. This way, it will
print the final value of data[i] while i is still valid.

                                                                                        restart »
```

**Figure 3.5**   The Debugging C Compiler's (DCC) Help tool

Personalisation in education presents a student-centred lens through which to view education, acknowledging that the one-size-fits-all approach common to massified learning environments may not be suitable for all. With a personalised learning system, pacing, assessment and even concepts are dynamic [9]. This is quite a departure for higher education, which typically features rigidity in concepts covered, and assessment timetables set years in advance.

Pre-transformer-based artificial intelligence, a type of AI which pre-dates the technology behind LLMs, is core to personalised learning. For all approaches of AI-based personalisation, datasets such as prior-student behaviours and outcomes, as well as individual student's progress, student engagement, and historical performance can be utilised by an algorithm to determine what comes next. For example, a student who breezes through knowledge-check quizzes could skip ahead to more challenging topics, while a student who is struggling can be provided with more in-depth revision materials on current topics.

Carnegie Learning's MATHiais an AI-powered math learning software adapts to each student's learning pace, providing personalised instruction and practice problems. It uses cognitive models to understand how students think about math concepts, adjusting difficulty and providing targeted feedback [?].

Furthermore, popular platforms like Duolingo[2] use AI to personalise language learning. The app adjusts the difficulty of exercises based on the user's recent performance, or performance in knowledge tests, ensuring that learners are constantly challenged but not overwhelmed. It also revisits vocabulary and grammar that learners struggle with, using spaced repetition techniques to enhance retention.

---

[2]Duolingo: https://www.duolingo.com/

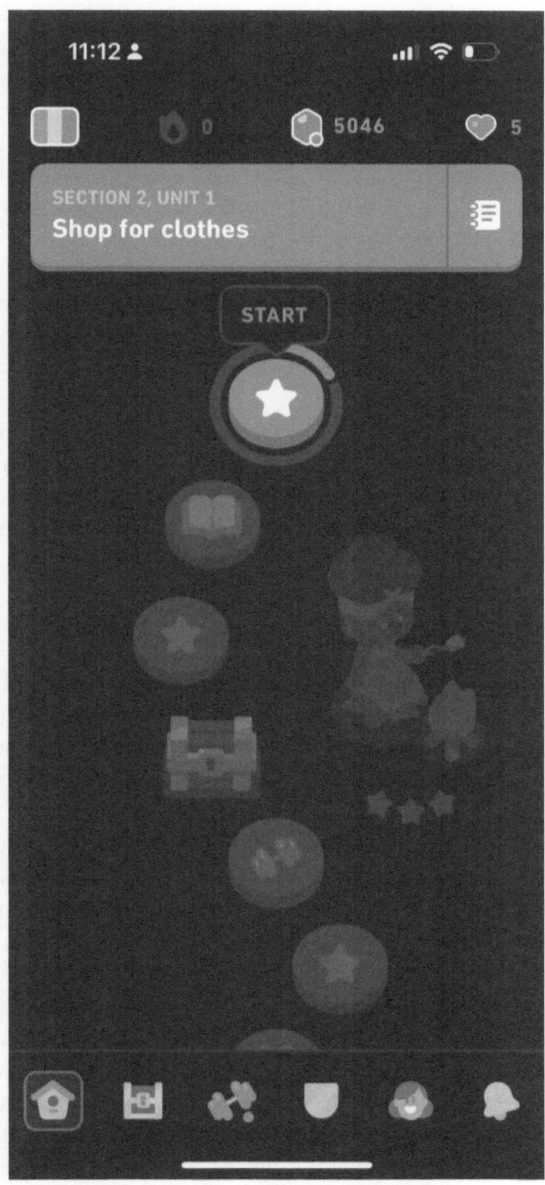

**Figure 3.6** The personalised Duolingo learning environment

Predictive analytics in education, an application of learning analytics, can identify at-risk students by analysing patterns in key metrics such as attendance, participation, and performance data. This proactive approach allows educators to intervene early, providing targeted support to help students succeed.

### 3.4.1  PERSONALISED, HIGHER EDUCATION

The challenge with implementing personalisation in higher education isn't so much a technical one as it is a systemic issue. Current university policies and structures often focus on standardised curricula and fixed schedules which don't easily adapt to the flexible, individualised approach of AI-driven personalised learning. Traditional assessment methods, like standardised, pre-scheduled exams and grading systems, are also not well-suited to accommodating personalised pacing and content.

Another challenge is ensuring that personalised learning pathways align with accreditation standards and degree requirements. Universities must ensure that these personalised experiences meet the necessary academic standards and learning outcomes expected of their programs. This might mean rethinking how credit hours and course completion are measured.

Despite these challenges, the benefits of personalised learning in higher education are substantial. It can increase student engagement, improve retention rates, and better accommodate diverse learning styles. As AI technologies continue to develop, integrating personalised learning into higher education is likely to become more common, offering a more flexible and student-centred approach.

### 3.5  GAMIFICATION: EDUCATION FOR THE TIKTOK GENERATION

Gamification is the application of game-design elements and principles in non-game contexts, such as education. It leverages elements like points, badges, and leaderboards to encourage participation and enhance the learning experience. The core idea is simple: make learning more enjoyable and fun by motivating extrinsic reward-centres.

From the student perspective, extrinsic motivation involves engaging in an activity to earn rewards or avoid negative outcomes, this is in contrast with intrinsic motivation, which describes self-motivated students doing something because it is inherently interesting, valuable or enjoyable. Looking back, higher education has typically relied upon the intrinsic motivation of students who are assured (repeatedly) by friends, family, and society, that they will be rewarded for their efforts.

Gamification is not new to higher education. Traditionally, higher education and society place significance on student results. Universities reward students with special titles for consistently achieving high grades (first class honours), and industry review student transcripts which contains a numbered grade. The sentiment goes that higher grades should improve a student's chances of getting that dream job. This is an example of extrinsic motivation, it is not the learning and achievement itself that is motivating the student, but the high weighted average mark (WAM). Within shifting job markets, rising costs of living, and shortened attention spans, perhaps pulling further at the extrinsic motivational heartstrings could serve as a way to motivate student learning.

Appropriate, technologically-powered applications of gamification in higher education include the use of points, badges, and leaderboards [16]. Points are a fundamental gamification element that can be awarded for completing tasks, answering questions correctly, or participating in class discussions. Ideally, a point-based system could be integrated into a learning management system to provide immediate feedback, track progress, and even be exchanged for small rewards.

Badges serve as a form of recognition for achieving specific milestones or mastering particular skills. They can represent various achievements, such as completing a course module, demonstrating proficiency in a subject, or displaying good study habits. Badges provide a sense of accomplishment, but also allow students to showcase their achievements to peers, fostering a sense of community and friendly competition. Moreover, the collection of badges can encourage students to explore different learning paths and challenge themselves in new areas.

Leaderboards are another effective gamification tool that can boost motivation by introducing a competitive element to learning. By ranking students based on their performance or participation, leaderboards can create a sense of excitement. Courses at UNSW's School of Computer Science and Engineering (CSE) such as Software Engineering Fundamentals have successfully utilised Leaderboards to anonymously rank students' software accuracy. Anonymity, or pseudo-anonymity is essential to avoid discouraging lower-performing students. Leaderboards can be made more inclusive by recognising different types of achievements, such as effort or improvement, not just top scores. This approach ensures that all students feel motivated and valued, regardless of their initial skill level.

Gamification has been in many other domains, including gaming itself to motivate particular behaviours and engagement. The very popular video game Dota 2 uses various gamification elements including badges, points, and leaderboards, with the former depicted in Figure 3.7.

**Figure 3.7** The Popular DotA 2's Badge System to Reward Player Progression

When thoughtfully integrated into the educational process, gamification elements like points, badges, and leaderboards can enhance student motivation, engagement, and overall learning outcomes.

## 3.6  ACADEMIC INTEGRITY AND MACHINE LEARNING

Recent developments in transformer-based machine learning (the technology which powers tools such as ChatGPT) has sent shockwaves into the assessment community. These systems can generate coherent, high-quality written content, making it easier for students to bypass the learning process and submit work that isn't their own. Since the output is novel, existing plagiarism detection systems such as TurnItIn are not able to successfully detect the misconduct. This poses a serious problem: how can teachers assure that students engaged in learning activities, while operating at the scale of modern higher education? In this section, we look to how technology can help address the very problem it helped create.

### 3.6.1  LEARNING ANALYTICS

Learning analytics is an application of data science techniques, accounting for the idiosyncrasies of the educational landscape [15]. Learning analytics have many applications, from automatically detecting at-risk students, to gaining the knowledge required to be able to effectively optimise courses and training.

The first forward-looking application of learning analytics we will explore is academic misconduct detection. By analysing writing patterns, engagement, source material, and linguistic styles, machine-learning-based verification systems are tasked with identifying potential instances of misconduct, such as engaging with contract cheating services, or offloading assessments to generative AI.

There are two major approaches to detecting academic misconduct. The first is via keystroke logging and clickstream data, which attempts to detect irregularities in behaviour within the learning environment as students work on assessments over time [22]. The approach, while simple and effective, has two major criticisms. First, the approach relies on students developing their assessment (essay, code writing, etc) within a designated environment. This could prove inequitable for students who use third-party authoring tools, for example for accessibility purposes [19]. The second criticism of this approach is surrounding general privacy, with many students, educators and privacy advocates worried that online invigilated exams are a type of surveillance [10].

The second approach to detecting academic misconduct with learning analytics is via style detection. Style detection is the algorithmic validation of style over time [7, 5], and hinges on the idea that each individual has idiosyncrasies in their output. Most work in style validation is in writing style, but similar approaches are being explored in code writing and other domains. The approach, while more complex and prone to false positives [6], has clear benefits compared to behaviour logging as it is less important where the authorship of assessments took place, and no privacy-violating monitoring is required. The final product (be it an essay, source code, or any other written work) can simply be validated against previous examples of a student's work.

These approaches offer a potential "way out" for the growing concern academics and educators have over the use of generative AI to produce novel works.

### 3.6.2 ONLINE INVIGILATION AND PSEUDO-INVIGILATION

The crammed lecture halls filled with nervous students hurriedly writing their final exams is a familiar picture for many around the world. In-person, invigilated examinations have served academic institutions for centuries, and for good reason— they offer high levels of assessment security. However, since the COVID-19 pandemic forced alternatives to in-person exams, Australian institutions are demonstrating reluctance in returning to in-person examinations. While there are many sound arguments in opposition of final exams for pedagogical purposes, it is clear that the high cost of running in-person exams is a key factor. Venue costs, staff costs, and materials all contribute to a relatively high cost for institutions to run on examinations.

As institutions looked to alternative approaches to examinations during the COVID-19 pandemic, online proctoring or online invigilation technology promised the best of both worlds: invigilated examinations that students could take from their bedrooms.

Online, invigilated examination software such as Proctorio [3] and ProctorU [4] were used extensively during pandemic-effected teaching periods. The tools work by constantly monitoring audio-visual feeds of the students' environments during an exam, and have human invigilators or machine learning algorithms analyse the feeds to ensure a) the person in the feed matches the photo ID of the enrolled student, and b) that the student is not appearing to receive assistance from someone else online or in the room.

Many educators and academics expressed significant concern with these proctored systems, citing data privacy violations, biases and discrimination allegations. In one report, media site The Verge explores an investigation of online proctoring systems which falsely flag students of colour to academic misconduct teams because the machine learning algorithms cannot detect a human in the frame [3]

'You're being watched and recorded, every breath'

As the dust has settled following the emergency response to COVID-19 teaching, it becomes clearer that the future of technologically-driven academic integrity will require privacy-friendly alternatives.

---

[3]https://proctorio.com/

[4]https://www.proctoru.com/

### 3.6.2.1 Case Study: Real Talk with Deep Speaker

Due to the serious concerns with full-blown proctoring approaches, academics explored more student and privacy-friendly alternatives. One innovative approach to maintaining academic integrity is speaker verification. This technology utilises voice recognition to verify a student's identity during oral examinations or assessments [18]. By ensuring that the student who registered for the course is the same person taking an online assessment, institutions can prevent impersonation and ensure that assessments reflect the student's own understanding and abilities. This method is less intrusive than other forms of surveillance.

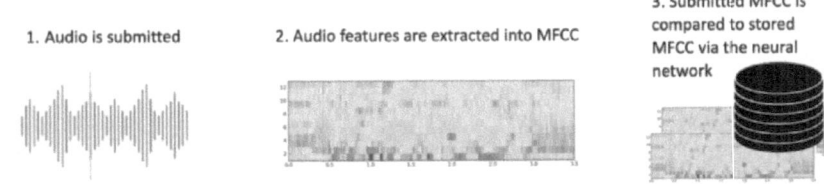

**Figure 3.8** The Deep Speaker System for Verifying Student Voice, as used in the Real Talk system [18]

The tool as developed and evaluated by [17], facilitated AI-invigilated oral assessments. Students were prompted to begin their online oral assessment by verifying that their microphone and speaker equipment was functional. Once ready, students were played back a pre-recorded audio question spoken by their teacher. The questions, while provided to all students for a particular assessment, asked questions specific to the student's work. For example, "Can you explain, line by line, the code your wrote for assessment A". Students then had to respond to the question in real time, with the AI system verifying the respondent's identity. The study found that the tool was successful in delivering scalable oral assessments in large computing courses, and paints a picture for a future, privacy-friendly approach to high-stake assessments.

### 3.6.3 FUTURE ASSESSMENT SECURITY

Contract cheating and generative AI tools have created new challenges for maintaining academic integrity in higher education. Meanwhile, the very technology which threatened assessment offers promising solutions to these challenges. Learning analytics, including keystroke logging and style detection, provide ways to verify student work without invasive surveillance. Online invigilation systems, while controversial, offer alternatives to traditional in-person exams. Less intrusive methods like speaker verification present a balance between integrity and privacy concerns.

As the education industry moves forward, it's clear that institutions have a variety of switches and levers which can be applied to design assessment of various levels of security and cost. More sophisticated and accurate style detection algorithms can monitor assessments conducted over time, while ethical approaches to learning analytics and online invigilation tools can be applied in high-stakes assessment environments.

Ultimately, the goal is to create an academic environment that embraces technological advancements while maintaining the integrity and value of education. As AI continues to evolve, so too must our approaches to academic integrity, balancing security, privacy, and equitable access to education.

## 3.7  TECHNOLOGY IN THE CLASSROOM

Higher education institutions are grappling with the challenge of encouraging students to return to campus. Online course materials such as recorded lectures, long commutes, and high costs of living are motivating students to engage asynchronously with their education. While this flexibility is positive for many students, educators are teaching to empty lecture halls thinking "what's the point?".

This section explores how technology can be integrated into the classroom to create immersive, collaborative and exciting learning environments that aren't available at home.

### 3.7.1  THE CONNECTED CLASSROOM

The concept of a connected classroom has emerged as a response to the evolving needs of modern education. Imagine a hybrid learning environment which can blend in-person and online students, creating an accessible and flexible learning experience.

*To ensure students and educators working remotely can fully participate in group collaboration and meetings, education workspaces will need technology to help*

**Figure 3.9**  Microsoft's imagining of the future classroom

*bridge the divide between the old, in-person models and the new, hybrid and remote spaces.*[5]

Connected classrooms are an amalgamation of existing audio-visual and networking technologies, and typically feature:

- Expansive video screens: Large displays to allow remote students to participate as if they were physically present in one-to-one scale, enabling face-to-face interactions with instructors and peers.
- High-quality audio systems: modern audio signal processing technologies such as room-aware, 3D audio helps place virtual speakers in a 3D environment
- Interactive whiteboards: These allow real-time sharing of content and annotations visible to all students, regardless of location.

While educators would enjoy seeing students returning to campus en-masse, issues such as geographic constraints and health issues present a number of barriers for students engaging only in in-person education. Future-looking, connected classrooms offer flexibility and higher-quality learning environments for all students, while preparing them for the increasingly remote future of work.

### 3.7.1.1   Case Study: UNSW's Classroom of the Future

The University of New South Wales Faculty of Engineering's AI-driven connected classroom is an advanced Microsoft Teams-connected classroom. The classroom allows dynamic multi-camera views, and instructors and students alike can easily interact with each other with equal ease.

> *the Digital Teaching Studio at UNSW Engineering, built in collaboration with Microsoft Surface, Steelcase, QSC, and Crestron Electronics, it is built from the ground up to make intelligent Microsoft Teams Room features sing. This may be the most sophisticated meeting room in the world, and it answers the challenge of the post-pandemic university – Associate Professor David Kellerman*

## 3.8   EXTENDED REALITY (XR) IN EDUCATION

Extended reality (XR) is a family of technologies, namely virtual reality (VR), augmented reality (AR) and other, similar technologies which seek to augment, replace, or enhance audio-visual sensory information.

This section explores how XR technologies can be applied in education to create mind-bending, eye-opening and transformative learning opportunities for students.

---

[5]https://learn.microsoft.com/en-us/microsoftteams/devices-for-education

**Figure 3.10** UNSW's Digital Teaching Studio

### 3.8.1 SIMULATION AND TRAINING

Recent developments and cost reductions paint an exciting future for extended reality, but the origins stretch back further than many realise. Flight simulators are an example of how technology revolutionised training and education.

Since as early as the 1930s, flight simulator technology has allowed pilots to experience realistic flight conditions, practice emergency procedures, and hone their skills without leaving the ground [2]. Modern flight simulators, with their high-fidelity graphics, motion platforms, and haptic feedback, represent an advanced form of XR that has been quietly shaping professional training for years.

Efficacy evaluations of simulator-based experiential learning goes back to the late 1980s, where water-based crash training was found to have occurred in 4 out of 5 helicopter pilots who survived real crashes [14].

We can draw valuable lessons from the flight simulator's evolution — from its early days as a niche training tool to its current status as an indispensable part of pilot certification. The proven track record of flight simulators in improving learning outcomes, ensuring safety, and providing cost-effective training paints an optimistic picture for many other safety critical fields.

Many children (often with the help of parents) around the world were tasked with building a Paper Maché model volcano at one point in their childhood. Other than being a fun, hands-on learning task— there must be a reason why educators have continued this volcanic tradition for so long. The answer may be simple: it's an **immersive, experiential and visual**[6] learning experience.

Just as the Paper Maché volcano has long served as a proxy for hands-on science, Extended Reality (XR) technologies could very well erupt as the modern equivalent.

---

[6]And, visiting a real volcano is typically unsuitable for many classroom teachers

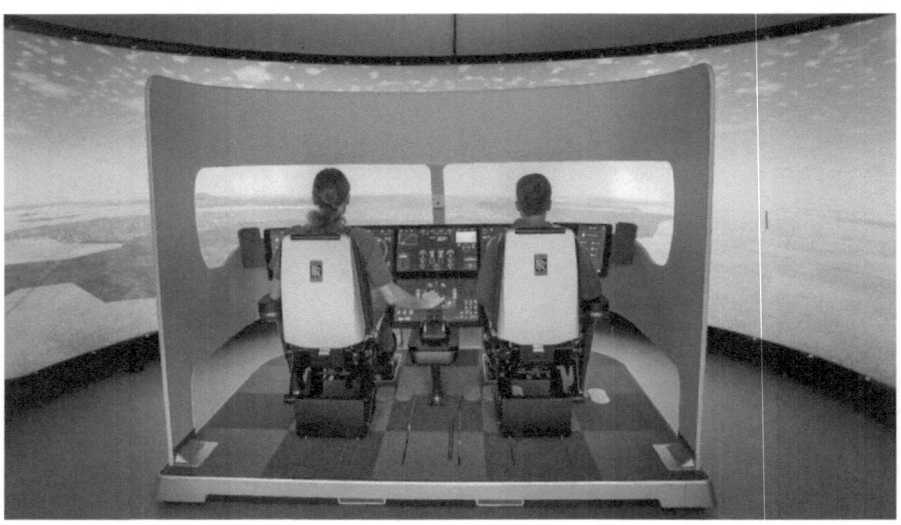

**Figure 3.11** A Modern Flight Simulator

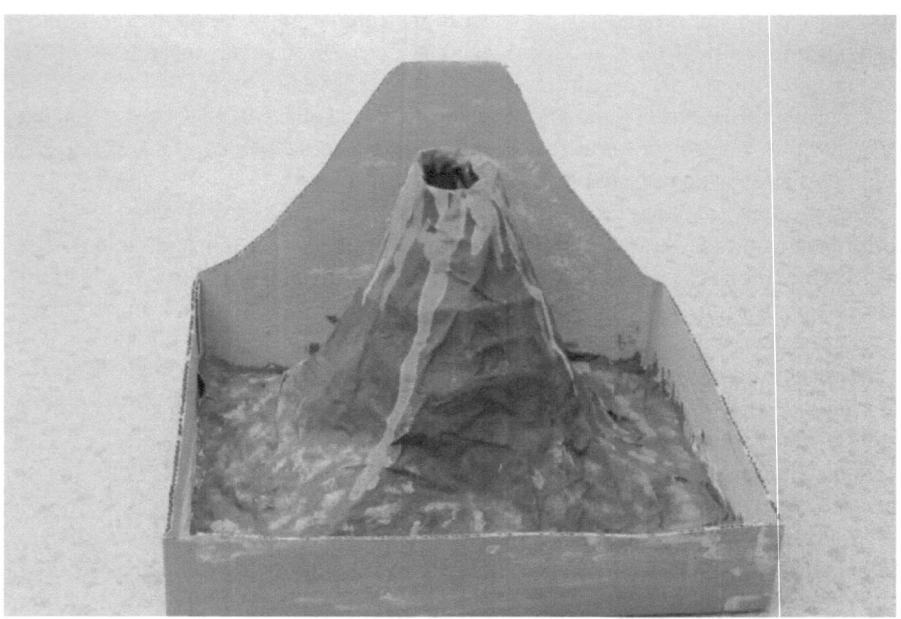

**Figure 3.12** Paper Mache volcano

While the traditional volcano model allows students to physically craft and observe a simulated eruption, XR takes this concept to new heights. Virtual Reality (VR), a subset of Extended Reality, can transport students to real volcanic environments, allowing wide-eyed students to stand at the base of an active volcano, feeling the rumble beneath their feet and witnessing the spectacle of an eruption in high-fidelity detail and scale.

With augmented reality technology (AR), picture overlays transform a classroom tabletop into a dynamic, 3D model of tectonic plate movements.

**Figure 3.13**   A student wearing VR goggles learning about gears

While generations of students have been captivated by their handcrafted volcanoes, XR has the similar potential to inspire students across a vast array of subjects, making it the 'paper maché volcano' of the 21st century – a versatile, engaging tool that brings learning to life in new ways.

As head mounted displays (HMD) (the most common form of Virtual Reality) have dramatically come down in cost, explorations into the adoption of VR in classrooms has begun. [13] analysed the organisational, institutional, contextual and practical challenges and opportunities in the implementation of HMD VR in K-12 school contexts. They found that while teachers envision the potential of VR technologies in the classroom, economic weakness is highlighted as the major obstacle. In Bring Your Own Devices (BYOD) classrooms, serious concerns surrounding equality and access still limit the potential of VR today.

Looking forward[7], we could extrapolate that costs will continue to drop until the technology is available to most students in developed nations [8]. Once accessibility

---

[7]and with a little help of Moore's law

is solved, the applications of VR in education are endless. [25] explores applications such as food digestion showing the process of how the human body digests food, to teaching concepts of electromagnetism and the magnetic field, as well as create experiential learning opportunities, such as transporting students back in time to prehistoric eras, sporting fields, or planets.

## 3.9   THE ROAD AHEAD

As we stand at the brink of what feels like a new era of education, we must not forget the lessons we have learned from a rich history of education technology. From the earliest flight simulators teaching life-saving skills, to the proliferation of education made possible via the simple cassette tape, the potential to transform lives remains as exciting as ever. Time and time again, educators and academics have been ready at the forefront of this revolution, together.

Looking forward, the biggest challenges facing education are the very same which were introduced by technology itself. Threats to academic integrity brought upon by generative AI perhaps place the most stress on a massified educational environment. In this sense, the road ahead is challenging. Institutions will need to maintain a focus on learning outcomes, protecting academic integrity, prioritising privacy, and perhaps sacrificing some of the massification it has so far enjoyed thanks to technology.

But as technology evolves, educators' ultimate goal remains unchanged: to nurture curious minds, foster critical thinking, and prepare students for the challenging world they will inherit. From the simple cassette tape, to million dollar flight simulators, technology remains just a tool in this most ancient of pursuits.

## REFERENCES

1. Elon Musk joins call for pause in creation of giant AI 'digital minds' — Artificial intelligence (AI) — The Guardian.
2. Flight simulator – Wikipedia.
3. Students of color are getting flagged to teachers because Proctorio testing software can't see them – The Verge.
4. The 50 Most Popular MOOCs of All Time (Updated For 2021) – Online Course Report.
5. Sadia Afroz, Michael Brennan, and Rachel Greenstadt. Detecting hoaxes, frauds, and deception in writing style online. *Proceedings – IEEE Symposium on Security and Privacy*, pages 461–475, 2012.
6. Nawaf Ali, Musa Hindi, and Roman V. Yampolskiy. Evaluation of authorship attribution software on a Chat bot corpus. *23rd International Symposium on Information, Communication and Automation Technologies, ICAT 2011*, 2011.
7. Alexander Amigud and Phillip Dawson. The law and the outlaw: is legal prohibition a viable solution to the contract cheating problem? *Assessment and Evaluation in Higher Education*, 45(1):98–108, 1 2020.
8. Paola Araiza-Alba, Therese Keane, and Jordy Kaufman. Are we ready for virtual reality in K–12 classrooms? *Technology, Pedagogy and Education*, 31(4):471–491, 8 2022.

9. Oyebola Olusola Ayeni, Nancy Mohd Al Hamad, Onyebuchi Nneamaka Chisom, Blessing Osawaru, Ololade Elizabeth Adewusi, Oyebola Olusola Ayeni, Nancy Mohd Al Hamad, Onyebuchi Nneamaka Chisom, Blessing Osawaru, and Ololade Elizabeth Adewusi. AI in education: A review of personalized learning and educational technology. *https://gsconlinepress.com/journals/gscarr/sites/default/files/GSCARR-2024-0062.pdf*, 18(2):261–271, 2 2024.

10. Phillip Dawson. Strategies for Using Online Invigilated Exams.

11. Deakin University. Remote learning at Deakin: from 1978 to now, 2021. Accessed: 2023-07-24.

12. Department of Education and Training. uCube – Higher Education Statistics. Technical report, 2018.

13. Göran Fransson, Jörgen Holmberg, and Claes Westelius. The challenges of using head mounted virtual reality in K-12 schools from a teacher perspective. *Education and Information Technologies*, 25(4):3383–3404, 7 2020.

14. Karsten Hytten. Helicopter crash in water: Effects of simulator Escape training. *Acta Psychiatrica Scandinavica*, 80:73–78, 1989.

15. Mohammad Khalil and Martin Ebner. What is Learning Analytics about? A Survey of Different Methods Used in 2013-2015. 6 2016.

16. Jonathon Meyers, Andrew Cain, Jake Renzella, and Alex Cummaudo. A Proposal for Integrating Gamification into Task-Oriented Portfolio Assessment. *Proceedings of 2018 IEEE International Conference on Teaching, Assessment, and Learning for Engineering, TALE 2018*, pages 1022–1027, 7 2018.

17. Jake Renzella, Andrew Cain, and Jean Guy Schneider. Real Talk: Illuminating Online Student Understanding with Authentic Discussion Tools. In *SIGCSE 2021 – Proceedings of the 52nd ACM Technical Symposium on Computer Science Education*, pages 886–892. Association for Computing Machinery, Inc, 3 2021.

18. Jake Renzella, Andrew Cain, and Jean-Guy Schneider. Verifying student identity in oral assessments with deep speaker. *Computers and Education: Artificial Intelligence*, 3:100044, 1 2022.

19. Lesley T. Sefcik, T. Veeran-Colton, M. Baird, C. Price, and S. Steyn. An examination of student user experience (UX) and perceptions of remote invigilation during online assessment. *Australasian Journal of Educational Technology*, 38(2):49–69, 2 2022.

20. Andrew Taylor, Jake Renzella, and Alexandra Vassar. Foundations first: Improving C's viability in introductory programming courses with the debugging C compiler. In *SIGCSE 2023 – Proceedings of the 54th ACM Technical Symposium on Computer Science Education*, volume 1, pages 346–352. Association for Computing Machinery, Inc, 3 2023.

21. Andrew Taylor, Alexandra Vassar, Jake Renzella, and Hammond Pearce. dcc - help: Transforming the role of the compiler by generating context-aware error explanations with large language models. In *SIGCSE 2024 Andrew Taylor, Jake Renzella, and Alexandra Vassar. Foundations first: Improving c's viability in introductory programming courses with the debugging c compiler Proceedings of the 55th ACM Technical Symposium on Computer Science Education*, volume 1, pages 1314–1320. Association for Computing Machinery, Inc, 3 2024.

22. Kelly Trezise, Tracii Ryan, Paula de Barba, and Gregor Kennedy. Detecting Academic Misconduct Using Learning Analytics. *Journal of Learning Analytics*, 6(3):90–104, 12 2019.

23. Karin Verspoor. 'Fighting fire with fire' — using LLMs to combat LLM hallucinations. *Nature 2024 630:8017*, 630(8017):569–570, 6 2024.

24. Jia-Yu Yao, Kun-Peng Ning, Zhen-Hui Liu, Mu-Nan Ning, and Li Yuan. LLM Lies: Hallucinations are not Bugs, but Features as Adversarial Examples. 10 2023.

25. Weiping Zhang and Zhuo Wang. Theory and Practice of VR/AR in K-12 Science Education—A Systematic Review. *Sustainability 2021, Vol. 13, Page 12646*, 13(22):12646, 11 2021.

# 4  Exploring the Integration of Design Thinking into the Engineering Discipline

*Alexandra Vassar*
School of Computer Science and Engineering, UNSW Sydney
Kensington, Australia

## 4.1  EXPLORING THE INTEGRATION OF DESIGN THINKING INTO THE ENGINEERING DISCIPLINE

Ask someone to describe where the term 'design' can be applied, and chances are their mind will gravitate towards aesthetics – the cut of a piece of clothing, the curves of furniture, the architectural elements of a house or the composition of an art piece. I would imagine that not many would name engineering in that list, even though it is a field that lies at the very heart of problem-solving, and design, as a discipline, is centred on understanding problems and crafting solutions. So too, the idea of using design thinking to guide definition of problems in engineering is gaining momentum, and represents a huge shift in how we approach technical education and problem-solving.

The marriage of design thinking and engineering recognises the fact that the challenges faced by modern engineers are not purely technical, but often involve complex human, social, and environmental factors that require a more integrated approach. And what can be more human than empathy – putting the people at the core of the solution first? Numerous case studies and real-world examples demonstrate the effectiveness of design thinking in tackling wicked problems, from improving healthcare delivery to addressing climate change concerns. One such example of this successful integration is the Mayo Clinic's OB Nest program, which used design thinking to explore a new, low-risk pregnancy care model [9]. Pregnancy care is usually focused on clinical outcomes, with a complex regiment of frequent medical appointments. On average, women with low-risk pregnancies are required to attend 12-14 appointments over a forty-week period. Using design thinking to empathise with expectant mothers and understand their needs in care models, the new model redistributes care based on individual patient needs by providing self-measurement tools, and continuous flexible access to a care team [9]. The result of de-medicalising prenatal care for low-risk pregnancies has led to improved experiences for women overall, placing as

DOI: 10.1201/9781032702797-4

much focus on the emotional experience, as on clinical outcomes. A by-product of this success is a benefit for cost savings.

The role of design in engineering has evolved significantly, and good design is no longer an afterthought, but a critical factor in determining the functionality and user acceptance of a proposed solution. Going hand in hand with this, is the ability to think creatively, which is becoming an increasingly valuable skill for engineers across all disciplines. Industry expectations for engineering graduates have also shifted accordingly. Employers now look for professionals who can not only apply technical knowledge but also navigate ambiguous problem spaces, understand their users, and generate innovative ideas. However, teaching design thinking skills within the engineering curriculum presents unique challenges in a discipline that is so heavily focused on technical capabilities [1].

Traditionally, engineering curricula is made up of subjects that offer clear-cut, formulaic approaches to problem-solving. Engineering design courses, which require a more nuanced and creative skill-set, are often not introduced until later in the degree program. This delay can lead to difficulties for students in understanding and practising engineering design, due to the contrast between traditional engineering curricula and design-based engineering courses which requires a significant shift from the convergent thinking emphasised in traditional engineering science to a blend of convergent and divergent thinking techniques [12].

While science-based subjects provide students with definitive "right" or "wrong" answers and strategic, formula-based approaches, design challenges often have multiple valid solutions depending on user needs and context. The breadth of this type of problem space can be a new and uncomfortable experience for some students who are accustomed to more structured problem-solving methods. However, this type of ambiguity and lack of clear cut solutions is important for developing our skills, and developing "outside-the-box" thinking. Early research into the integration of design thinking into engineering has shown that student teams who consistently challenge assumptions throughout the design process tend to perform better than those who adhere rigidly to initial concepts [12].

Other work has found positive project performance with the incorporation of design thinking practices [36]. The development of divergent thinking cannot be gained by merely slotting a design subject, as an afterthought, into the engineering curriculum – a multifaceted approach is needed. Scattered across the curriculum, internships provide real-world exposure, makerspaces offer hands-on experiential learning, project-based courses simulate real open-ended problem spaces and focus on early development of important soft skills. By embedding Design Thinking principles throughout the curriculum, engineering educators can foster a mindset that embraces ambiguity, encourages creative problem-solving, and prepares students for the complex, interdisciplinary challenges they will face in their professional careers. More than that, these subjects provide students with a space to experiment and to choose projects in which they have an interest.

## 4.2 DESIGN THINKING

The process of design is never simple. Imagine a series of nesting dolls. Who are these nesting dolls for? Are they for little hands, or big hands? In either case, each one has to be just the right size to fit into the next one. Thinking about who these dolls would be for would change how hard they are to open, and would also affect the patterns on the dolls themselves. Each two halves of a doll must meet precisely to have visual continuity. Who knew that such a simple toy would involve so much thinking, and the thinking can only start when we establish who these nested dolls are destined for. Similarly in real life, design involves thinking about a target audience, whilst also considering the multiple levels of interacting elements within a system, which may be nested or connected to another system and to another and so on.

Central to the principle of design is the ability to engage in [20]. However, as a discipline, design thinking did not emerge until the later part of the twentieth century, when Rowe used the term 'Design Thinking', as a title of his book [37]. In the ensuing decades, the process has moved from being an innovation buzzword to widely diffused practice [25, 32]. Multiple models have emerged that have described design thinking [10], with the community agreeing that a framework is needed to sustain the process across a variety of industries. The perceptions of design thinking are diverse, some describe it as a mindset or as a group of characteristics and principles [34, 12]; others consider it to be more as a process with distinct phases [32, 24, 31]. Liedtka mentions that despite the calls for the adoption of the design thinking process, "even the term itself is a subject of controversy among its practitioners and advocates." [25, p. 926]. In fact, there appears to still be some substantial differences in the definition of the design thinking process, and agreement on its virtues [32, 18, 7, 6, 17].

The tension perhaps centres upon the varied origin of the term [17]. Whilst design scholars have described the process extensively in design contexts [23], the term has only in the last decade become widely recognised in management practice as a process of creative problem solving [25]. Micheli *et. al.* in their systematic literature review of the process, propose eleven key principal attributes of design thinking [32]. One of the most commonly occurring themes in literature as related to the design thinking process is creativity and innovation [32]. Other commonly occurring themes are the user centredness of the process, frequently cited as a core feature of design thinking [7], its ability to problem-solve effectively, iteration and experimentation of design thinking, interdisciplinary collaboration, abductive reasoning, and tolerance of ambiguity and failure, amongst others.

Despite the debate, design thinking, as a non-prescriptive approach to problem solving, is most well known for its categorisation into phases. Although there are variations on the names and number of phases included, when the most frequently cited models are considered a certain degree of commonality emerges [32]. Design Thinking is a non-linear, user-centric ideology and process that provides a solution-based approach to problem solving, consistently considering how the solution meets the needs of the user [34]. It is widely known to tackle "wicked" problems, ill-defined problems that are essentially unique and that have no immediate or ultimate test of a solution. Solutions to these wicked problems are not true-or-false, but rather good-or-bad [27]. These kinds of problems require creative out of the box thinking and solutions.

A number of frameworks define the process, but a number of distinct stages can be seen across all the frameworks. One of the common, core steps that we start with in the design thinking process is working through empathy to understand the user and their needs (to empathise). This helps us to define the problem, where the gathered insights from our empathy are synthesised to clearly articulate a core problem that needs to be addressed. The latter half of the process involves generating ideas – and is hence a judgement free zone. Following the ideating, a selection of ideas that are considered to be the most promising are turned into prototypes, allowing the exploration of different possibilities and the identification of potential issues early on in the design process. Finally, the prototypes are put to the test, however, the process does not end there! This is an iterative process, which means that we collect feedback from our users through all the stages, and apply it to help redefine the problem and define a solution. The process is simultaneously abductive (what is it that we are trying to solve), inductive (how are we trying to solve this problem?) and deductive (what is the result that we are looking for in our problem solving?) [10]. This means that all parts of the equation are considered starting with understanding what the actual problem is that is being solved. Throughout the process, however, the main aspect of the design thinking process is its focus on the needs of the user whilst also being practical and flexible with using some trial and error methods [10].

You may be surprised to find out that in 2009, the company AirBnB, that provides homestay accommodation across the world, was close to going bankrupt. Within the startup game, they were just another idea that was getting swallowed up, with company revenue at just $200 a week [13]. The three co-founders of the business spent hours poring over the search results to understand why the business was just not growing, and what caught their attention is that the photos of the properties were just not up to par. People were using their phone cameras or using other images that were often the wrong resolution, were blurry, or were not appropriate to showcase the properties. It is no wonder that customers did not book properties when they did not even know for sure what those properties looked like! Surprisingly the team decided to take matters into their own hands, and travelled to New York to spend some time with the hosts of properties and to help them take higher resolution and more professional photographs of their properties. The team at this point was really going off a hunch, but this hunch was rooted in a higher understanding the needs of their customer base. A week later, the revenue doubled – the first financial improvement the company has seen in approximately eight months [13]. AirBnb has grown steadily since then to a multi-billion dollar online platform. However, without that moment where the founders found themselves empathising with their customer and learning more about the customer's needs that was a real turning point in the future of the company.

It is not hard to see why design thinking really works. Solving a problem for a group of people, who are involved in first understanding the problem – surely this screams as a recipe for success. The other day I walked past a series of postcards that

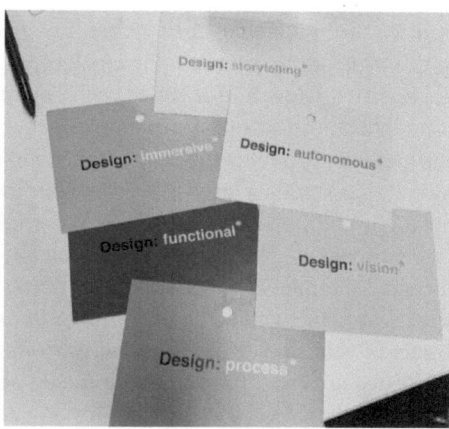

**Figure 4.1** A series of postcards introducing the concepts of Design Thinking to students

were advertising the virtues of design and design thinking and were inviting students to find out more about these key concepts (Figure 4.1). What was most interesting about this set of postcards, is that perhaps the designers themselves did not consider the principles of design thinking when designing these. Despite their aesthetic value, it looks like the "empathise" step was forgotten with some questionable contrast appearing on a series of the cards. For example, the postcard that goes on to explain functionality as part of the process of design thinking has a dark text on a dark background, and ironically the postcard with vision of design thinking has a light text on a light background, therefore making it very hard to envision at all. This is just a simple example of what can happen when the key concepts of design thinking are not taken into consideration.

## 4.3 DESIGN IN ENGINEERING EDUCATION

From experience, I was an Engineering student about twenty years ago. Just two decades back, there was no design thinking or even really design being taught at university as part of the engineering curriculum. The courses were full of assessments and exams, that were broadly made up of clear-cut problems, where there was most definitely a correct answer. This put emphasis on rote learning, memorising facts and formulas and reciting those back. I found it to be fairly uninspiring. This continued until I was in the third year of university and by sheer accident had chosen Human Computer Interaction as an elective. This was my first encounter with user-centric thinking, iterative design processes, and with an introduction to creativity in problem solving. This was a turning point for me, as up until this point, I had contemplated changing degrees. But here, I finally got a glimpse of why I had decided to go into engineering, and what kind of problem solving I found to be particularly fascinating! It just made so much sense to me to involve the user, and to focus on iterating through the stages until an optimal solution (note that it may not be perfect) be reached through trial and error processes.

It makes sense that it was only a matter of time, before we seriously started considering incorporating this type of thinking into the curriculum. Running for the first time in 2020, at the University of New South Wales each engineering discipline now requires students to complete a core second-year course focused on applying design thinking to real-world problems. From having taught this course myself twice, I find that undergraduate engineering students are often thrown by the course – they don't quite know where to place it and how to go about the material. In the software engineering discipline, whilst most students go into the course with the idea that they will be able to "fly through" the material, once they are doing the course, they find that the large problem space and the wicked nature of the proposed problems actually leads to a large investment of time and effort. I would like to think that this may be a turning point for the students, as it was for me, and some do email me in later years describing their enjoyment of the process and asking for advice about other projects they are doing where they want to apply the same process.

But these types of courses may have a huge part to play in engineering education. Traditional engineering education often focuses heavily on technical skills and theoretical concepts, sometimes at the expense of real-world applications. Design thinking addresses this by shifting the focus to empathy. Empathising with users helps to define the problem initially, and to re-imagine a solution that maintains user-centeredness. Students learn to consider the human aspects of engineering problems, not just technical specifications. Bridging the gap between theoretical knowledge and practical application, the most important element of these courses is it ignites something magical in our future engineers – there is nothing like the feeling of ideating and working together to solve difficult problems – probably the very reason they first enrolled in engineering.

So the question remains as to what effects if any are there to integrating design thinking practices into engineering curriculum has on student learning outcomes. Pedagogical theory seems to support the principals of design thinking – in fact, the main characteristics of design thinking, such as collaboration and iteration, are relevant to pedagogical theories and cognitive psychology. The concepts of collaboration being beneficial to learning have been outlined as early as the 1970s, as part of Vygotsky's social learning theory [44], the concept of iterations builds into our growth mindset and theories of the self [11], which has also been associated with higher achievement in studies and greater resilience in students [46]. The iterative nature of design thinking – involving stages like empathising, defining, ideating, prototyping, and testing – teaches students to embrace failure as a learning opportunity and to continually refine their ideas. This further builds into the growth mindset, and aligns with industry, where innovation and continuous improvement are paramount. By encouraging multiple iterations and rapid prototyping, design thinking helps students develop resilience and adaptability, crucial traits for success in the fast-paced world of engineering.

A vital aspect of these types of courses, and the process of ideating is the ability to work together with others, this may be within your own discipline, or across several disciplines. Any course with teamwork will illicit very strong reactions from students and educators alike (not always positive). There are plenty of memes making their way round disavowing the virtues of teamwork, and plenty more that centre of constantly being let down by your teammates. Memes aside, in real life, engineering challenges rarely exist in isolation; they often intersect with economic, social, and environmental concerns. This complexity often necessitates collaboration in industry and beyond, and design thinking fosters this collaborative spirit inherently. For those that do get to have a positive experience in a collaborative environment, where all students have come to learn and to engage with the process and the project, they get to experience the Mecca of ideas. Teams are often composed of individuals with varied backgrounds, skills, and experiences and this combination is more likely to generate innovative solutions. For those teams, where things are not as collegial as they would want, students develop the communication and interpersonal skills necessary for success in the workplace, in addition to potential conflict resolution skills. There are however, also pedagogical theories supporting teamwork and collaborative learning [19, 42].

Collaborative learning introduces the concept of a collective working memory, based on the principles of cognitive load theory, where the cognitive load of a task is shared between members of the group [42]. As Kirschner (2018) [19] posits, this shared cognitive resource provides team members with a dynamic scaffold of information, drawn not from external sources, but from the interactions of the team itself. This collective memory becomes a readily accessible repository of knowledge, available precisely when needed, thereby significantly enhancing learning opportunities. For this reason, teams can tackle more complex problems than individuals working alone. The collective knowledge and skills of a team allow for a more thorough exploration of challenges and potential solutions. The collaborative nature of this process also fosters a culture of continuous learning and adaptation, as team members share, critique, and build upon each other's ideas throughout the design thinking journey. This iterative, team-based approach not only enhances the quality of outcomes but also accelerates the overall design process.

Moreover, integration of design thinking skills helps to develop critical soft skills amongst students, which are often under-emphasised in traditional engineering curricula. Good communication skills are developed, as students are required to consistently and clearly articulate their ideas to their peers. Aspects of creative thinking, and thinking "outside-the-box" are encouraged, thereby helping to develop vital creativity skills. And lastly, problem-solving skills are practices as students are given problems with ill-defined domains, common to real-life engineering problems. Together, these help to develop resilience and a mindset that values challenges.

Diversity within the discipline and within teams is an important factor in driving innovation and creating an inclusive environment for all. For years, the discipline of Engineering has been known to have a large gender imbalance [43]. In Australia, only 15% of graduates from STEM are women [14]. Research has explored the reasons for this imbalance, with various literature showing that females prefer the social and humanitarian side of engineering – solving problems that benefit humanity [3, 15, 30]. The implementation of design thinking into the engineering curriculum, where the human-centred approach is valued, could be one way in which engineering programs can appeal to students who might otherwise be deterred by a purely technical focus. Fostering diversity has long been a goal in Engineering, and increasing the number of women in STEM professions has a long history of attempts – perhaps applying the design thinking process could also drive the solution to this wicked problem.

### 4.3.1 MAKERSPACES

The Maker Movement is a rapidly growing trend, where a group of people, or singular persons create products [21]. One of my favourite definitions, is given by Martin [28, p.30], and describes the maker movement as "...a community of hobbyists, tinkerers, engineers, hackers, and artists who creatively design and build projects for both playful and useful ends...". A lot of maker-centred learning has most often been aligned with STEM subjects [39]. There is still a great deal of debate questioning what makers learn, and how that learning is achieved [39]. There are however, pedagogical theories to back the use of such spaces and position them as important in the overall learning process. For example, constructivism is based around the idea that students learn by doing [5], this means students use the environment around them and the information available to them to construct their knowledge – all integral to the makerspace. Cognitive theories centring around embodied cognition, also move to propel makerspaces and their place as important with regard to how students construct knowledge through movement – connecting their environment, body and knowledge [41]. There is however, evidence that explicit instruction and learning must take place prior to the making, in order for making to have a positive effect on learning outcomes [42].

This move towards incorporating design thinking into the curricula at our large universities in Australia has resulted in the creation of design studios and makerspaces across campuses. These types of spaces provide the physical infrastructure necessary to implement design thinking principles effectively. They not only enhance technical skills but also foster creativity, collaboration, and innovation – qualities essential for future engineers. I have often found myself strongly wishing that these types of spaces existed when I was a student, and I am well known to get lost in the makerspace for hours experimenting with different ideas and building things – perhaps one of the greatest reasons for why I became an engineer in the first place. The Engineering makerspace at UNSW is always a hub of activity, fostering a community of makers and innovators within the engineering department and beyond. I love having a chat with the different personalities who use the makerspace, and particularly the people that run the makerspace itself – they always have a project moving, which is exciting to discuss! Around December of 2023, these makerspaces start to wind down and clear out for the holiday break, and this is my favourite time to get lost in the space. An abundance of small off-cuts, people making their home-made gifts, sunshine in the air (we are in Australia after all!) – together this really makes for a somewhat magical atmosphere.

More seriously, despite providing me a way to use off-cuts and make ridiculously sized earrings, these spaces play a crucial role in modern engineering education, particularly in the context of design thinking. They serve as catalysts for creativity, innovation, and hands-on learning. The design of our makerspace encourages students to have open space for interaction, free exchange of ideas, and overall the feeling that you get when you walk into this space, with the dull scent of sawdust surrounded by what feels like creativity all around you plays a significant role in also getting the students excited about the opportunities that exist. Makerspaces often bring together students from various engineering disciplines and even other fields, such as industrial design or business. This cross-pollination of ideas fosters interdisciplinary thinking, which is important for solving complex real-world problems. These types of meetings are important for students to remove themselves from one-sided thinking, and to embrace different types of ideas and solutions. Makerspaces are also ideal for project-based learning, a key component of design thinking – unless a few people are operating the saws at once, in which case the space gets a little bit loud! We do have desks and tables set up in an alley outside, which allows students to work on long-term projects, simulating real-world engineering challenges (whilst also getting to be in the fresh air, which they sometimes forget to do as the term goes on!). With access to tools like 3D printers, laser cutters, and CNC machines, students can quickly prototype their ideas. This rapid iteration is a key principle of design thinking and is a huge part of the iterative lifecycle. This gives students a good baseline for which tools are appropriate at each stage of prototype development and allow experimentation without the fear of failure. Students can try out unconventional ideas and learn from both successes and failures.

Of course, these types of spaces do not come without their challenges also. Establishing and maintaining these spaces requires significant investment in equipment and staff. The UNSW makerspace has a positive environment, and it shows in the way you are always greeted when you enter the space and helped.

## 4.3.2 GAME DESIGN

I wanted to touch on another course that I teach and absolutely love teaching – Game Design. This is an interesting branch of design, as the game studies did not become formally recognised as a legitimate academic discipline until recently, and the establishment of a cohesive framework became an important part of the process [35]. Literature offers multiple insights into methods for game design [8]. Bridging the gap between theoretical frameworks and the actual practical aspects of game design, some methods underline the importance of the iterative lifecycle and suggest the use of Prototype/Playtest/Evaluate/Refine lifecycle, which aligns with design thinking processes [38]. This method highlights the importance of the act of play itself, as it is the only means through which meaningful feedback is achieved, which makes it vital that this part of the cycle is not just an afterthought (as testing often is). Expanding on this, and now including the process of ideation, Schell [40] presents a playcentric iterative methodology that closer resembles the design thinking process, with stages of Ideation, Prototyping, Testing and Evaluation. Both authors underline the importance of empathising with the player first, and using this as a way to set specific player experience goals early on in the design process to continue to guide ideas and exploration of design. However, much of the complexity in this field of design is due to the diversity of definitions, language, and experiences, which makes it difficult to drive a unified framework. Cormio et al. [8] in their interview with forty game designers, found that interviewees all acknowledges the presence of shared steps that structure the game design process and highlight the importance of an overall game design framework to ensure that development steps are not fragmented through misunderstanding.

In our Game Design course, I am influenced by the design thinking process itself, and I encourage the use of the play-centric framework in the design of games. We also make full use of makerspaces, however, only after explicit instruction of concepts and ideas to ensure that students have the grounding of theory and a communal framework available to establish initial ideas. Interestingly, in the last offering of this small fourth-year course at UNSW, students arrived expecting to start coding their games. These students live and breathe games and yet they have never really thought about the very elements that make up a game *per se*, the building blocks and the design of a game itself. There appeared to be little understanding of iteration, and even less understanding of the importance of centring their design on the player. When I question what it is that they would expect to code, they often become overwhelmed, largely because they have not considered the actual design of the thing itself.

The iterative nature of design thinking aligns well with the realities of game development. Games are rarely, if ever, perfect on the first attempt. They require constant refinement, and balancing. Design thinking embraces this, encouraging designers to view each iteration as an opportunity for improvement. This might involve playing with the game mechanics, refining the user interface, or adjusting the difficulty curve of the game. Even after a game's release, this iterative process often continues through updates and potential expansions. This type of iteration at the very heart of the process encourages experimentation, creative thinking, and consistent playtesting.

Before this can begin, game designers must understand their players, their motivations, and their behaviours. This understanding goes beyond simple demographics; it may involve creating detailed player personas and mapping out the emotional journey that a player might experience whilst experiencing the game. By putting themselves in the players' shoes, designers can craft experiences that resonate with players, creating games that are not just played, but felt. The first time that I played a game called "To the Moon"[1], the opening score just tugged at the heart strings. The premise of the story was an experience that was felt, and the feelings were enough to forgive some of the gaps in the storyline.

The process of empathising with players, thinking about different types of players, also encourages game designers to consider broader issues of accessibility and inclusivity. By keeping the diverse needs of players in mind, designers can create

---

[1] https://www.nintendo.com/us/store/products/to-the-moon-switch/

games that are enjoyable for a wider audience. In 2020, the Last of Us Part II started winning awards for the designers innovations in the accessibility space. There was finally a game that considered the vast range of abilities and catered to its players. Since then, accessibility has become more and more important in game design. Sites, such as Can I Play That? [2] rate games in terms of their vision, audio, cognitive, and motor accessibility They are an important piece of the puzzle that highlights the importance of designing well-rounded games. More recently, Forza Motorsport [3] has won Accessibility Awards with their Blind Driving Assists. These provide audio indicators for driving across different sections of tracks, acceleration and deceleration cues, shifting cues, and even cues for driving the wrong way. Other features like assisted steering, automatic shifting, and assisted braking and full screen reader support allow blind and low vision players to be as independent as they wish to be.

Design thinking also helps game designers navigate the ethical considerations inherent in their work. Games have the power to influence behaviour and shape perceptions. By taking a holistic, empathetic approach, designers can create games that not only entertain but also promote positive behaviour and contribute positively to society. As one exercise in our class, we used four games and analysed them for their inclusivity to begin with. Although not something that you think about first however, we found a real lack of inclusive characters in most of board games. Interestingly enough, we used one board game, which did have an updated version and the updated version levelled up with their inclusivity of characters – it is fantastic to see that game designers are now starting to think about these issues and are putting them at the forefront. In our exercise, I think everyone was fairly surprised at this finding, but a follow-up exercise of reimagining these games in an inclusive atmosphere sparked some amazing ideas, stories of being left out and being included, and the important role that games can play in creating welcoming environments. Ideation in game design is where creativity truly flourishes. Designers can start to brainstorm innovative game mechanics, explore unique narrative structures, consider inclusive characters, accessibility options, and novel visual styles. This phase encourages thinking outside the box, challenging conventional wisdom about what games can be and how they can be played. It's often in this stage that the most groundbreaking ideas emerge, ideas that can redefine genres or create entirely new ones.

## 4.4 INDUSTRY PERSPECTIVES ON DESIGN IN ENGINEERING

The need to understand traversal competencies in the engineering curricula was first proposed in 1996, when Boeing in their job advertisement asked for "good communication skills: written, verbal, graphic, listening, ability to think both critically and creatively, curiosity and a desire to learn – for life, and profound understanding of the importance of teamwork..." [29]. As engineering problems are becoming more complex and multifaceted – more "wicked" [27], such competencies are not

---

[2] https://caniplaythat.com/

[3] https://www.accessibility.org.au/forza-motorsport-drives-innovation-with-accessibility-features/

just desired, but often expected of our engineering graduates and are often part of accreditation bodies requirements, such as Engineers Australia. In Computing, the Association for Computing Machinery curriculum guidelines list the application of the interplay between theory and practice, good communication, ability to work as part of the team, as some of the many desired characteristics of engineers in the computing field [33]. It thus becomes increasingly crucial that our engineering curriculum is able to impart such competencies, as the gap between academic preparation and professional expectations continues to evolve. There is an assumption, that academia needs to rethink classic forms of engineering education, and prepare students for the modern workplace by ensuring that they are able to lead and manage groups, creatively solve problems and solve ever day problems effectively [1]. Many industry leaders have identified a significant skills gap between recent engineering graduates and the competencies required in the modern workplace. While graduates often possess strong technical knowledge, they frequently lack the practical design skills, interdisciplinary thinking, and holistic problem-solving abilities that are essential in today's complex engineering projects. In a constantly changing world, life-long learning competencies have become even more important, but are often the least integrated into the engineering curriculum [4]. Engineering curriculum though remains fairly stagnant, and industry continues to bear the burden of training workforce that emerges from academia.

In response to this challenge, leading companies are increasingly collaborating with universities to enhance design education in engineering programs. These partnerships take various forms, from guest lectures and industry-sponsored projects to curriculum development and research collaborations. For instance, companies like IBM, Google, IDEO, and Autodesk have established partnerships with universities to integrate design thinking and user-centred design principles into engineering courses [26]. These collaborations often involve bringing real-world design challenges into the classroom, allowing students to work on authentic projects and receive feedback from industry professionals. Some companies are going a step further by co-developing entire courses or degree programs with universities. For example, Dyson has partnered with several universities to create engineering degrees that emphasise practical design skills alongside traditional engineering theory [2]. These industry-academic partnerships not only help to align curriculum with industry needs but also provide students with valuable exposure to current industry practices and technologies.

Internships and co-op programs are another important component in bridging the gap between academic learning and professional practice [16]. These experiential learning opportunities allow students to apply their theoretical knowledge to real-world problems, develop practical soft skills, and gain insight into industry expectations [22]. Many companies view internships as an essential part of their recruitment strategy, using these programs to identify and nurture talent while simultaneously helping to shape the skills of future engineers. Additionally, internships provide opportunities for students to work in multidisciplinary teams, mirroring the collaborative nature of professional work environments. In the computing discipline, students greatly valued the ability to learn on the job and apply their knowledge to actual real life projects during their internships [33]. Similar practices are underway in other engineering disciplines.

As the field of engineering continues to evolve, these partnerships between industry and academia will play an increasingly important role in ensuring that engineering graduates are equipped with the skills necessary to meet the challenges of our future technological landscape.

## 4.5 CHALLENGES AND OPPORTUNITIES IN ENGINEERING DESIGN EDUCATION

The last few years have seen an increased interest in generative AI, propelled by the release of OpenAI's ChatGPT. Large Language Models (LLMs), such as Chat-GPT, are based upon transformer architecture, and at their core exploit the fact that language follows a specific orderly structure. These models are trained over large quantities of text scraped from the internet. Huge strides have been made in the quality of output of these models, improvements in pattern recognition, data analysis, and even creative tasks like image generation and text composition have been consistently seen. There are, however, limitations to what can be produced by LLMs, which, despite their sophistication, operate within the constraints of their training data and predefined algorithms.

Design thinking is inherently a human-centric process that relies heavily on empathy, innovation, and creativity – qualities that are, as yet, uniquely human. For example, the first stages of the design thinking process, requires one to empathise require a deep, intuitive understanding of human emotions, experiences, and unspoken needs. While AI can analyse vast amounts of user data, it lacks the emotional intelligence and lived experience necessary to truly empathise with users. This human touch is crucial in identifying subtle, often unsaid problems that play such an important role in coming up with innovative solutions.

Similarly, the next stages of the design process, ideation, also show limitations of AI. True innovation often involves making unexpected connections, challenging established norms, and thinking outside-the-box. Despite the ability of LLMs to generate seemingly creative output, these models are fundamentally bound by the patterns and information present in their training data. They can combine existing ideas in novel ways, but they cannot truly innovate in the sense of creating something entirely new or revolutionary. Human creativity, on the other hand, can draw from a vast well of experiences, emotions, and abstract thinking to produce genuinely original ideas.

Prototyping and testing phases of design thinking also highlight the importance of human involvement. While AI can assist in generating prototypes or analysing test data, it cannot fully grasp the tactile, experiential aspects of interacting with a physical prototype. Humans can quickly pivot their approach based on subtle feedback, intuition, or changing circumstances. They can read between the lines, understand implicit information, and make judgement calls based on complex, often contradictory factors. This is not yet possible to replicate, and still requires a vast well of human input. Human designers bring a level of intuition and sensory perception to these stages that AI cannot replicate. They can sense when something 'feels right' or identify potential issues that may not be apparent in data alone.

Navigating ethical considerations, cultural sensitivities, and social implications requires human judgement and human values play an important role. AI, lacking consciousness and moral reasoning capabilities, cannot independently make the ethical decisions often required in the design process. This is not even considering the inherent bias and racial/gender stereotyping often present in LLM-generated output [45]

Whilst AI can be a powerful tool in helping to augment and support the design thinking process, it cannot fully replicate or replace the human elements that make this methodology so effective (yet!). The essence of design thinking lies in its deeply human approach to problem-solving, drawing on empathy, creativity, and innovation in ways that current AI technology cannot match. As we continue to advance in AI development, it's crucial to recognise these limitations and focus on leveraging AI as a complement to, rather than a replacement for, human-driven design thinking. Given the irreplaceable human elements in design thinking, it becomes paramount to incorporate this methodology into engineering curricula. By teaching design thinking, we equip future engineers with a powerful set of tools that complement their technical expertise. This human-centred approach encourages engineers to look beyond purely technical solutions and consider the broader context of their work, including social, ethical, and environmental implications. Design thinking also fosters the development of crucial soft skills such as empathy, creativity, and adaptability – qualities that are increasingly valued in the professional world but are often underemphasised in traditional engineering education. Moreover, as AI and automation continue to advance, these uniquely human skills become even more critical, differentiating human engineers from AI systems. This integrated approach to engineering education can help to produce well-rounded professionals who are better equipped to tackle wicked problems, ensuring that the human touch remains at the heart of engineering innovation even as technology continues to evolve.

## 4.6 CONCLUSION

To help us create well rounded engineering graduates, to ensure that our students are able to think outside of formulaic responses, it is important to incorporate design education into the engineering curriculum. This needs to be done with early curriculum integration, and in a multifaceted approach. Firstly, integrating real-world, interdisciplinary projects into the curriculum allows students to apply design thinking to complex, real world problems, which are often open-ended with multiple potential solutions. These types of problems help to bridge the gap between theory and practice, and help students to practice their soft skills. Further to this, the potential for closer collaborations between different engineering disciplines, amongst other disciplines such as business, psychology, and the arts provides a more realistic experience to students. This also exposes students to diverse perspectives. These types of hands-on, experiential learning opportunities can also include internships, which provide students practical experience in applying design thinking principles to real-world engineering problems. Alongside technical competencies, which are often at the core of engineering curriculum, a strong emphasis on developing soft skills such as empathy, communication, and teamwork are essential. Not only are these skills at the core of the design thinking process, but they work to improve the overall qualities of our graduates. The use of the design thinking process in engineering can help to encourage a culture of innovation and risk-taking, where failure is viewed as a learning opportunity rather than a setback, mirroring real-world design processes. Finally, developing assessment methods that effectively evaluate design thinking skills, moving beyond traditional exams to include project-based assessments and portfolios, ensures that students' abilities in this area are properly recognised and developed.

## REFERENCES

1. Fernando Almeida and José Morais. Strategies for Developing Soft Skills Among Higher Engineering Courses. *Journal of Education*, 203(1):103–112, 1 2023.
2. Tom Banks. Dyson says his new school will "embrace creativity" and teach business skills. *Design Week*, 2015.
3. A. Barco, R. M. Walsh, A. Block, K. Loveys, A. McDaid, and Broadbent E. Teaching Social Robotics to Motivate Women into Engineering and Robotics Careers. In *14th ACM/IEEE International Conference on Human-Robot Interaction*, volume 22, pages 518–519, Daegu, Korea (South), 2019. Institute of Electrical and Electronics Engineers Inc.
4. Una Beagon, Klara Kövesi, Brad Tabas, Bente Nørgaard, Riitta Lehtinen, Brian Bowe, Christiane Gillet, and Claus Monrad Spliid. Preparing engineering students for the challenges of the SDGs: what competences are required? *European Journal of Engineering Education*, 48(1):1–23, 2023.
5. Mordechai Ben-Ari. Constructivism in Computer Science Education. Technical report, 1998.
6. Michael B. Beverland, Sarah J.S. Wilner, and Pietro Micheli. Reconciling the tension between consistency and relevance: design thinking as a mechanism for brand ambidexterity. *Journal of the Academy of Marketing Science*, 43(5):589–609, 9 2015.
7. Tim Brown. *Change by Design: How Design Thinking Transforms Organizations and Inspires Innovation*. HarperCollins, New York, 2009.
8. Laura Cormio, Catia Giaconi, Maura Mengoni, and Tommaso Santilli. Exploring game design approaches through conversations with designers. *Design Studies*, 91-92, 3 2024.
9. Marnie J Meylor de Mooij, Rachael L Hodny, Daniel A O'Neil, Matthew R Gardner, Mekayla Beaver, Andrea T Brown, Barbara A Barry, Lorna M Ross, Amy J Jasik, Katharine M Nesbitt, Susan M Sobolewski, Susan M Skinner, Rajeev Chaudhry, Brian C Brost, Bobbie S Gostout, and Roger W Harms. OB Nest: Reimagining Low-Risk Prenatal Care. *Mayo Clinic Proceedings*, 93(4):458–466, 2018.
10. Kees Dorst. The core of 'design thinking' and its application. *Design Studies*, 32(6):521–532, 11 2011.
11. Carol S. Dweck. *Self-theories: Their Role in Motivation, Personality, and Development*. Psychology Press, 1st edition, 1999.

12. Clive L. Dym, Alice M. Agogino, Ozgur Eris, Daniel D. Frey, and Larry J. Leifer. Engineering design thinking, teaching, and learning. In *Journal of Engineering Education*, volume 94, pages 103–120. Wiley-Blackwell Publishing Ltd, 2005.

13. S Ellis. How Design Thinking Transformed Airbnb from a Failing Startup to a Billion Dollar Business. 2015.

14. Camilla R. Fisher, Christopher D. Thompson, and Rowan H. Brookes. Gender differences in the Australian undergraduate STEM student experience: a systematic review. *Higher Education Research and Development*, 39(6):1155–1168, 9 2020.

15. Jane Goodyer and B Soysa. A New Zealand National Outreach Program-Inspiring Young Girls in Humanitarian Engineering. *International Journal for Service Learning in Engineering, Humanitarian Engineering and Social Entrepreneurship*, 12(2):1–14, 2017.

16. Roger G. Hadgraft and Anette Kolmos. Emerging learning environments in engineering education. *Australasian Journal of Engineering Education*, 25(1):3–16, 1 2020.

17. Ulla Johansson-Sköldberg, Jill Woodilla, and Mehves Cetinkaya. Design thinking: Past, present and possible futures. *Creativity and Innovation Management*, 22(2):121–146, 2013.

18. Lucy Kimbell. Design practices in design thinking/1 Design practices in design thinking. *European Academy of Management*, 5:1–24, 2009.

19. Paul A. Kirschner, John Sweller, Femke Kirschner, and Jimmy R. Zambrano. From Cognitive Load Theory to Collaborative Cognitive Load Theory. *International Journal of Computer-Supported Collaborative Learning*, 13(2):213–233, 6 2018.

20. Joyce Hwee Ling Koh, Ching Sing Chai, Benjamin Wong, and Huang-Yao Hong. *Design Thinking for Education: Conceptions and Applications in Teaching and Learning*. Springer, Singapore, 2015.

21. Dora Konstantinou, Antigoni Parmaxi, and Panayiotis Zaphiris. Mapping research directions on makerspaces in education. *Educational Media International*, 58(3):223–247, 2021.

22. A. D. Lantada. Engineering education 5.0: Continuously evolving engineering education. *International Journal of Engineering Education*, 36(6):1814–1832, 2020.

23. B Lawson and K Dorst. *Design expertise*. Routledge, 2013.

24. Michel T Leger, Anne-Marie Laroche, and Diane Pruneau. Using design thinking to solve a local environmental problem in the context of a university civil engineering course - an intrinsic case study. *Global Journal of Engineering Education*, 22(1):6–12, 2020.

25. Jeanne Liedtka. Perspective: Linking Design Thinking with Innovation Outcomes through Cognitive Bias Reduction, 11 2015.

26. Rongxin Liu, Carter Zenke, Charlie Liu, Andrew Holmes, Patrick Thornton, and David J. Malan. Teaching CS50 with AI: Leveraging Generative Artificial Intelligence in Computer Science Education. In *SIGCSE 2024 - Proceedings of the 55th ACM Technical Symposium on Computer Science Education*, volume 1, pages 750–756. Association for Computing Machinery, Inc, 3 2024.

27. Johanna Lönngren and Katrien van Poeck. Wicked problems: a mapping review of the literature. *International Journal of Sustainable Development and World Ecology*, 28(6):481–502, 2021.

28. Lee Martin. The promise of the maker movement for education. *Journal of Pre-College Engineering Education Research*, 5(1):30–39, 2015.

29. John McMasters and Lee Matsch. Desired attributes of an engineering graduate - An industry perspective. In *Advanced measurement and ground testing conference*, page 2241, 1996.

30. P. Meiksins, P. Layne, K. Beddoes, and J. Deters. Women in engineering: A review of the 2019 literature. *SWE Magazine*, 65(2):4–38, 2019.

31. Christoph Meinel and Timm Krohn. *Design Thinking in Education: Innovation Can Be Learned*. Springer International Publishing, 1 2022.

32. Pietro Micheli, Sarah J.S. Wilner, Sabeen Hussain Bhatti, Matteo Mura, and Michael B. Beverland. Doing Design Thinking: Conceptual Review, Synthesis, and Research Agenda. *Journal of Product Innovation Management*, 36(2):124–148, 3 2019.

33. Mia Minnes, Sheena Ghanbari Serslev, and Omar Padilla. What Do CS Students Value in Industry Internships? *ACM Transactions on Computing Education*, 21(1), 3 2021.

34. Charles Owen. Design Thinking: Notes on its Nature and Use. 2007.

35. Paul Ralph and Kafui Monu. Toward a Unified Theory of Digital Games. *The Computer Games Journal*, 4(1):81–100, 2015.

36. Kristiana Roth, Dietfried Globocnik, Christiane Rau, and Anne Katrin Neyer. Living up to the expectations: The effect of design thinking on project success. *Creativity and Innovation Management*, 29(4):667–684, 12 2020.

37. Peter G Rowe. *Design thinking*. MIT Press, 1987.

38. Katie Salen Tekinbas and Eric Zimmerman. *Rules of Play: Game Design Fundamentals*. MIT Press, 2003.

39. Michael Schad and W. Monty Jones. The Maker Movement and Education: A Systematic Review of the Literature, 1 2020.

40. Jesse Schell. *The art of game design: a book of lenses*. Morgan Kaufmann Publishers Inc., San Francisco, CA, USA, 2008.

41. Lawrence Shapiro and Steven A. Stolz. Embodied cognition and its significance for education. *Theory and Research in Education*, 17(1):19–39, 3 2019.

42. John Sweller, Jeroen J.G. van Merriënboer, and Fred Paas. Cognitive Architecture and Instructional Design: 20 Years Later, 6 2019.

43. Sonia Verdugo-Castro, Alicia García-Holgado, and Mª Cruz Sánchez-Gómez. The gender gap in higher STEM studies: A systematic literature review, 8 2022.

44. Lev Vygotsky. Play and its role in the mental development of the child. In M. Cole, editor, *Soviet development psychology*, pages 76–99. White Plains, NY, 1977.

45. Laura Weidinger, Jonathan Uesato, Maribeth Rauh, Conor Griffin, Po Sen Huang, John Mellor, Amelia Glaese, Myra Cheng, Borja Balle, Atoosa Kasirzadeh, Courtney Biles, Sasha Brown, Zac Kenton, Will Hawkins, Tom Stepleton, Abeba Birhane, Lisa Anne Hendricks, Laura Rimell, William Isaac, Julia Haas, Sean Legassick, Geoffrey Irving, and Iason Gabriel. Taxonomy of Risks posed by Language Models. In *ACM International Conference Proceeding Series*, pages 214–229. Association for Computing Machinery, 6 2022.

46. David S Yeager and Carol S Dweck. Supplemental Material for What Can Be Learned From Growth Mindset Controversies? *American Psychologist*, 2020.

# 5 How the Metaverse and Brain Computer Interfaces can Revolutionise the Education Industry

*Ali Darejeh*
School of Computer Science and Engineering, UNSW Sydney
Kensington, Australia

*Sara Mashayekh*
School of Education, UNSW Sydney
Kensington, Australia

## 5.1 HOW THE METAVERSE AND BRAIN COMPUTER INTERFACES CAN REVOLUTIONISE THE EDUCATION INDUSTRY

The rapid advancements in metaverse and immersive technologies have ushered in a transformative era for the education industry, particularly within the fields of engineering and medical science. The metaverse, a virtual world developed to enable people to interact in a simulated environment using immersive technologies including virtual reality (VR) and augmented reality (AR), is expected to provide a fully immersive experience. Users will interact with each other in real-time, similar to the physical world. The metaverse, anticipated to be the next major technological advancement, is being developed by some of the world's largest companies.

This chapter explores the profound effects of metaverse and immersive technologies on pedagogical approaches, skill development, and knowledge acquisition in critical sectors, including engineering and medical science, delving into the ways these technologies revolutionise the learning experience for students and foster a more interactive and engaging educational environment.

In the field of engineering, the metaverse and immersive technologies have proven instrumental in enhancing practical learning experiences. Through realistic simulations and scenarios, students engage in hands-on training, applying theoretical knowledge to real-world situations. The immersive nature of these technologies facilitates a deeper understanding of complex engineering concepts, ultimately preparing students for industry challenges.

DOI: 10.1201/9781032702797-5

Also, in the field of medical science, metaverse and immersive technologies have emerged as a powerful tool for medical training, providing students with realistic surgical simulations, anatomy visualisations, and patient interactions. This not only enhances the technical skills of medical students but also cultivates a sense of empathy and understanding crucial for effective patient care.

The integration of metaverse and immersive technologies into educational curricula offers a dynamic and adaptable approach to learning. These technologies transcend geographical constraints, enabling remote access to high-quality educational resources and collaborative learning experiences. Engineering and medical science students can engage in virtual laboratories, collaborative projects, and interactive lectures, fostering a globalised educational community.

## 5.2 WHAT THE METAVERSE IS

The concept of the metaverse has transcended its origins in science fiction and has rapidly become a transformative force with diverse applications across various industries. The metaverse is a virtual reality space that transcends the traditional boundaries of online interaction, creating a digital universe where users can engage with a computer-generated environment and interact with each other in real-time. It goes beyond conventional two-dimensional internet experiences by offering immersive, three-dimensional environments where users can navigate, communicate, and collaborate seamlessly. In essence, the metaverse is a collective virtual shared space that encompasses the sum of all virtual worlds, virtual reality technology, and the internet itself, providing a comprehensive and interconnected digital experience [38].

The gateway to the metaverse is virtual reality (VR) technology, immersing users in simulated environments that closely replicate real-world scenarios. Users can engage with these simulated environments using head-mounted displays (HMD), motion tracking, and haptic feedback devices, enhancing the overall sense of immersion [51], [39].

Within the metaverse, users can create personalised avatars, representing themselves in the digital realm, and engage in various activities ranging from socialising and gaming to business meetings and educational experiences. Virtual currencies, blockchain technology, and decentralised systems are also integral components of the metaverse, providing users with a sense of ownership and security within the digital space. As the metaverse continues to evolve, it holds the promise of transforming the way we perceive and interact with the digital realm, offering new possibilities for entertainment, communication, and collaboration on a global scale. The metaverse is not confined to a single platform or application but is an interconnected network of virtual spaces, accessible through various devices and platforms. It has the potential to revolutionalise the way we work, socialise, and consume information by blending the physical and digital worlds seamlessly [41].

Technology companies and innovators are investing heavily in the development of the metaverse, aiming to create a more immersive and interconnected online experience. For example, Meta (formerly Facebook) has developed an application called Horizon Workrooms that is a VR platform designed for collaboration and communication in a digital space. Users can create personalised avatars and participate in virtual meetings, workshops, and presentations. The platform aims to provide an immersive and interactive environment for remote teams and professionals, leveraging the capabilities of VR technology for a more engaging work experience. This is a part of Meta's broader vision to create a metaverse, a collective virtual shared space that integrates various aspects of the digital world.

The metaverse offers a multitude of opportunities to reshape traditional practices and introduce innovative solutions. From gaming and entertainment to education, business collaboration, healthcare, social interaction, and training simulations, the metaverse has proven to be a dynamic and versatile platform [31].

## 5.3  THE EXPANDING REACH OF THE METAVERSE

The metaverse has significantly impacted the gaming and entertainment industries by introducing innovative applications. Virtual worlds, characterised by immersive digital environments, have become the foundation for gaming and social interaction, providing users with a unique and engaging experience. Furthermore, the metaverse facilitates the hosting of live events such as virtual concerts, and conferences creating new avenues for entertainment and cultural exchange within a dynamic digital space [13].

The metaverse is also reshaping the landscape of business and collaboration by introducing virtual offices and workspaces. This allows for remote collaboration and meetings, fostering seamless communication among team members regardless of physical location. Additionally, conferences and trade shows hosted within the metaverse provide businesses with a platform for virtual exhibitions, networking, and showcasing products, leading to more inclusive and efficient global collaborations [76].

In the healthcare sector, the metaverse has proven invaluable for medical training and telemedicine. Simulating medical procedures within a virtual environment enables realistic training scenarios for healthcare professionals, enhancing their skills and preparedness. Telemedicine services, facilitated by the metaverse, enable virtual consultations and healthcare services, offering patients more accessible and flexible medical care.

The metaverse has revolutionalised social interaction by offering virtual spaces for networking and gatherings. Social networking within the metaverse provides individuals with the opportunity to connect with others in immersive digital environments. Furthermore, virtual gatherings, including parties, meetups, and events, have become a popular way to foster social connections in a digital realm, transcending physical boundaries [75].

In the realm of simulation, the metaverse plays a crucial role in military training and emergency response training. Simulating military scenarios within the metaverse allows for realistic and immersive training experiences, preparing military personnel for various situations. Similarly, emergency response training benefits from virtual simulations, offering first responders a controlled environment to train, practice and enhance their skills in managing emergency situations effectively [43].

In the field of education, the metaverse offers transformative applications. Virtual classrooms have emerged as a powerful tool for conducting classes, workshops, and training sessions in an immersive digital environment, breaking down geographical barriers and enhancing accessibility. Simulations within the metaverse provide realistic scenarios for hands-on training and skill development, offering students practical experiences in a controlled and interactive setting. In line with the goals of this book chapter, centred on examining how the metaverse is applied in education, our exploration will focus on different facets within the education domain in the forthcoming section [44].

## 5.4 APPLICATIONS OF THE METAVERSE IN EDUCATION

In the realm of education, the metaverse presents an exciting frontier with the potential to revolutionalise the way students learn and educators teach. It achieves this by simulating various environments, tools, and events, fostering collaboration between students in a virtual world. In the next paragraphs, we will discuss various applications of the metaverse in different academic majors including history, geography, geology, science, medical, engineering.

In history education, the metaverse can serve as a powerful tool for recreating historical events and periods. Students can step into virtual reconstructions of ancient civilizations, witness key historical moments, and interact with virtual historical figures. For example, a history class might virtually visit the ancient city of Rome during the height of the Roman Empire or experience the signing of important historical documents. Such immersive experiences deepen students' historical knowledge and foster a more profound connection to the past.

In the realm of history education, researchers have employed metaverse technologies for various purposes. Gaafar [28] created a metaverse-like environment to teach History of Architecture courses, simulating fully immersive virtual replicas of various heritage buildings. Agustini *et. al.* [2] developed a metaverse environment for students to explore and interact with prehistoric objects. Son *et. al.* [68] established a metaverse museum covering the period from the time of excavation to the Heungdeoksa Temple in the Koryeo Dynasty, adorned with photos of excavated artifacts. In the Heungdeoksa Temple map, the photo data were systematically published, reflecting the stages of metal type production. Chehab, A., & Nakhal, B. [11] created a metaverse to facilitate a virtual tour of the main historic buildings of Beirut City center, allowing students to examine the potential restoration of this historic site. Additionally, Cabero-Almenara, Llorente-Cejudo, & Martinez-Roig [10] developed a virtual reality version of the Church of the Annunciation in Seville for teaching History of Art. In geography, the metaverse offers a groundbreaking platform for immersive exploration and understanding of the world. Students can embark on virtual field trips, navigating realistic 3D environments to study diverse landscapes, ecosystems, and cultural landmarks [56]. For instance, a geography class could explore the Amazon rainforest, witness natural phenomena like volcanic eruptions, or visit historical sites around the globe. Such experiences provide a tangible sense of place, fostering a deeper appreciation for geographical concepts and cultural diversity.

In the realm of geography education, researchers have harnessed metaverse technologies for diverse purposes. In their work, Habibah *et. al.* [30] pioneered a VR environment for teaching eco-spatial and estuary conservation concepts in Geography, providing a viable alternative to challenging field trips. Furthermore, Tsou and Mejia [72] conducted an analysis on the applications of metaverse and virtual reality in cartography. Hagge [32] and Shakirova, Said and Konyushenko [61] evaluated the effect of learning geography through the VR version of Google Earth app to virtually visit places relevant to that day's lecture. In other studies, Shen *et. al.* [63] and Prisille and Ellerbrake [56] investigated the impact of 360-degree virtual reality videos designed for geography immersion learning. While their system may not strictly meet the criteria for a metaverse, they employed virtual reality to examine how 3D videos within the VR setting can impact students' emotions and learning-an element commonly associated with the metaverse environment.

Another field similar to geography that can benefit from the metaverse is geology and mining education. It allows students to virtually explore the Earth's composition, geological formations, and natural processes. Virtual reality simulations can recreate geological phenomena like earthquakes, allowing students to witness and analyze these events in a safe and controlled environment. This hands-on approach enhances students' understanding of geological concepts, making the subject more engaging and accessible. In mining education, it can also be beneficial for learning about the mining process and understanding safety considerations at mining sites [69].

As an instance of applying the metaverse in geology and mining, Miao *et. al.* [50] introduced a virtual reality-based system for learning mining operations. The application scheme enables virtual-real mapping, real-time interaction, and enhances learning in coal mining operations. This includes understanding the workface environment and mining knowledge related to coal shearer, scraper conveyor, stage loader, crusher, hydraulic support, belt conveyor support, and emulsion pump station. In a separate study, Janiszewski *et. al.* [35] designed two virtual reality (VR) learning system focused on rock engineering, geology, and mining education. This system was developed to facilitate training in structural mapping and rock mass characterisation. Abdelrazeq *et. al.* [1] created a virtual reality (VR) learning platform designed to replicate mining sites, providing students with a virtual tour to enhance their understanding of the challenges associated with mining. Chenrai and Jitmahantakul [14] developed a VR environment for geoscience classrooms, offering high-school students a unique way to explore geological features through immersive 360-degree scenes. In a study by Antoniou et. al. [5], they integrated a VR application with a Geographic Information System tool for mapping and data collection in volcanic areas, specifically in Santorini (Metaxa mine). Furthermore, Tibaldi *et. al.* [71] introduced a VR environment allowing students to explore volcanic regions, facilitating measurements of various geological parameters such as orientation, dip, inclination, azimuth, area, and thickness.

In the area of science including chemistry, physics, and biology, the metaverse's impact extends beyond traditional laboratories. Students can engage in virtual experiments and simulations, such as exploring the microscopic world or conducting physics experiments in a virtual lab [29]. This approach allows for a more interactive and dynamic learning experience, where students can manipulate variables and observe outcomes in real-time. For instance, in a chemistry class, students could experiment with virtual chemical reactions, enhancing their understanding of fundamental scientific principles.

In the realm of chemistry, Reeves, Crippen, and McCray [59] pioneered a virtual reality based chemistry lab, empowering students to conduct diverse experiments using virtual materials and lab equipment. Cortes Rodriguez *et. al.* [17] designed an application enabling students to explore the 3D molecular structures of various materials within a virtual reality environment. Dinther, Putter, and Pepin [73] created a virtual reality application presenting 360° video lessons tailored for secondary school students. Edwards *et. al.* [24] introduced the VR Multisensory Classroom, an immersive learning space where learners can construct hydrocarbon molecules using hand movements, experiencing tactile feedback through gloves with sensors and hand-tracking via the Leap Motion system. Ramírez and Bueno [58] implemented a virtual reality learning tool for organic chemistry, utilising immersive technology to facilitate the creation of chemical compound molecules. Fung *et. al.* [27] developed a virtual reality application for Environmental Chemistry Education, simulating overseas field trips. Ferrell *et. al.* [26] engineered a VR system allowing students to practice pulling methane molecules through carbon nanotubes in an introductory organic chemistry course.

In the field of physics, Georgiou, and Ioannou [29] designed a virtual reality (VR)-based learning system aimed at instructing high-school students on the Special Theory of Relativity. Daineko *et. al.* [18] created a VR-based physics lab, providing students with the capability to solve a variety of practical physics tasks. Pirker *et. al.* [55] assessed students' learning outcomes using Maroon VR, an immersive room-scale physics laboratory environment in virtual reality, designed for conducting diverse physics experiments. Bogusevschi, Muntean, and Muntean [9] introduced a VR Physics educational application tailored to teach the water cycle in nature. Additionally, Šiđanin *et. al.* [80] developed a VR application designed for learning and conducting experiments in nuclear physics.

In the field of biology, Choi and Kim [16] developed a VR application to illustrate the functioning of the digestive system to students. Bennett and Saunders [7] designed a VR application specifically for a cell biology course, providing students with a virtual tour of the cell and its surroundings within the human body. In a related investigation, Thompson *et. al.* [70] crafted a VR application to educate students on cell structure and characteristics. Paxinou *et. al.* [53] and Paxinou *et. al.* [54]conducted assessments to gauge the effectiveness of OnLabs, a VR-based virtual biology lab, on students' learning performance in utilising biology laboratory equipment such as microscopes.

Hemme *et. al.* [33] pioneered the development of a comprehensive suite of virtual and augmented reality applications designed to instruct students on various biomedical science concepts. This suite encompasses the visualisation of molecules, elucidation of the mechanism of action of anticancer drugs, cell culture techniques, and nanotechnology applications. Medical education in the metaverse involves realistic simulations that provide invaluable training for future healthcare professionals. Through virtual reality, medical students can practice surgeries, diagnose virtual patients, and navigate medical scenarios in a risk-free environment, fostering a more practical and experiential learning approach. For example, a medical science class might use the metaverse to simulate heart or brain surgery, allowing students to hone their skills before entering an operating room. This hands-on, immersive approach enhances practical knowledge and confidence among medical students, preparing them with the skills needed for real-world situations. Additionally, the metaverse facilitates collaborative research efforts, enabling scientists and medical professionals to work together across borders, sharing data and insights seamlessly.

In the realm of medical education, Singh *et. al.* [65] conducted a comparison between the effects of virtual reality (VR) and traditional videos in teaching communication skills to medical science students working with clinical partners in healthcare settings. Lopez *et. al.* [46] assessed students' learning performance using a VR simulator for cardiology and neurology studies. Additionally, Alharbi *et. al.* [4] designed a VR-based learning system for the anatomy course, focusing on evaluating students' knowledge retention. Chen *et. al.* [12] developed a VR-based learning platform for nursing education, allowing simulations of various scenarios in patient care. In another study, Behmadi *et. al.* [6] created a VR-based learning application to teach start triage lessons in emergency situations to medical students.

In the field of engineering, the metaverse offers a dynamic platform for innovative learning experiences. Students can design and prototype products in virtual environments, simulating real-world engineering challenges. Virtual reality enables them to visualise and test their creations, fostering a more creative and iterative design process. For instance, an engineering class might collaborate in a virtual space to design and optimise a sustainable energy solution, leveraging the metaverse's capabilities for real-time collaboration and experimentation. Engineers can use virtual reality to create and manipulate 3D models, simulate the behaviour of structures and systems, and test various scenarios without the need for physical prototypes. This interconnected approach accelerates the design process, reduces costs, and enhances innovation by facilitating global collaboration among engineering teams, allowing experts from different parts of the world to contribute their expertise in real-time [66]. In the expansive realm of engineering education, several pioneering studies have harnessed the power of VR to augment learning experiences. Kumar et al. (2021) contributed significantly by designing a VR-based learning system tailored for biochemical engineering education, with a specific focus on membrane reactors. In a parallel effort, Salah et al. (2019) introduced a groundbreaking VR-based learning system aimed at enhancing comprehension of Industry 4.0 concepts, particularly the reconfigurable manufacturing system (RMS). This innovative approach empowers engineering students to anticipate RMS design intricacies, interact with the system, understand its operation, and critically evaluate its performance.

Moving forward, Yang *et. al.* [79] offered an innovative perspective with a virtual reality learning environment dedicated to urban railway vehicle engineering students.

This environment provides invaluable insights into the disassembly and assembly processes of a bogie. Vergara *et. al.* [74] further enriched the field by developing virtual reality learning environments tailored for material engineering students. These environments offer a comprehensive suite of virtual experiments, spanning tensile testing, compression testing, X ray evaluation, ultrasonic testing, Rockwell hardness testing, crystal lattices analysis, and Vickers hardness testing.

Continuing on this trajectory, Wu *et. al.* [77] took a unique approach with an avatar-based communication VR platform. This platform enables engineering students to collaborate within a building information modelling (BIM) system, fostering problem identification from individual perspectives and instilling global engineering collaboration skills essential for international students in the realm of building design. Singh et al. (2021) contributed to the landscape by developing a VR-based learning environment specifically tailored for electrical engineering students, offering prior training on electronics laboratory hardware, including the oscilloscope.

In the automotive sector, Hernández-Chávez *et. al.* [34] introduced a VR application for students in Automotive Systems Engineering within the context of Education 4.0. This application provides 3D models of primary components of a four-stroke combustion engine and a mechanical workshop scenario, enabling students to manipulate the engine's key parts. Shifting gears, Pérez *et. al.* [57] explored the simulation of a manufacturing robot through a VR application. It enabled users to control the virtual robot using VR controllers, featuring implemented mathematical models for effective control within the virtual realm.

Finally, in military education, the integration of the metaverse can revolutionise training methodologies, offering immersive and realistic experiences for personnel. Military forces worldwide can utilise metaverse platforms to simulate intricate combat scenarios in immersive virtual battlefields. This allows soldiers to participate in lifelike training exercises that closely emulate real battlefield conditions. Virtual environments, powered by metaverse technology, allow aviators to refine their skills in realistic and dynamic scenarios, providing a cost-effective and safe alternative to traditional training methods. The metaverse facilitates interactive and collaborative training sessions, enhancing situational awareness and decision-making skills crucial for military and aviation professionals.

In the realm of military education, several groundbreaking studies have utilised advanced technologies to enhance training effectiveness and address critical challenges faced by armed forces personnel. Du *et. al.* [23] pioneered the development of a scenario-based mixed-reality platform, catering to the training needs of both technical and non-technical skills in battlefield first aid contexts. Complementing this innovation, Jindal *et. al.* [36] engineered a dynamic battlefield simulator, immersing users in diverse combat scenarios and facilitating physical interaction among players for enhanced training experiences. Meanwhile, Kim, Min, and Kim (2021) [40] delved into the educational realm with their VR-based system, offering insights into weapon usage while comparing the educational efficacy of VR, real equipment, and video resources. Dalladaku *et. al.* [19] ventured into flight simulation VR applications, evaluating their impact on army pilots' learning performance vis-a-vis traditional methods.

Chen, Chiu, and Mao [12] addressed soldiers' resilience and recovery through stress management techniques in military training, emphasizing the importance of holistic well-being in combat readiness. Additionally, Choi *et. al.* [16] advocated for the establishment of military safety training facilities using VR applications, highlighting the pivotal role of hands on training in preventing accidents and suicides within the armed forces. Lastly, Jones *et. al.* [37] explored the potential of VR-based interventions in mitigating symptoms of PTSD among Canadian Armed Forces personnel, shedding light on innovative approaches to address mental health challenges in military settings. These studies collectively represent a significant advancement in military education and training methodologies, harnessing the power of technology to optimise readiness and resilience among service members.

As these examples illustrate, the metaverse is redefining education across disciplines by fostering creativity, collaboration, and practical skills. It serves as a transformative force, offering immersive and interactive experiences that bridge the gap between theory and practice. From geography and geology to history, science, medical education, and engineering, the metaverse enhances learning across a wide array of subjects. As this technology continues to evolve, its applications in education are set to expand, presenting new and exciting possibilities for both learners and educators. The next section provides a snapshot of successful metaverse projects conducted by researchers and their colleagues at UNSW.

## 5.5  OUR SUCCESSFUL METAVERSE EXPERIENCE FOR UNIVERSITIES

Universities face challenges in providing high-tech and costly engineering and medical lab equipment to all students. Metaverse and virtual Reality (VR) offer a cost-effective solution by simulating lecture theatres and lab environments. Studies recognise VR's potential for low-cost education [1]. Its immersive nature elevates user motivation [3], positively influencing perception in STEM courses [4, 8] by simulating laboratory environment to offer safe practice [5].

While a couple of projects and studies have developed metaverse platforms for different purposes, to the best of our knowledge, no existing application has developed a multiplayer metaverse world that fully simulates an entire university campus, lecture theatres and lab environments with functional equipment, such as manufacturing robots or medical science labs employing Polymerase Chain Reaction (PCR) machines, to enable students to collaborate with each other in the virtual lab environment. Also, there is no study that evaluated the effect of metaverse on cognitive load of students in medical science and engineering laboratories.

In response to this gap, we developed our own metaverse platform and conducted four different experiments, to evaluate the effect of Metaverse in Medical Science and Engineering students cognitive load while performing lab procedures. Two experiments are related to the medical science and another two to mechanical Engineering.

## 5.5.1 THE PURPOSE OF OUR RESEARCH PROJECTS

### EXPERIMENT 1:

The primary objective of this research was to simulate a multiplayer medical science laboratory environment in VR, exploring its effectiveness in teaching Polymerase Chain Reaction (PCR) procedures. The sub-objectives were as follows:

1. Evaluate participants' perceptions and attitudes toward using VR simulations for learning PCR procedures by collecting qualitative data through post-questionnaires and interviews.
2. Assess participants' cognitive load during PCR procedures after receiving VR training compared to training in a physical lab.

### EXPERIMENT 2:

The purpose of this project was to evaluate the efficiency of the sense of immersion in virtual reality in medical science laboratory experiments. The sub-objectives were as follows:

1. Compare users' cognitive load between the VR version and the same version using a regular computer display.
2. Assess participants' perceptions and attitudes toward using the simulation to learn PCR procedures in the VR version compared to the same version using a regular computer display.

### EXPERIMENT 3:

The purpose of this experiment was to compare a virtual and real-world mechanical engineering laboratory, analysing the impact on users' cognitive load in the virtual environment. The project served two sub-purposes:

1. Evaluate participants' perceptions and attitudes toward using VR simulations for learning manufacturing composite through qualitative data collected from post-questionnaires and interviews.
2. Assess participants' cognitive load during manufacturing composite procedures after receiving VR training compared to training in a physical lab.

### EXPERIMENT 4:

The purpose of this project aligned with that of the 3rd experiment. However, in this experiment, instead of simulating the process of making composites, we simulated an expensive piece of equipment found in mechanical engineering labs: a manufacturing robot. The sub-objectives were as follows:

1. Evaluate participants' perceptions and attitudes toward using VR simulations for learning how to work with a manufacturing robot through qualitative data collected from post-questionnaires and interviews.
2. Assess participants' cognitive load during working with a manufacturing robot after receiving VR training compared to training in a physical lab.

## 5.5.2 OUR METAVERSE PLATFORM

In our metaverse platform we recreated the university campus as a form of a virtual city, including distinct buildings representing schools like Computer Science, Mechanical Engineering, and Medical Science, mirroring the layout of the physical campus. Within this virtual campus, students can interact with each other through their avatars, engaging in discussions, collaborative work in labs, and attending lectures together in the VR lecture theatres. Each building in the city represents a specific academic discipline, allowing students to access the respective labs and facilities by navigating to the corresponding buildings.

**Figure 5.1**  The metaverse city environment and user's avatar

A key highlight of this project is the simulation of laboratory environments, providing students with access to expensive equipment that might not be readily available to all. Through this virtual environment, students can work with a wide range of lab equipment, including expensive and potentially hazardous instruments, within a safe and controlled setting. The dynamic nature of the equipment allows for authentic interactions and hands-on experiments, replicating the experience of using real-world machinery. They are functional tools, and students can grab, assemble, and conduct various experiments using them. For instance, we have successfully simulated a manufacturing robot and car engine from the School of Mechanical Engineering, a Programmable logic controller (PLC) from the School of Electrical Engineering and a

Polymerase Chain Reaction (PCR) machine from the School of Medical Science, offering students unparalleled opportunities for practising (see Figures 5.2 and 5.3).

**Figure 5.2**   The medical science lab and the PCR machine

**Figure 5.3**   The mechanical engineering lab

In addition to the labs and the university campus, the metaverse provides, Virtual Lecture Theatres for Conducting Online Classes where students can attend either live online sessions or access recorded lectures (See Figure 5.4). These lecture theatres can serve as a replacement for telecommunication applications, such as Zoom or Microsoft Teams, as they offer a sense of immersion, enabling students to interact

**Figure 5.4**  The lecture theatre

with both their peers and the lecturer. Moreover, since students can see themselves in the same environment, this setup can lead to better learning outcomes.

### 5.5.3  OUR METAVERSE ARCHITECTURE

The platform has been meticulously developed using a combination of the Unreal engine and the Unity game engine and Unity XR interaction toolkit, enabling seamless functionality on both Windows and Android-based headsets, such as HTC VIVE Pro and Meta Quest headset. The simulated equipment was designed using Blender and imported into Unity. To promote collaboration and enhance the learning experience, the system has been designed as a multiplayer environment, allowing multiple students to log in simultaneously and interact with one another. To achieve this, the Photon plugin has been seamlessly integrated into the platform, facilitating real-time communication and synchronisation among users across various locations.

## 5.6  FINDINGS

The combined results of these case studies highlight the transformative implications of the metaverse in higher education, particularly in addressing challenges related to resource constraints and enhancing learning outcomes across medical and engineering disciplines. By leveraging a custom-developed metaverse platform, we demonstrated the potential of virtual reality (VR) and immersive technologies to replicate complex laboratory environments, enabling hands-on practice with expensive and potentially hazardous equipment. For instance, the PCR machine simulation in medical science and the manufacturing robot simulation in mechanical engineering offered students an accessible, safe, and cost-effective alternative to traditional labs, aligning with prior studies that emphasise the educational value of VR in different fields ([49] [60]).

For example, Mergen, Graf, & Meyerheim, [49] found that VR-based simulations in medical education allow students to practice procedures without the risks associated with real-life practice, thereby enhancing learning outcomes. Similarly, in mechanical engineering, VR simulations are reported to enable students to engage with manufacturing processes in a controlled environment, facilitating a deeper understanding of complex systems [60]. Both these studies reported accessibility, repeatability, cost-effectiveness, and improved skill development as advantages of metaverse use.

A key finding across the experiments was the reduction of cognitive load experienced by students when using the metaverse compared to traditional settings. This supports earlier research by Makransky and Lilleholt [48], which found that immersive VR environments reduced extraneous cognitive load, allowing learners to focus more effectively on core tasks. They emphasise that VR enhances procedural learning and emotional engagement, findings consistent with our observations that medical students reported improved understanding and confidence in performing PCR procedures. However, while Makransky and Lilleholt [48] observed long-term engagement benefits, our study primarily highlighted short-term cognitive load reductions, indicating a need for further longitudinal research to assess skill retention and transferability.

The collaborative aspects of the metaverse platform further underline its potential to revolutionalise education. The inclusion of multiplayer functionality and virtual lecture theatres enabled students to engage in peer learning and interactive discussions, creating a more dynamic and participatory learning environment. This aligns with the findings of several studies that reported that VR-based collaborative platforms significantly boosted student motivation and engagement ([45] [52] [64]). Additionally, Lawson McLean, & Lawson McLean [42] demonstrated that real-time collaboration in VR enhanced teamwork and problem-solving skills, outcomes mirrored in our experiments where engineering students collaboratively optimised virtual manufacturing processes. Unlike traditional online tools like Zoom, these virtual spaces provided a sense of presence and interactivity that added value to the learning experience, a distinction also noted by Tsou and Mejia [72].

The metaverse's scalability and versatility have broad implications for interdisciplinary education. By simulating university campuses and incorporating specialised facilities for fields like computer science, mechanical engineering, and medical science, the platform fosters creativity and innovation across disciplines. This mirrors findings by Sharma et. al. [62], who highlighted the metaverse's potential to bridge gaps between theoretical and practical knowledge across diverse fields. Furthermore, our case studies highlighted how virtual labs and lecture theatres provided an effective alternative for students in rural or remote areas, addressing accessibility issues-a key aspect of democratising education ([31] [51]). This is particularly relevant in resource-limited settings, where VR can offer equitable access to high-quality resources that might otherwise be unavailable.

Despite these promising results, challenges remain, including the affordability and accessibility of VR hardware for students. Previous studies ([3] [15] [22]) have similarly identified hardware costs as a significant barrier to widespread adoption. Additionally, while our findings indicate immediate cognitive and procedural benefits, further research is needed to explore the long-term impact of metaverse-based learning on knowledge retention and the transferability of skills to physical settings. Expanding the scope to include soft skills training, such as communication and ethical decision-making, as suggested by Mahindru *et. al.* [47] could provide a more holistic understanding of the metaverse's educational potential.

Moving forward, integrating advanced technologies like artificial intelligence to adapt simulations to individual learning needs and exploring the scalability of the metaverse across diverse educational contexts could unlock its full potential.

## 5.7   DISCUSSION

As it can be seen from the findings of these case studies, the metaverse represents a transformative shift in education, addressing long-standing challenges and unlocking new opportunities across disciplines. By leveraging immersive technologies like virtual reality and augmented reality, it enables accessibility and democratisation of education, enhances cognitive and procedural learning, fosters collaboration and interactivity, and drives interdisciplinary innovation. These not only underscore the metaverse's potential to bridge gaps in geographical, financial, and logistical constraints but also highlight its ability to redefine how students learn, engage, and collaborate in shared digital spaces. This section explores these categories in depth, drawing insights from case studies and existing literature to illuminate the metaverse's broad implications for higher education.

### 5.7.1   ACCESSIBILITY AND DEMOCRATISATION OF EDUCATION

The metaverse presents a groundbreaking opportunity to democratise education, addressing geographical, financial, and logistical barriers that have long hindered equitable access to quality learning. By simulating university campuses, laboratories, and lecture theatres, the metaverse enables learners from remote or underfunded institutions to access high-quality resources otherwise unavailable to them. Biswas *et. al.* [8] emphasise that virtual reality can bridge gaps in accessibility by offering immersive and interactive environments, even in resource-limited settings. Similarly, Similarly, Dede *et. al.* [21] argue that immersive technologies can transform education by providing learners with equitable opportunities for engagement, regardless of their physical location or financial constraints. Our findings align with these perspectives, particularly in the context of simulated labs for medical and engineering students. For instance, virtual Polymerase Chain Reaction (PCR) machines and manufacturing robots provided students in our case studies with access to expensive equipment, enabling them to practice in a cost-effective and risk-free environment.

This democratisation is especially relevant in the context of global educational inequalities. By transcending the physical boundaries of traditional classrooms, the metaverse allows students to participate in collaborative learning experiences with peers and experts from around the world, fostering an inclusive and interconnected academic landscape.

### 5.7.2  ENHANCING COGNITIVE AND PROCEDURAL LEARNING

A key strength of the metaverse lies in its capacity to enhance cognitive and procedural learning through immersive environments that reduce cognitive load. Makransky and Lilleholt [48] found that VR environments minimise extraneous cognitive demands, allowing learners to focus on core tasks. Similarly, Jovanović and Milosavljević [38] highlighted how immersive simulations improve procedural understanding and emotional engagement. These findings are reflected in our case studies, where medical and engineering students reported reduced cognitive load when practising complex tasks in the metaverse. For example, students practising PCR procedures or working with manufacturing robots demonstrated improved confidence and understanding compared to traditional methods.

By enabling learners to repeatedly engage with interactive simulations, the metaverse fosters skill acquisition and retention. However, as noted by Yang *et. al.* [78], further longitudinal research is required to evaluate the long-term effectiveness of VR-based learning on skill transferability to physical settings. This need for extended research underscores the potential of the metaverse to act not only as a supplemental tool but as an integral component of modern education.

### 5.7.3  COLLABORATION AND INTERACTIVITY

Collaboration and interactivity are foundational aspects of the metaverse's educational potential. Unlike traditional online tools like Zoom or Microsoft Teams, the metaverse offers immersive, multiplayer environments where students can engage in real-time collaboration. Paulsen *et. al.* (2024) [52] found that VR-based collaborative platforms significantly boost student motivation and foster teamwork, and also demonstrated that multiplayer VR environments enhance problem-solving skills by promoting interactive peer learning.

Our platform's multiplayer functionality and virtual lecture theatres exemplify these collaborative benefits. In our case studies, engineering students effectively worked together to troubleshoot and optimise virtual manufacturing processes, while medical students engaged in interactive discussions during simulated lab procedures. These features not only enhanced engagement but also prepared students for the collaborative demands of modern industries. The ability to simulate real-world teamwork scenarios within the metaverse positions it as a transformative tool for fostering professional readiness.

### 5.7.4  INTERDISCIPLINARY INNOVATION

The metaverse's scalability and versatility enable it to transcend disciplinary boundaries, fostering interdisciplinary innovation and creative problem-solving. By simulating diverse academic environments, from medical labs to engineering work-shops, the metaverse provides a shared digital space for students from various dis-ciplines to collaborate. This aligns with findings from several studies that note the metaverse's potential to bridge theoretical and practical knowledge across fields, pro-moting innovative solutions to complex problems ([20] [25] [67].

In our platform, students from computer science, mechanical engineering, and medical science explored simulations that encouraged interdisciplinary thinking. For example, engineering students collaborated on renewable energy solutions, integrat-ing principles from electrical and mechanical engineering. This holistic approach not only enhances technical competencies but also cultivates critical thinking and adapt-ability—skills essential for tackling global challenges. Expanding metaverse appli-cations to include interdisciplinary projects could unlock its full potential, fostering a more integrated and innovative educational experience.

## 5.8 CONCLUSION

The metaverse represents a transformative shift in education, offering innovative solutions to traditional challenges, such as limited access to resources, logistical constraints, and learner disengagement. By simulating real-world environments and equipment, the metaverse enables learners to practice complex tasks in a safe, cost-effective manner while reducing learner's cognitive load. Virtual labs allow students to engage with expensive or hazardous equipment like PCR machines in medical sci-ence or manufacturing robots in engineering, addressing resource limitations faced by many institutions. These immersive simulations bridge the gap between theoret-ical knowledge and practical application, fostering deeper understanding and skill acquisition.

Additionally, the metaverse enhances collaboration and interactivity through its multiplayer features and virtual lecture theatres, which go beyond traditional online-learning tools by providing a sense of presence and engagement. This environment facilitates teamwork, problem-solving, and peer learning, preparing students for the collaborative demands of modern industries. Furthermore, the metaverse democra-tises education by offering equitable access to high-quality resources, particularly for students in remote or underserved regions. Virtual campuses and labs allow learners worldwide to participate in lifelike simulations and engage with peers and instruc-tors, breaking down geographical and financial barriers.

Despite its promise, the metaverse's widespread adoption faces challenges, in-cluding the affordability of VR hardware and the need for infrastructure investments. Overcoming these barriers will require strategic partnerships between governments, educational institutions, and private enterprises. Moreover, the integration of ad-vanced technologies like Artificial Intelligence (AI) offers the potential to further personalise learning, catering to diverse educational needs and goals and need to be studied.

Looking forward, the metaverse's ability to democratise education, reduce cogni-tive barriers, and enhance interdisciplinary learning positions it as a cornerstone of innovation in the global educational landscape. By addressing current challenges and continuing to expand its applications, the metaverse can redefine how knowledge is shared, acquired, and applied, paving the way for a more inclusive, engaging, and future-ready approach to education.

## REFERENCES

1. A. Abdelrazeq, L. Daling, R. Suppes, Y. Feldmann, and F. Hees. A virtual reality educational tool in the context of mining engineering-the virtual reality mine. In *Inted2019 Proceedings*, pages 8067–8073. IATED, 2019.
2. K. Agustini, I. M. Putrama, D. S. Wahyuni, and I. N. E. Mertayasa. Applying gamification technique and virtual reality for prehistoric learning toward the metaverse. *International Journal of Information and Education Technology*, 13(2):247–256, 2023.
3. R. Alfaisal, H. Hashim, and U. H. Azizan. Metaverse system adoption in education: a systematic literature review. *Journal of Computers in Education*, 11(1):259–303, 2024.
4. Y. Alharbi, M. Al-Mansour, R. Al-Saffar, A. Garman, and A. Alraddadi. Three-dimensional virtual reality as an innovative teaching and learning tool for human anatomy courses in medical education: A mixed methods study. *Cureus*, 12(2), 2020.
5. V. Antoniou, F. L. Bonali, P. Nomikou, A. Tibaldi, P. Melissinos, F. P. Mariotto, and M. Whitworth. Integrating virtual reality and gis tools for geological mapping, data collection and analysis: An example from the metaxa mine, santorini (greece). *Applied Sciences*, 10(23):8317, 2020.
6. S. Behmadi, F. Asadi, M. Okhovati, and R. E. Sarabi. Virtual reality-based medical education versus lecture-based method in teaching start triage lessons in emergency medical students: Virtual reality in medical education. *Journal of Advances in Medical Education & Professionalism*, 10(1):48, 2022.
7. J. A. Bennett and C. P. Saunders. A virtual tour of the cell: Impact of virtual reality on student learning and engagement in the stem classroom. *Journal of Microbiology & Biology Education*, 20(2):10–1128, 2019.
8. P. Biswas, P. Orero, M. Swaminathan, K. Krishnaswamy, and P. Robinson. Adaptive accessible ar/vr systems. In *Extended Abstracts of the 2021 CHI Conference on Human Factors in Computing Systems*, pages 1–7, 2021.
9. D. Bogusevschi, C. Muntean, and G. M. Muntean. Teaching and learning physics using 3d virtual learning environment: A case study of combined virtual reality and virtual laboratory in secondary school. *Journal of Computers in Mathematics and Science Teaching*, 39(1):5–18, 2020.
10. J. Cabero-Almenara, C. Llorente-Cejudo, and R. Martinez-Roig. The use of mixed, augmented and virtual reality in history of art teaching: A case study. *Applied System Innovation*, 5(3):44, 2022.
11. A. Chehab and B. Nakhal. Exploring virtual reality as an approach to resurrect destroyed historical buildings-an approach to revive the destroyed "egg building" through vr. *Architecture and Planning Journal (APJ)*, 28(3):17, 2023.
12. S. T. Chen, P. L. Chiu, and C. C. Mao. Bringing virtual reality into military mental health education: A pilot study on stress management course. In *Advances in Usability, User Experience, Wearable and Assistive Technology: Proceedings of the AHFE 2020 Virtual Conferences*, pages 705–711. Springer International Publishing, 2020.
13. S. Cheng. *Metaverse*, pages 1–23. Springer Nature Switzerland, 2023.
14. P. Chenrai and S. Jitmahantakul. Applying virtual reality technology to geoscience classrooms. *Review of International Geographical Education Online*, 9(3):577–590, 2019.

15. M. Chi, Y. Chen, Y. Xu, and Y. Wu. Modelling barriers to metaverse adoption in the hospitality and tourism industry. *Information Technology & Tourism*, pages 1–33, 2024.

16. S. O. Choi, Y. S. Min, S. I. Kim, and J. G. Ghoi. A study on establishment of safety training center based on virtual reality and augmented reality technology for military safety and suicide accident prevention. *Journal of Internet Computing and Services*, 21(2):139–148, 2020.

17. F. J. Cortes Rodriguez, G. Frattini, F. Teixeira Pinto Meireles, D. A. Terrien, S. Cruz-Leon, M. Dal Peraro, and L. A. Abriata. Molecularwebxr: Multiuser discussions about chemistry and biology in immersive and inclusive vr. *bioRxiv*, pages 2023–11, 2023.

18. Y. Daineko, M. Ipalakova, D. Tsoy, Z. Bolatov, Z. Baurzhan, and Y. Yelgondy. Augmented and virtual reality for physics: Experience of kazakhstan secondary educational institutions. *Computer Applications in Engineering Education*, 28(5):1220–1231, 2020.

19. Y. Dalladaku, J. Kelley, B. Lacey, J. Mitchiner, B. Welsh, and M. Beigh. Assessing the effectiveness of virtual reality in the training of army aviators. In *Proceedings of the 2020 Annual General Donald R. Keith Memorial Capstone Conference*, page 40, 2020.

20. R. Damaševičius and T. Sidekerskienė. Virtual worlds for learning in metaverse: a narrative review. *Sustainability*, 16(5):2032, 2024.

21. C. Dede, J. Richards, and B. Saxberg. *Virtual, Augmented, and Mixed Realities in Education*, pages 1–16. Springer Singapore, 2017.

22. S. Dhingra. Metaverse adoption: a systematic literature review and roadmap for future research. *Global Knowledge, Memory and Communication*, 2024.

23. W. Du, X. Zhong, Y. Jia, R. Jiang, H. Yang, Z. Ye, and Z. Zong. A novel scenario-based, mixed-reality platform for training nontechnical skills of battlefield first aid: Prospective interventional study. *JMIR Serious Games*, 10(4):e40727, 2022.

24. B. I. Edwards, K. S. Bielawski, R. Prada, and A. D. Cheok. Haptic virtual reality and immersive learning for enhanced organic chemistry instruction. *Virtual Reality*, 23:363–373, 2019.

25. M. A. Fadhel, A. M. Duhaim, A. S. Albahri, Z. T. Al-Qaysi, M. A. Aktham, M. A. Chyad, and Y. Gu. Navigating the metaverse: unraveling the impact of artificial intelligence—a comprehensive review and gap analysis. *Artificial Intelligence Review*, 57(10):264, 2024.

26. J. B. Ferrell, J. P. Campbell, D. R. McCarthy, K. T. McKay, M. Hensinger, R. Srinivasan, and S. T. Schneebeli. Chemical exploration with virtual reality in organic teaching laboratories. *Journal of Chemical Education*, 96(9):1961–1966, 2019.

27. F. M. Fung, W. Y. Choo, A. Ardisara, C. D. Zimmermann, S. Watts, T. Koscielniak, and R. Dumke. Applying a virtual reality platform in environmental chemistry education to conduct a field trip to an overseas site. *Learning in a Digital World: Perspective on Interactive Technologies for Formal and Informal Education*, pages 213–238, 2019.

28. A. Gaafar. Metaverse in architectural heritage documentation & education. *Advances in Ecological and Environmental Research*, 6(10):66–86, 2021.

29. Y. Georgiou, O. Tsivitanidou, C. Eckhardt, and A. Ioannou. Work-in-progress—a learning experience design for immersive virtual reality in physics classrooms. In *2020 6th International Conference of the Immersive Learning Research Network (iLRN)*, pages 263–266. IEEE, 2020.

30. K. Habibah, A. K. Putra, S. Nilsson, and C. Vielhaber. Digital estuaries: Exploring the pedagogical benefits of virtual reality media in geography and spatial analysis. *Jambura Geo Education Journal*, 4(2):187–198, 2023.

31. R. Hadi Mogavi, J. Hoffman, C. Deng, Y. Du, E. U. Haq, and P. Hui. Envisioning an inclusive metaverse: Student perspectives on accessible and empowering metaverse-enabled learning. In *Proceedings of the Tenth ACM Conference on Learning@ Scale*, pages 346–353, 2023.

32. P. Hagge. Student perceptions of semester-long in-class virtual reality: Effectively using "google earth vr" in a higher education classroom. *Journal of Geography in Higher Education*, 45(3):342–360, 2021.

33. C. L. Hemme, R. Carley, A. Norton, M. Ghumman, H. Nguyen, R. Ivone, and B. Cho. Developing virtual and augmented reality applications for science, technology, engineering and math education. *BioTechniques*, 0, 2023.

34. M. Hernández-Chávez, J. M. Cortés-Caballero, Á. A. Pérez-Martínez, L. F. Hernández-Quintanar, K. Roa-Tort, J. D. Rivera-Fernández, and D. A. Fabila-Bustos. Development of virtual reality automotive lab for training in engineering students. *Sustainability*, 13(17):9776, 2021.

35. M. Janiszewski, L. Uotinen, J. Merkel, J. Leveinen, and M. Rinne. Virtual reality learning environments for rock engineering, geology and mining education. In *ARMA US Rock Mechanics/Geomechanics Symposium*, pages ARMA–2020, 2020.

36. P. Jindal, V. Khemchandani, S. Chandra, and V. Pandey. A multiplayer shooting game based simulation for defence training. In *2021 International Conference on Computational Performance Evaluation (ComPE)*, pages 592–597. IEEE, 2021.

37. C. Jones, L. Smith-MacDonald, A. Miguel-Cruz, A. Pike, M. van Gelderen, L. Lentz, and S. Brémault-Phillips. Virtual reality-based treatment for military members and veterans with combat-related posttraumatic stress disorder: protocol for a multimodular motion-assisted memory desensitization and reconsolidation randomized controlled trial. *JMIR Research Protocols*, 9(10):e20620, 2020.

38. A. Jovanović and A. Milosavljević. Vortex metaverse platform for gamified collaborative learning. *Electronics*, 11(3):317, 2022.

39. G. Karthick, B. Rebecca Jeyavadhanams, S. Ling, A. Kiyani, and N. Somasiri. Immersive learning using metaverse: Transforming the education industry through extended reality. In *International Conference on Micro-Electronics and Telecommunication Engineering*, pages 447–456. Springer Nature Singapore, 2023.

40. D. H. Kim, S. H. Min, and Y. H. Kim. A study of effectiveness on military training of army anti-aircraft weapon using virtual reality. *The Journal of the Korea Contents Association*, 21(5):499–507, 2021.

41. T. Kim, J. Planey, and R. Lindgren. Theory-driven design in metaverse virtual reality learning environments: Two illustrative cases. *IEEE Transactions on Learning Technologies*, 16(6):1141–1153, 2023.

42. A. Lawson McLean and A. C. Lawson McLean. Immersive simulations in surgical training: analyzing the interplay between virtual and real-world environments. *Simulation & Gaming*, 55(6):1103–1122, 2024.

43. H. Lee, D. Woo, and S. Yu. Virtual reality metaverse system supplementing remote education methods: Based on aircraft maintenance simulation. *Applied Sciences*, 12(5):2667, 2022.

44. H. Lin, S. Wan, W. Gan, J. Chen, and H. C. Chao. Metaverse in education: Vision, opportunities, and challenges. In *2022 IEEE International Conference on Big Data (Big Data)*, pages 2857–2866. IEEE, 2022.

45. X. P. Lin, B. B. Li, Z. N. Yao, Z. Yang, and M. Zhang. The impact of virtual reality on student engagement in the classroom—a critical review of the literature. *Frontiers in Psychology*, 15:1360574, 2024.

46. M. Lopez, J. G. C. Arriaga, J. P. N. Álvarez, R. T. González, J. A. Elizondo-Leal, J. E. Valdez-García, and B. Carrión. Virtual reality vs traditional education: Is there any advantage in human neuroanatomy teaching? *Computers & Electrical Engineering*, 93:107282, 2021.

47. R. Mahindru, A. Kumar, G. Bapat, A. D. Rroy, Kavita, and N. Sharma. Metaverse unleashed: Augmenting creativity and innovation in business education. *Engineering Proceedings*, 59(1):207, 2024.

48. G. Makransky and L. Lilleholt. A structural equation modeling investigation of the emotional value of immersive virtual reality in education. *Educational Technology Research and Development*, 66(5):1141–1164, 2018.

49. M. Mergen, N. Graf, and M. Meyerheim. Reviewing the current state of virtual reality integration in medical education-a scoping review. *BMC Medical Education*, 24(1):788, 2024.

50. B. Miao, S. Ge, and Y. Guo. Construction of digital twin system for intelligent mining in coal mines. *Metaverse*, 3(2):16, 2022.

51. P. Onu, A. Pradhan, and C. Mbohwa. Potential to use metaverse for future teaching and learning. *Education and Information Technologies*, 29(7):8893–8924, 2024.

52. L. Paulsen, S. Dau, and J. Davidsen. Designing for collaborative learning in immersive virtual reality: a systematic literature review. *Virtual Reality*, 28(1):63, 2024.

53. E. Paxinou, M. Georgiou, V. Kakkos, D. Kalles, and L. Galani. Achieving educational goals in microscopy education by adopting virtual reality labs on top of face-to-face tutorials. *Research in Science & Technological Education*, 40(3):320–339, 2022.

54. E. Paxinou, C. T. Panagiotakopoulos, A. Karatrantou, D. Kalles, and A. Sgourou. Implementation and evaluation of a three-dimensional virtual reality biology lab versus conventional didactic practices in lab experimenting with the photonic microscope. *Biochemistry and Molecular Biology Education*, 48(1):21–27, 2020.

55. J. Pirker, M. Holly, I. Lesjak, J. Kopf, and C. Gütl. Maroonvr—an interactive and immersive virtual reality physics laboratory. In *Learning in a Digital World: Perspective on Interactive Technologies for Formal and Informal Education*, pages 213–238, 2019.

56. C. Prisille and M. Ellerbrake. Virtual reality (vr) and geography education: Potentials of 360° 'experiences' in secondary schools. *Modern Approaches to the Visualization of Landscapes*, pages 321–332, 2020.

57. L. Pérez, E. Diez, R. Usamentiaga, and D. F. García. Industrial robot control and operator training using virtual reality interfaces. *Computers in Industry*, 109:114–120, 2019.

58. J. Á. Ramírez and A. M. V. Bueno. Learning organic chemistry with virtual reality. In *2020 IEEE International Conference on Engineering Veracruz (ICEV)*, pages 1–4. IEEE, 2020.

59. S. M. Reeves, K. J. Crippen, and E. D. McCray. The varied experience of undergraduate students learning chemistry in virtual reality laboratories. *Computers & Education*, 175:104320, 2021.

60. B. Salah, M. H. Abidi, S. H. Mian, M. Krid, H. Alkhalefah, and A. Abdo. Virtual reality-based engineering education to enhance manufacturing sustainability in industry 4.0. *Sustainability*, 11(5):1477, 2019.

61. N. Shakirova, N. Said, and S. Konyushenko. The use of virtual reality in geo-education. *International Journal of Emerging Technologies in Learning (iJET)*, 15(20):59–70, 2020.

62. A. Sharma, L. Sharma, and J. Krezel. Bridging theory into practice: An investigation of the opportunities and challenges to the implementation of metaverse-based teaching in higher education institutions. In *International Conference on Human–Computer Interaction*, pages 173–189. Springer Nature Switzerland, 2024.

63. Y. Shen, Z. Wang, M. Li, J. Yuan, and Y. Gu. An empirical study of geography learning on students' emotions and motivation in immersive virtual reality. In *Frontiers in Education*, volume 7, page 831619. Frontiers, 2022.

64. K. Silseth, R. Steier, and H. C. Arnseth. Exploring students' immersive vr experiences as resources for collaborative meaning making and learning. *International Journal of Computer-Supported Collaborative Learning*, 19(1):11–36, 2024.

65. A. Singh, D. Ferry, A. Ramakrishnan, and S. Balasubramanian. Using virtual reality in biomedical engineering education. *Journal of Biomechanical Engineering*, 142(11):111013, 2020.

66. M. Soliman, A. Pesyridis, D. Dalaymani-Zad, M. Gronfula, and M. Kourmpetis. The application of virtual reality in engineering education. *Applied Sciences*, 11(6):2879, 2021.

67. M. M. Soliman, E. Ahmed, A. Darwish, and A. E. Hassanien. Artificial intelligence powered metaverse: analysis, challenges and future perspectives. *Artificial Intelligence Review*, 57(2):36, 2024.

68. Jungmyoung Son, Soohee Woo, Jeong Hye Han, and Jong-Jun Kim. Development and application of social studies content based on augmented virtual metaverse: Jikji simche yojeol. *Journal of Digital Contents Society*, 2023.

69. P. Stothard. Mining metaverse–a future collaborative tool for best practice mining. *Mining Technology*, 132(3):165–178, 2023.

70. M. M. Thompson, A. Wang, C. Uz Bilgin, M. Anteneh, D. Roy, P. Tan, and E. Klopfer. Influence of virtual reality on high school students' conceptions of cells. *Placeholder Journal Name*, 2020.

71. A. Tibaldi, F. L. Bonali, F. Vitello, E. Delage, P. Nomikou, V. Antoniou, and M. Whitworth. Real world–based immersive virtual reality for research, teaching and communication in volcanology. *Bulletin of Volcanology*, 82:1–12, 2020.

72. M. H. Tsou and C. Mejia. Beyond mapping: Extend the role of cartographers to user interface designers in the metaverse using virtual reality, augmented reality, and mixed reality. *Cartography and Geographic Information Science*, pages 1–15, 2023.

73. R. van Dinther, L. de Putter, and B. Pepin. Features of immersive virtual reality to support meaningful chemistry education. *Journal of Chemical Education*, 100(4):1537–1546, 2023.

74. D. Vergara, J. Extremera, M. P. Rubio, and L. P. Dávila. Meaningful learning through virtual reality learning environments: A case study in materials engineering. *Applied Sciences*, 9(21):4625, 2019.

75. H. Wang, H. Ning, Y. Lin, W. Wang, S. Dhelim, F. Farha, and M. Daneshmand. A survey on the metaverse: The state-of-the-art, technologies, applications, and challenges. *IEEE Internet of Things Journal*, 10(16):14671–14688, 2023.

76. Y. Wang, Z. Su, N. Zhang, R. Xing, D. Liu, T. H. Luan, and X. Shen. A survey on metaverse: Fundamentals, security, and privacy. *IEEE Communications Surveys & Tutorials*, 25(1):319–352, 2022.

77. T. H. Wu, F. Wu, C. J. Liang, Y. F. Li, C. M. Tseng, and S. C. Kang. A virtual reality tool for training in global engineering collaboration. *Universal Access in the Information Society*, 18:243–255, 2019.

78. C. Yang, J. Zhang, Y. Hu, X. Yang, M. Chen, M. Shan, and L. Li. The impact of virtual reality on practical skills for students in science and engineering education: a meta-analysis. *International Journal of STEM Education*, 11(1):28, 2024.

79. J. Yang, F. Liu, J. Wang, Z. Kou, A. Zhu, and D. Yao. Effect of virtual reality technology on the teaching of urban railway vehicle engineering. *Computer Applications in Engineering Education*, 29(5):1163–1175, 2021.

80. P. Šiđanin, J. Plavšić, I. Arsenić, and M. Krmar. Virtual reality (vr) simulation of a nuclear physics laboratory exercise. *European Journal of Physics*, 41(6):065802, 2020.

# 6 UX Design Guided by Cognitive Load Theory

*Nadine Marcus*
School of Computer Science and Engineering, UNSW Sydney
Kensington, Australia

*Alexandra Vassar*
School of Computer Science and Engineering, UNSW Sydney
Kensington, Australia

## UX DESIGN GUIDED BY COGNITIVE LOAD THEORY

Jacob Nielsen has provided a list of 10 general principles for Interaction Design that are widely employed by UX (user experience) designers. These heuristic design principles serve to support the design of more usable interfaces. Cognitive load theory, which focuses on scientifically based empirical approaches to designing instructions and interfaces that minimize the burden on our limited capacity to process new or unfamiliar information, underpins the effectiveness of these principles. Using these principles in design therefore helps to guide the design in such a way that users can focus on the goals of the task at hand, rather than being distracted by the extraneous load of interacting with a poorly designed interface. Cognitive load theory posits that we have a limited working memory responsible for processing new information, and a vast store of familiar information stored within our long-term memories. Working memory, often referred to as our consciousness, is constrained both in terms of the amount of new information it can process at a time, as well as the time this information can remain in our consciousness. We can overcome some of these processing limitations by relying on our vast stores of prior knowledge stored in our long-term memories. By designing interfaces that aim to reduce constraints on our limited working memories and rather tap into resources stored in long-term memory, users will benefit from these design principles. This chapter aims to theoretically ground each of Nielsen's heuristics within cognitive load theory principles, explaining why the practical guidelines are so effective in improving interface design. We will also provide an overview of relevant empirically validated cognitive load effects. Establishing this connection between the theory and the usability guidelines can help users of the heuristics better understand why they work and enable designers to more broadly and intuitively implement good design practices. It should be noted that while heuristic design principles and evaluation are a useful tool in the early stages

DOI: 10.1201/9781032702797-6

of the interaction design lifecycle, they should not replace thorough usability testing later in the design lifecycle.

## 6.1  INTRODUCTION

Usability heuristics are one of the most widely used methods that guide the design and evaluation of interactive interfaces, ensuring that interface design is comprehensive, simple, and user-friendly. The method is particularly useful for desktop interfaces. Used as part of a heuristic evaluation, these rules of thumb can be used to identify usability problems in a system's interface design. Whilst they are not comprehensive, they cover a wide range of common issues that may affect the user experience. There are several different heuristics sets available for design and evaluation [28, 11, 25]. However, one of the most widely used heuristics guidelines were developed by Jacob Nielsen [20], based on years of experience in the field of human-computer interaction. Heuristics were not an entirely new concept, but were distilled from existing practice and research in usability. They were designed to be easy to remember and apply, making them accessible to practitioners in the field. While these rules of thumb are very practical, they also work because they tap into our cognitive strengths. The longevity of these heuristics is in part due to their broad applicability and the fact that they address fundamental issues in user interaction that go beyond specific technologies or trends. One of the other reasons, however, for this longevity is that these heuristics can tap into our understanding of cognitive architecture, specifically our limited working memory capacity. This chapter aims to improve our understanding of the value and durability of these original ten heuristics for good user experience and interface design, by linking them to cognitive load theory [19]. If we can better understand why the heuristics work so well then it can further facilitate their application. The heuristics work because they essentially reduce the load on our limited working memories and so make information easier to process and understand.

However, it is important to understand the context in which the heuristics were originally developed by Jakob Nielsen [21]. Nielsen had access to a database of 249 usability problems from 11 different projects, as well 101 usability principles that could explain the design flaws. He used a factor analysis to distil the principles down to 10 factors that explained most of the problems. This led to the 10 usability heuristics with the largest explanatory power, that have been extensively used for the past 30 years. Now that we understand how he derived these heuristic principles that are so widely used in the UX design domain, we will now tie this into a discussion of *why* these principles work, based on our understanding of human cognitive architecture.

We begin with an overview of cognitive load theory and then use this understanding to expand on why and how each heuristic can work to improve UX design.

## 6.2  COGNITIVE LOAD THEORY

Cognitive load theory is an empirically validated theory that relates to how our cognitive architecture is used to support the learning and understanding of new information

[35]. Cognitive load theory assumes a very limited working memory used to process new and unfamiliar information and an unlimited long-term memory used to store vast amounts of information over time and focuses on interactions between the two memory systems. Working memory, often referred to as our consciousness, is constrained by both the amount of new information it can process at one time, as well as the time the information remains in our consciousness. We overcome some of these processing limitations by relying on vast stores of prior knowledge stored in our long-term memories, in the form of schemas. Schemas are cognitive constructs that allow us to process large amounts of information by organizing information according to how it will be used [38]. Schemas allow us to process vast amounts of familiar information in a single unit. Moreover, the more knowledge you have in a domain the more information a single schema may contain. And the more practiced a schema is the more automated it becomes, and the less processing capacity it consumes [32]. Automated information can be processed without conscious attention and is often difficult to suppress, such when one is walking along a familiar route but aiming to arrive somewhere new and rather finds oneself walking in automatic mode to the usual destination. Schemas help reduce the burden on our limited working memories and the more automated they are the less of a burden they are on our limited processing resources. Prior knowledge can thus support our learning and reduce the burden on our limited cognitive resources.

Moreover, more recent updates of the theory by Sweller [33] also allude to the evolutionary and biological aspects of our cognitive architecture that impact the way we learn. He alludes to the important distinction between biologically primary knowledge that we have evolved to acquire (such as facial recognition and learning to walk) and so does not need to be taught; and biologically secondary knowledge (such as mathematics and learning to write) that need to be explicitly taught to be learned. The purpose of our education system is to acquire biologically secondary knowledge, and we can use primary skills and knowledge (such as human movement or collaborating with others) to support the acquisition of new secondary knowledge and skills. Tapping into primary knowledge when users are overloaded can be a helpful strategy. Cognitive load theory is focused on empirically validated strategies to support the acquisition of biologically secondary information within educational institutions.

Furthermore, Sweller [37] focuses on five biologically primary principles that relate to how we acquire knowledge and provide a framework for the cognitive architecture that underlies cognitive load theory. Amongst these principles, The Information Store Principle details the large store of information that we require to function in the natural world. The Borrowing and Reorganising Principle focusses on the bulk of information stored in long term memory that comes from other people – this principle is particularly useful in the context of educational collaborative practices. The third principle, Randomness as Genesis Principle, focusses on the generation of novel information during problem solving. Severe limitations of working memory when processing new information, with recent evidence showing depletion of working memory after cognitive effort [7]. And finally, the Environmental Organising and

Linking Principle focusses on the unlimited long-term memory and the environmental cues that can be generated to process information appropriate to that environment in our long-term memories. In summary, explicit instruction is necessary as we have evolved to learn from others via the borrowing and reorganising principle. This information needs to be organised in such a way as to reduce working memory load, because this load is most evident when processing new information (narrow limits of change). When we learn from others, we can reduce our cognitive load in comparison to generating our own novel information (randomness as genesis). Once we have obtained and stored the information in our long-term memory (information store), the limitations of working memory no longer apply, and the stored information can be transferred between long term and working memory via the organizing and linking principle. However, for the purposes of this chapter we will just focus on these basic tenets of the theory mentioned above that are most relevant to our discussions.

Novice users rely on limited working memories to help them interact with new interfaces, and keeping the strain on limited working memory resources to a minimum is particularly important for them. In contrast, experts have huge amounts of familiar information stored in their long-term memories which they can retrieve as automated schemas when needed, and are less constrained by working memory limitations. Those that design interfaces are often experts and so less aware of these limitations, but need to be mindful of the needs of the novices they are also designing for [12]. Moreover, when we design interfaces with the aim to reduce the strain on working memory (WM) and rather try to tap into familiar resources stored in long-term memory (LTM), all users will benefit. With this in mind, we begin an exploration of how to design interfaces that can also consider our novice users with limited working memory resources available to them.

### 6.2.1 DIFFERENT TYPES OF COGNITIVE LOAD

Also relevant to Cognitive Load Theory is the fact that there are three types of cognitive load. The first type of load is intrinsic load which is the load related to the inherent complexity of the information itself. This load is fixed and is related to the type of information the user is dealing with, and the concept of element interactivity [16]. This concept of element interactivity is dependent on how many elements are interacting in the presented information and is related to the prior knowledge of the person who is taking in information. For example, when learning to read English, the myriad of new letter formations and interpretations would constitute a high element interactivity, whereas for someone that knows how to read English, the characters would present as a single element and would therefore have a low element interactivity. Examples of high intrinsic load content that involve high element interactivity include learning the grammar of a new language, as there are many elements that need to be considered simultaneously, such as word order, tense, pronouns and so on. In contrast, learning the vocabulary of a new language is still a difficult task but each new word can be learnt individually and so the intrinsic load and level of interacting elements is low. However, intrinsic load is also impacted by the prior knowledge of the users and if they already have knowledge in the domain, it is less likely to have an impact on users. Someone who is fluent in a language no longer thinks about the rules of the grammar or how to construct a sentence (as this information has been automated), in contrast to someone who is still learning the language. Therefore, it is always important to know something about the users your design is aimed for. The higher the intrinsic load of the content presented to your users, the more important it is to reduce extraneous load.

Extraneous load is the load that relates to how the information is presented. This load is not fixed and can be altered by using different information presentation techniques, with a goal of using techniques that reduce the load on the user or the learner. We will be discussing some of these techniques as well. And lastly there is germane load which relates to the load associated with creating schemas and automating them and so learning. Whereas we aim to reduce extraneous load, especially if the intrinsic load is high, we rather aim to increase the germane load or the load associated with acquiring new knowledge [38]. However, since no instructional consequences of germane load have been identified, it is more recently often not even considered [34].

## 6.3    RELEVANT COGNITIVE LOAD EFFECTS

We will now discuss some different cognitive load effects that have been empirically discovered as ways to reduce extraneous load and so improve the understanding and processing of new and unfamiliar information. These effects are methods that can be used to improve information presentation and reduce load on the learners and users.

### 6.3.1    WORKED EXAMPLE EFFECT

The Worked example effect was one of the first cognitive load effects to be empirically validated. It relates to fact that problem solving can overload working memory and make it more difficult to transfer information to long-term memory and so learn. Novice learners learn better by rather studying worked out problem solutions to unfamiliar problems. Sweller and Cooper [36] provided empirical evidence for this effect using algebra problems, followed by many other researchers in different domains including banking, design, medical field and English essay writing [9, 26, 27, 30, 14]. Providing an example of how to use an unfamiliar interface, or guidance as it is navigated for the first time, are instances of using the worked example effect to improve understanding. Moreover, as users progress to an intermediate level of knowledge providing a partially completed worked out example that steers users as to how to solve the problem has been found to be an effective way to support the scaffolding of new knowledge acquisition [35].

### 6.3.2    SPLIT ATTENTION EFFECT

The next cognitive load effect is the split attention effect, where Tarmizi and Sweller [41] found that certain mathematical worked examples needed to be restructured to be effective. In particular, information that was physically split up and needed to be mentally integrated was more difficult to learn from. Physically integrating mutually referring sources of information (such as diagrams and text, or even text and text) so that learners do not have to engage in unnecessary mental integration, has been empirically shown to lead to better learning for novices in many domains ranging from geometry [43], to an engineering programming language and education reports [6], and also including meteorological tasks [17], and many more. The split attention effect relates to the fact that we need to physically integrate mutually referring sources of related information, so that users or learners do not have to engage in unnecessary mental integration. Having information split across multiple screens or windows that need to be navigated to search for related information, would be an example of split attention that should be avoided for users of an interface.

### 6.3.3   REDUNDANCY EFFECT

The next relevant cognitive load effect is the Redundancy effect, where information that is not essential to learning has been found time and time again to have negative consequences. Rather than being neutral, having to process non-essential information uses up valuable resources and can impair learning and understanding of new information. Moreover, for novice users of an interface having to process redundant content is likely to lead to information overload. This effect was empirically discovered by Chandler and Sweller [5] using electrical engineering and biology materials but has been replicated in many, many domains including paper folding, geometry tasks [4] and in teaching orthopedic and physiotherapy content [23] to name just a few. Including non-essential and extra information in an interface means the user must still read and process it, which can lead to cognitive overload.

### 6.3.4   MODALITY EFFECT

The modality effect is slightly different to the other effects, as it works by effectively expanding working memory. If two sources of information both need to be included for information to be understood, then having some of the information in an auditory format rather than all in a written format can enhance learning. This effect works because our visual and auditory processors are partially independent and so it allows for some information to be offloaded into a different processor and so not overload the visual component of working memory. Mousavi et al. [18] were the first to discover this effect using geometry materials and it has been replicated by many others as summarised by Ginns [10] in his meta-analysis. The important thing to be aware of is that the auditory component must not be too long or complex and it should be coordinated in time with the visual information.

### 6.3.5   TRANSIENT INFORMATION EFFECT

The transient information effect follows next as it occurs when transient information, like auditory content or animations, which are only available for a few seconds and then disappear, lead to cognitive overload. Transient information, like speech, does not remain but rather is constantly replaced with newer content and so if it is too long and too complex it may overwhelm our limited processing capacities. Tabbers et al. [40], and then Leahy et al. [15] found evidence for this effect with auditory information that was too long and complex leading to inferior performance when compared to visual information alone. In contrast, non-transient information (like written text or static graphics) is available to be revisited when needed. Singh et al. [29], found transient effects when comparing spoken to written text for learning, but found it could be moderated for the spoken information using segmentation and pauses. Moreover, Wong et al. [44] also found negative effects of transient information for both long and complex animated and audio content. We need to design materials and interfaces to be mindful of how transient information can lead to cognitive overload. Audio should not be too long or complex, and should ideally be under user control to pause, rewind and slow down, and similarly for instructional animations.

### 6.3.6   HUMAN MOVEMENT EFFECT

While the transient information effect can explain why users learn less from dynamic information (like animations) than static content, the Human Movement effect refers to the fact that it is better to use animations rather than statics to teach concepts that involve some form of human movement. This effect was discovered by Ayres, et el. [3] and Wong et al. [45] where they found superior learning outcomes when learning human motor skills (paper folding, knot tying) using instructional animations. We have an innate ability to learn by observing and learning human movement related content by observation can tap into this ability (as described by Van Gog et al. [42]). We learn how to tie a shoelace or throw a ball while watching others carry out these tasks, and animations that are designed with this in mind, can potentially reduce cognitive load and lead to improved user experiences. However, because we have an innate ability to learn by observing we sometimes overgeneralise this and include non-human movement related animations too liberally in our interfaces, and so potentially overload our users with transient information. Animations thus need to be included into interfaces with care and we should focus on animating content that has a human movement component associated with it.

### 6.3.7   EXPERTISE REVERSAL EFFECT

Another relevant cognitive load effect that has been empirically validated in numerous domains is the expertise reversal effect (see Kalyuga et al. [12]). This effect occurs when the format of information presentation that is best for experts is the opposite of what is best for novices and occurs because of the vast store of knowledge and schemas that experts in a domain, have acquired (e.g. [13, 7]). As an example of this, novices learn best by studying worked out examples, while experts may learn best by solving problems in a domain; additionally, novice users of an interface may want access to lots of help and extra tips, while experts may find this extra information unnecessary. The experts often design course materials and interfaces and so may make assumptions about what is best for the users and need to be mindful to thus include user testing of a range of different users in the design process.

## 6.3.8   GUIDANCE FADING EFFECT

The guidance fading effect refers to gradually fading the guidance provided to the user when their knowledge or skills grow. This greatly relates to the previous effect because the integration of detailed instructional guidance, such as the those provided in worked examples, for users whose schemas and structures are already well developed, will require additional cognitive resources to process and add an unnecessary load on the architecture [1, 26, 2]. Thus, we want to aim to gradually reduce the amount of help provided to the user as they gain more experience with the interface. This also applies to worked examples, where we also want to fade out the steps as expertise of the user increases. The assumption supporting this effect is that our working memory capacity will be able to deal with an increase in demands, and a gradual reduction in problem solving guidance as expertise develops to thus cope with increased problem-solving demands [31].

There are many more cognitive load effects that have been discovered via empirical research as summarised by Sweller, et al. [39], but the ones mentioned above are the most relevant to Usability, UX and Interface design. We note that applying these cognitive load effects to reduce extraneous load is most important when the intrinsic load of the information being presented to the users is already high and so the users are already potentially cognitively overloaded.

## 6.4   APPLICATION OF COGNITIVE LOAD THEORY TO EACH HEURISTIC

In this next section we aim to make it clear why each of the rules of thumbs developed by Nielsen [22, 19] manage to make good use of our cognitive resources, often by reducing the load on our limited working memories, and so make information easy to process and make sense of. This in turn supports the user in the use an interface or a system that involves less load and is thus easier to use. This will be of most benefit for novice users, but everyone will benefit from an easy-to-use interface, that places less load on our working memories. We will describe each heuristic and then why it works from a cognitive load perspective.

### 6.4.1   VISIBILITY OF SYSTEM STATUS

The first heuristic of Visibility of System Status relates to always keeping user informed about what is happening in a timely manner, using appropriate feedback [19]. This heuristic works because effective and useful feedback increases the chance that users will learn from their mistakes, more easily learn how to use the system, and ultimately integrate new knowledge into their existing schemas. Moreover, from a cognitive load perspective it reduces the need for users to search for information and work out what is happening. Search uses up cognitive resources and so results in less resources available for other valuable cognitive activities such as learning and understanding. An example includes letting users know how long a task will take to complete and that it is currently in the process of being executed (Figure 6.1).

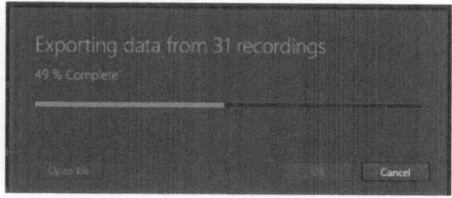

**Figure 6.1** An example of Visibility of System Status heuristic. Being able to understand and view the progress of the system task reduces cognitive load

## 6.4.2 MATCH BETWEEN THE SYSTEM AND REAL WORLD

The second heuristic of Match between the System and the Real World involves speaking the user's language using words, phrases and concepts that are familiar rather than system-oriented terms and jargon [19]. If we can design a system that uses familiar language and concepts, this then allows the users to apply their prior knowledge and schemas to the task at hand and can help to reduce cognitive load. Moreover, an interface or system will be easier to use and understand if the information is presented in a way that is more familiar to users. This relies on avoiding jargon and unfamiliar terminology and keeping the language simpler and more user friendly. Ultimately, this heuristic relies on linking new information to users' prior knowledge to ultimately reduce the cognitive load of using an interface or a new system. An instance of this principle could involve using tools and icons that resemble items in the real world (Figure 6.2).

**Figure 6.2** An example of Match between System and Real World. Email icons resemble the objects in the real world (for example Delete has an icon of a rubbish bin) to reinforce our understanding of what the command does and reduce cognitive load of learning the interface

## 6.4.3 USER CONTROL AND FREEDOM

The third heuristic of providing User Control and Freedom relates to providing users with ways to easily escape from places they unexpectedly find themselves, by providing clearly marked 'exits' or ways to undo things [19]. By giving the users clear control of what they are doing, this allows their cognitive resources to be focussed on what they are aiming to achieve and reduces unwanted distractions. It also has the potential to avoid the split attention involved with the user having to try to navigate many screens and possible options to work out where they want to be. The caveat to this is that giving users too many ways to do the same thing can be confusing and lead to redundancy and should thus be avoided. Giving users control of what they are doing allows their cognitive resources to be focussed on the goal and not on other unnecessary and potentially redundant tasks. For instance, users should always be able to easily navigate to the home page of a website or exit of a system whenever needed. As a further example, folder navigation should allow the user to go back one step at any time, by providing a clear direction in which they can move (Figure 6.3).

**Figure 6.3**    The OneDrive folder navigation menu allows the user to go back one step at any time, by providing clear visibility of location and nesting

### 6.4.4   CONSISTENCY AND STANDARDS

The fourth heuristic of Consistency and Standards alludes to the importance of not making users wonder if different words, situation, or actions mean the same thing [19]. If we use consistent terminology, colours, layout, actions, fonts and the like it makes it much easier for users to know where to expect to find things and what different actions and situations are likely to mean. In addition, once users become familiar with the layout, colours, actions, terminology and so on, it becomes easier to find information and to interact with an interface. In essence, consistency allows users to more easily acquire schemas of where to find things and how things operate. It is good practice to not only ensure good consistency and standards within your own system, but also to consider the meanings of certain icons, colours, key presses and so on in other systems so as not to overload and confuse your users. User testing allows you to get a good understanding of your users' prior knowledge and thus consider it in your design choices. Examples of good consistency and standards include using acronyms or key presses to mean the same things as in other website and systems, locating navigation panes in a consistent location across all your interfaces, and using icons and colours in the same manner and to mean the same thing across all your interfaces within your system. One of the most persistent examples of this consistency and standards is the use of the old floppy disk as an icon for the action 'Save'. Despite the fact, that most younger people now have never used or even seen a floppy disk, they are still able to recognise this icon easily due to the consistency in its use.

On a visit to a State National Park recently, we came across a fire safety lift to take us down to the train station, we encountered a rather confusing lift button sequence (Figure 6.4). We wondered how many times someone called the firehouse by accident instead of just calling the lift to them. This lack of consistency and adherence to regular lift panels is an example of why the use of such heuristics provides guidelines that improve the design of things, whilst also reducing our cognitive load. In the case of an emergency, one doesn't want to have to choose from three possible buttons that may need to be pressed, rather one wants to be directed straight away to an emergency button, as one would not have a lot of cognitive resources to dedicate to this type of choice, in the case of emergency.

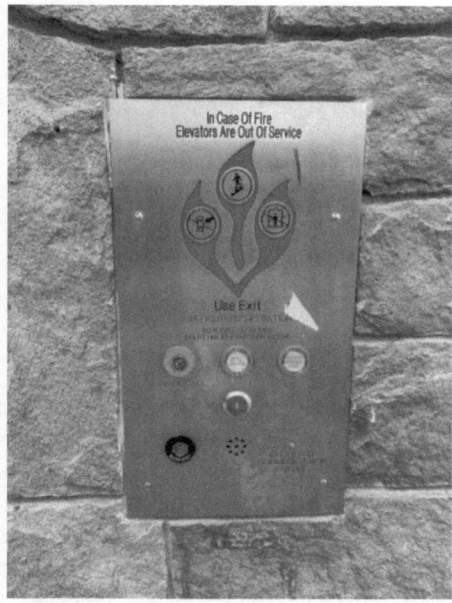

**Figure 6.4**   An elevator to move visitors from national park ground level down into the metro level below ground

### 6.4.5   HELP USERS RECOGNIZE, DIAGNOSE, AND RECOVER FROM ERRORS

This fifth heuristic involves using plain language to describe the nature of the problem and suggest a way to solve it [19]. Some of the error messages presented to users can be confusing and not helpful to solving the error. Effective and useful feedback can increase the chances that a user will learn from their mistake and integrate new knowledge into their existing schemas. Moreover, familiar language increases the chance that the user will understand the information presented to them, and not be overloaded by the problem they have encountered. Good error messages help reduce the load associated with problem solving by providing hints towards an effective solution and in essence help the users by providing a partially worked out solution to their problem or error encountered, which relates to the empirically validated worked example completion effect [35]. A helpful error message provides a description of what and where the issue is and may suggest a potential solution. Avoid unhelpful error messages that contain jargon and don't suggest how to recover from the issue.

For example, an example of a Learning Management system, which provides an error message when an incorrect user name or password have been entered (Figure 6.5), this can be further improved by providing a step to let the user know what to do if the password is forgotten.

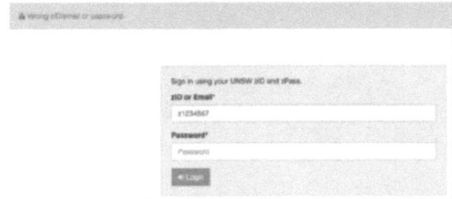

**Figure 6.5** This Learning Management System provides an error message when incorrect username or password have been entered. This message would also benefit from specifying what to do if you do not remember your password

### 6.4.6   ERROR PREVENTION

Error prevention alludes to designing an interface in a way that errors are prevented from occurring in the first place [19]. This sixth heuristic is effective from a cognitive load perspective as when a user makes an error, cognitive resources are used up by trying to understand and then fix the problem, rather than being devoted to the task at hand. If errors can be avoided in the first place, then all cognitive resources can be devoted to the task which will lead to faster learning and better use of a users' attention and limited cognitive resources. To achieve this goal, good user testing of an interface is needed, so that issues can be identified early on and resolved. Tips for how to design interfaces to prevent errors include avoiding confusing and redundant links, providing reminders and hints for common errors (such as reminders to attach a file or fill out a field in a form) as well using good consistent terminology, links, layout, and actions. For example, the AirBnB calendar picker dates will grey out any dates that are not available to prevent them from being chosen (Figure 6.6).

### 6.4.7   RECOGNITION RATHER THAN RECALL

The seventh heuristic is relying on Recognition rather than Recall, which involves making objects, actions, and options visible at the appropriate time [19]. If there is less information that needs to be remembered this can reduce the burden on our limited WM, which in turn can reduce the chance of making errors and can also make the interface and system easier to use and interact with. If the design can help minimise the load on our memories, this can also facilitate making good decisions. This heuristic works because we are much better at recognising a choice from an array of options than trying to recall an item stored in our long-term memories. Examples of how to apply this include using menus with familiar layouts and items instead of forcing users to type in their choices, making search histories available to your users

**Figure 6.6**   The Airbnb date picker does not let you choose dates that are in the past or dates that are unavailable, as check-in dates, showing good error prevention and thereby lowering cognitive load

and including previous selections when entering data. For example, a menu summarising recently accessed files is an example of recognising what you may need (Figure 6.7), whilst a password request is an example of pure recall, which has the potential to overburden the user (Figure 6.8).

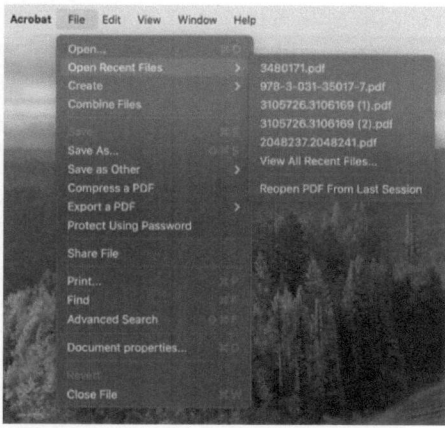

**Figure 6.7**   An example of "Recognise", where all recent files are kept separately for easier access, thereby reducing cognitive load that would otherwise be required to search for the right files

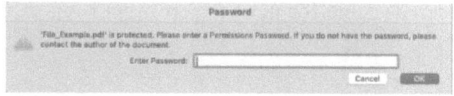

**Figure 6.8**   An example of "Recall" – there is nothing that you can recognise the password by here, thereby using heavy cognitive resources to recall a password

### 6.4.8 FLEXIBILITY AND EFFICIENCY OF USE

Flexibility and efficiency of use is the eighth heuristic, which involves providing accelerators that are invisible to novice users, but that allow more experienced users to carry out tasks more efficiently [19]. This principle relies on the fact that the needs of novice and expert users are not the same and are almost the opposite, as per the expertise reversal effect, as described above [12]. Accelerators or short-cuts would require extra processing capacity for inexperienced or novice users who are still learning to use an interface or a system, so it is better to make them invisible. In contrast, accelerators, short-cuts, customised layouts, and macros all allow expert users to more easily automate basic functions and therefore work more efficiently and effectively. Examples of how to better cater for novices are training wheel systems, where certain system functionality is not available or greyed out in a menu system [24]; while for experts having short cut key presses like Ctrl+C for copying in a word processor and macros in spreadsheets, can facilitate and speed up their workflow and allow experts to work more productively (Figure 6.9).

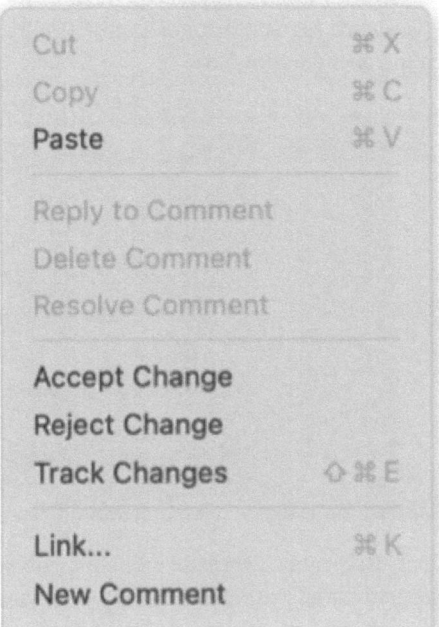

**Figure 6.9** Having a right click menu where novices can choose what they want to do, but also making shortcuts available for more expert users is an example of Flexibility and Efficiency of Use

### 6.4.9   AESTHETIC AND MINIMALIST DESIGN

Creating an Aesthetic and minimalist design is the ninth heuristic and involves avoiding the use of information that is irrelevant and rarely needed [19]. This heuristic in essence refers to the Redundancy effect, as per above [5], where non-essential information is not neutral but rather requires extra processing and so increases the load on our limited working memories. If information is well laid out and easy to read and find, this reduces the amount of search needed to interact with an interface and find relevant information. Search using up our working memory capacity and so leaves less capacity to devote to understanding, decision making and learning. So, when we design an interface, we should only be including the essential information and should eliminate redundant information as processing it uses up our limited cognitive resources (Figure 6.10). For instance, websites that only include the essential information are much easier to use and navigate and thus more likely to lead to customers returning to use them again. Prior to Google, search engines were often cluttered with recent news, weather, and other information that was not necessary for the ultimate functionality of search. The Google search engine was able to optimize this principle by putting front and centre the essence of search and focusing on that single functionality without including the redundant information.

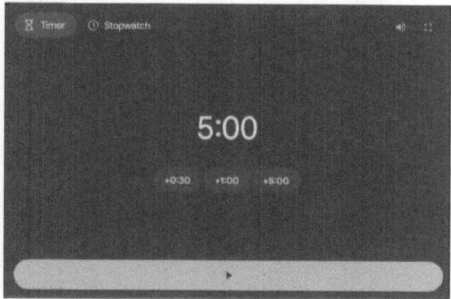

**Figure 6.10**   As an example, the Google countdown timer screen only has the counter, and three choices for adding extra time to this counter that would be frequently used (not adding an extra second for example, which would be redundant). The Start button is also well located, overall, the timer serves the purpose well with no redundancy on the screen to unnecessarily use up limited cognitive resources of the user

### 6.4.10   HELP AND DOCUMENTATION

The tenth and final heuristic is to provide Help and documentation, which alludes to providing your users with information that can be easily searched and providing help in a concrete set of steps that can be easily followed [19]. Help and system documentation that is easy to locate, understand and use makes it much easier to learn how to use the system. Information that is easier to learn uses up less of our cognitive resources and so is less of a burden on our limited working memories. A useful tip is to ensure help systems provide meaningful headings and cues that make it easy to search for and locate relevant information. A good help system is easily available and includes step to by step instructions that are easy to follow, for example, the Google calendar below allows a user to understand what each category is for by showing concise greyed out wording explanations (Figure 6.11).

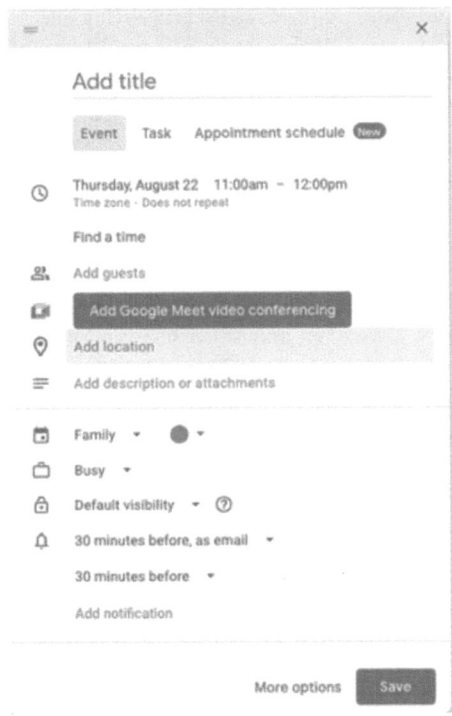

**Figure 6.11**    The Google calendar add an Event has short descriptions that provide guidance on what the user is meant to enter, thereby reducing cognitive load of the user trying to add an event and now knowing which sections require what information

An important consideration when applying any of these ten design heuristics is that good design will always make the use of a system more enjoyable and less frustrating for your users. From a cognitive load perspective, this good design is particularly important for more complex and multifaceted systems that are high in intrinsic cognitive load and so are already challenging users limited cognitive resources. It is also particularly important that these principles are considered when designing for novice or less experienced users, who are cognitively overloaded because everything is new and unfamiliar. Although most users do not stay novices for too long, if you only design for and user test with intermediate or experienced users some of these complexities and their impacts on your most cognitively overloaded group of users could be missed [8]. This highlights the importance of also considering users experience and expertise, and so cognitive load, when designing your interface and the user testing.

## 6.5  CONCLUSION

Nielsen's ten heuristics encompass a range of different guidelines and are very well regarded and used within the field of UX design. There have been different variations of heuristics and different sets of heuristics based on similar principles that can be used for evaluation of interfaces, as they allow scoring. The key message from this chapter is that Nielsen's heuristics have survived the test of time as they ultimately reduce the load on our limited processing capacities and thereby improve overall interface design. If we as designers can better understand why they are effective, we can then more intuitively use and apply them into interface design. While the heuristics were not specifically designed with a focus on the nature of our cognitive architecture, they have in essence been so successfully used and applied over many decades because they tap into the nature of our cognitive architecture and make information easier to process and make sense of.

## REFERENCES

1. Robert K Atkinson, Sharon J Derry, Alexander Renkl, and Donald Wortham. Learning from Examples: Instructional Principles from the Worked Examples Research. *Review of Educational Research*, 70(2):181–214, 2000.
2. Robert K Atkinson, Alexander Renkl, and Mary Margaret Merrill. Transitioning From Studying Examples to Solving Problems: Effects of Self-Explanation Prompts and Fading Worked-Out Steps. *Journal of Educational Psychology*, 95(4):774–783, 2003.
3. Paul Ayres, Nadine Marcus, Christopher Chan, and Nixon Qian. Learning hand manipulative tasks: When instructional animations are superior to equivalent static representations. *Computers in Human Behavior*, 25(2):348–353, 3 2009.
4. Janette Bobis, John Sweller, and Martin Cooper. Cognitive load effects in a primary-school geometry task. *Learning and Instruction*, 3(1):1–21, 1993.
5. Paul Chandler and John Sweller. Cognitive Load Theory and the Format of Instruction. *Cognition and Instruction*, 8(4):293–332, 12 1991.
6. Paul Chandler and John Sweller. The split-attention effect as a factor in the design of instruction. *British Journal of Educational Psychology*, 62(2):233–246, 1992.
7. Ouhao Chen, Slava Kalyuga, and John Sweller. When instructional guidance is needed. *Educational and Developmental Psychologist*, 33(2):149–162, 12 2016.
8. A. Cooper, R. Reimann, D. Cronin, and C. Noessel. *About face: the essentials of interaction design*. John Wiley & Sons, 2014.
9. Graham Cooper, John Sweller, Christopher Farnsworth, St Paul', Christian Brothers, Ronald Clarke, Walter Mastus, John Mackie, Davidson High, Tony Wells, John Potter, and Tony Locastro. Effects of Schema Acquisition and Rule Automation on Mathematical Problem-Solving Transfer. Technical Report 4, 1987.
10. Paul Ginns. Meta-analysis of the modality effect. *Learning and Instruction*, 15(4):313–331, 2005.
11. Toni Granollers. Usability Evaluation with Heuristics, Beyond Nielsen's List. In *International Conference on Advances in Computer-Human Interactions (ACHI 2018)*, 3 2018.
12. Slava Kalyuga, Paul Ayres, Paul Chandler, and John Sweller. The expertise reversal effect, 2003.

13. Slava Kalyuga, Paul Chandler, Juhani Tuovinen, and John Sweller. When problem solving is superior to studying worked examples. *Journal of Educational Psychology*, 93(3):579–588, 2001.

14. Suna Kyun, Slava Kalyuga, and John Sweller. The effect of worked examples when learning to write essays in english literature. *Journal of Experimental Education*, 81(3):385–408, 7 2013.

15. Wayne Leahy and John Sweller. Cognitive load theory, modality of presentation and the transient information effect. *Applied Cognitive Psychology*, 25(6):943–951, 11 2011.

16. Nadine Marcus, Martin Cooper, and John Sweller. Understanding Instructions. Technical Report 1, 1996.

17. Roxana Moreno and Richard E. Mayer. Cognitive principles of multimedia learning: The role of modality and contiguity. *Journal of Educational Psychology*, 91(2):358–368, 6 1999.

18. Seyed Yaghoub Mousavi, Renae Low, and John Sweller. Reducing Cognitive Load by Mixing Auditory and Visual Presentation Modes. *Journal of Educational Psychology*, 87(2):319–334, 1995.

19. Jacob Nielsen. Heuristic evaluation. In Jacob Nielsen and R. L. Mack, editors, *Usability Inspection Methods*. John Wiley & Sons, New York, 1994.

20. Jacob Nielsen. 10 Usability Heuristics for User Interface Design, 1995.

21. Jacob Nielsen. How I Developed the 10 Usability Heuristics. Jakob Nielsen on UX., 2024.

22. Jakob Nielsen. Enhancing the explanatory power of usability heuristics. In *Proceedings of the SIGCHI Conference on Human Factors in Computing Systems*, pages 152–158, 1994.

23. F. D. Pociask and G. R. Morrison. Controlling split attention and redundancy in physical therapy instruction. *Educational Technology Research and Development*, 56:379–399, 2008.

24. J. Preece, Y. Rogers, and H. Sharp. *Interaction Design: Beyond Human Computer Interaction*. United Kingdom: John Wiley & Sons, 2002.

25. Costin Pribeanu. A Revised Set of Usability Heuristics for the Evaluation of Interactive Systems. *Informatica Economica*, 21(3/2017):31–38, 9 2017.

26. Alexander Renkl. Learning from worked-out examples: A study on individual differences. *Cognitive Science*, 21(1):1–29, 1997.

27. Arianne Rourke and John Sweller. The worked-example effect using ill-defined problems: Learning to recognise designers' styles. *Learning and Instruction*, 19(2):185–199, 4 2009.

28. B. Shneiderman. *Designing the user interface: Strategies for effective human-computer interaction*. Boston: Addison-Wesley, Inc., 1987.

29. Anne Marie Singh, Nadine Marcus, and Paul Ayres. The transient information effect: Investigating the impact of segmentation on spoken and written text. *Applied Cognitive Psychology*, 26(6):848–853, 11 2012.

30. Robin Stark, Veronika Kopp, and Martin R. Fischer. Case-based learning with worked examples in complex domains: Two experimental studies in undergraduate medical education. *Learning and Instruction*, 21(1):22–33, 2 2011.

31. John Sweller. *Cognitive Load Theory*, volume 55. Elsevier Inc., 7 2011.

32. John Sweller. Cognitive Load Theory. In S. Tindall-Ford, S. Agostinho, and John Sweller, editors, *Advances in Cognitive Load Theory: Rethinking Teaching*. Routledge, 1st edition, 2019.

33. John Sweller. The Role of Evolutionary Psychology in Our Understanding of Human Cognition: Consequences for Cognitive Load Theory and Instructional Procedures. *Educational Psychology Review*, 34(4):2229–2241, 12 2022.

34. John Sweller. The Development of Cognitive Load Theory: Replication Crises and Incorporation of Other Theories Can Lead to Theory Expansion. *Educational Psychology Review*, 35(4), 12 2023.

35. John Sweller, Paul Ayres, and Slava Kalyuga. The Worked Example and Problem Completion Effects. In *Cognitive Load Theory. Explorations in the Learning Sciences, Instructional Systems and Performance Technologies*, volume 1. Springer, New York, 2011.

36. John Sweller and Graham A. Cooper. The Use of Worked Examples as a Substitute for Problem Solving in Learning Algebra. *Cognition and Instruction*, 2(1):59–89, 1985.

37. John Sweller and Susan Sweller. Natural information processing systems. *Evolutionary Psychology*, 4(1), 2006.

38. John Sweller, Jeroen J G Van Merrienboer, and Fred G W C Paas3. Cognitive Architecture and Instructional Design. *Educational Psychology Review*, 10(3):251–296, 1998.

39. John Sweller, Jeroen J.G. van Merriënboer, and Fred Paas. Cognitive Architecture and Instructional Design: 20 Years Later, 6 2019.

40. Huib K. Tabbers, Rob L. Martens, and Jeroen J.G. Van Merriënboer. Multimedia instructions and cognitive load theory: Effects of modality and cueing. *British Journal of Educational Psychology*, 74(1):71–81, 2004.

41. Rohani Ahmad Tarmizi and John Sweller. Guidance During Mathematical Problem Solving. *Journal of Educational Psychology*, 80(4):424–436, 1988.

42. Tamara van Gog, Fred Paas, Nadine Marcus, Paul Ayres, and John Sweller. The mirror neuron system and observational learning: implications for the effectiveness of dynamic visualizations. *Educational Psychology Review*, 21(1):21–30, 3 2009.

43. Mark Ward and John Sweller. Structuring Effective Worked Examples. *Cognition and Instruction*, 7(1):1–39, 1990.

44. Anna Wong, Wayne Leahy, Nadine Marcus, and John Sweller. Cognitive load theory, the transient information effect and e-learning. *Learning and Instruction*, 22(6):449–457, 12 2012.

45. Anna Wong, Nadine Marcus, Paul Ayres, Lee Smith, Graham A. Cooper, Fred Paas, and John Sweller. Instructional animations can be superior to statics when learning human motor skills. *Computers in Human Behavior*, 25(2):339–347, 3 2009.

# 7 Ripple Down Rules and Classification

*Eric Martin*
School of Computer Science and Engineering, UNSW Sydney
Kensington, Australia

## 7.1 RIPPLE DOWN RULES AND CLASSIFICATION

Fields and subfields, often use variations on the same concepts and techniques, even if that is not always known to researchers working in their own domain of expertise. For instance, consider three subfields of Artificial intelligence: knowledge acquisition, knowledge representation, and . As particular techniques, they use Ripple Down Rules (RDR), belief revision based on preferential models, and learning in the limit with bounded mind changes, respectively. All three techniques are related to the topological concept known as the difference hierarchy. In this chapter, we show how developing a clear understanding of how RDR works, results in notions and questions on the basis of which such relationships naturally emerge.

## 7.2 PRACTICAL RIPPLE DOWN RULES

One aspect of knowledge acquisition is capturing human expertise. Recognising that it is an iterative process, that now and then requires revisions to what has been gathered so far, it is important to first, design a framework that makes the exercise as easy and effective as possible. Ripple Down Rules (RDR) is such a framework, developed at the School of Computer Science and Engineering (CSE) at the University of New South Wales (UNSW) by a former Head of School, Paul Compton [1]. Adapted from [5], Figure 7.2 shows an example of an RDR tree, the key structure of the RDR framework, at a very early stage of knowledge acquisition from medical experts.

Each node of the tree comes with a set of conditions, meant to be evaluated as either true or false, and a conclusion—here, a reference to a particular diagnosis. That set is empty for the root of the tree, associated with a default conclusion. Each node has up to two children, connected to their parent either with an *elif* edge or with an *unless* edge; the latter kind of edge and only the latter leaves from the root. Decision trees only have implicit *elif* edges between siblings. This is illustrated in Figure 7.1 w.r.t. to the toy example of deciding whether to play golf: if the outlook is sunny then consider the level of humidity, elif it is overcast then decide to play, elif it is rainy then consider the strength of the wind.

DOI: 10.1201/9781032702797-7

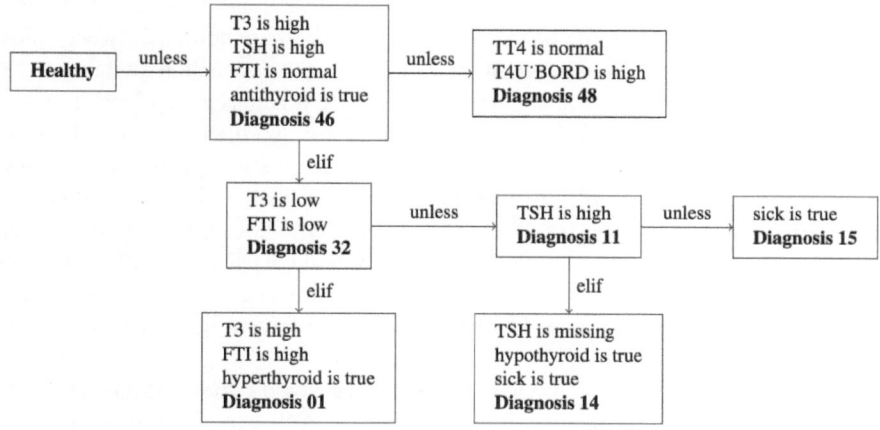

Each *unless* edge of an RDR tree, connecting a node *A* to a node *B*, often corresponds to having extended the tree from a stage where *A* was a leaf to the next stage, with *B* becoming a leaf, following the realisation that the conclusion associated with *A*'s condition is not always correct. Rather than fixing at least part of the tree, and possibly the whole tree, adding an *unless* edge amounts to applying a patch, leaving everything as it is except for... an exception node being added to the tree. An earlier stage of the RDR tree fragment given as an example likely did not have the leaf associated with "Diagnosis 48". Processing a case that would lead to the conclusion that "Diagnosis 46" should not apply, despite the fact that the case satisfies the associated condition, the RDR framework would not fix that condition and then possibly, probably, the condition associated with "Diagnosis 32", and the condition associated with "Diagnosis 01"; instead, the condition associated with "Diagnosis 48" plays the role of a patch, applied to the condition associated with "Diagnosis 46". While it might appear that the procedure is "messy" and could result in a tree that is way larger than it optimally has to be, evidence supports the claim that it is the other way around.

**Figure 7.1**

Whereas decision trees are built from nothing but *elif* conditions, nonmonotonic reasoning is developed on the basis of nothing but *unless* conditions. Tweety flies, unless it is found out to be a penguin, in which case the conclusion switches to "it does not actually fly", as the standard example goes. Whereas exceptions are usual built in by design in nonmonotonic reasoning, as a way to effectively, straight away bet for the most likely conclusion, accepting to later give it up and opt for a new conclusion as a new piece of information is being received, and then possibly give that second conclusion up as well for a third one, or why not for the first one again, as still another piece of information is being received, the RDR methodology reflects the more candid acknowledgement that one makes mistakes, but that's okay, it is enough to apply patches; no need to get back to the drawing board and start from scratch.

From a conceptual point of view, the RDR framework first appears as pretty straightforward. But "the devil is in the details". A well explained data structure, a well explained algorithm is perfectly well "understood", until one decides to implement it, then leading to the realisation that after all, this, and that, is not totally clear and further thinking is required. In this chapter, we will properly get into the formal details of the RDR framework. Also, "understand" is usually too crude a notion: from a level of understanding that happens to be shallow to start with, it is often possible for the understanding to get deeper and deeper by discovering connections to other notions or techniques. We just alluded to relationships between RDR and nonmonotonic reasoning. But there is much more. Once we've got all formal details right, a number of natural questions come to mind, that prompt for notions and techniques that directly relate to the preferential models of belief revision, to the mind changes of formal learning theory and its classification paradigm, to the difference hierarchies in topology, to the distinction between determinism and nondeterminism, between exponential and non-exponential complexity.

For lack of space, we won't be able to fully present the relevant notions from belief revision, formal learning theory, topology, complexity theory, and establish relationships in full generality and in great depth. Rather, we will define nothing but the notions that we need to formalise and study RDR, just pointing out to corresponding concepts in other fields, hoping to trigger the readers' curiosity and leaving it to them to further explore the relationships. At the very least, we hope that readers will appreciate how simple notions can turn out to be fruitful and related to a broad body of knowledge, provided they are properly captured formally.

## 7.3  LOGICAL BACKGROUND

### 7.3.1  GENERAL BACKGROUND

First, some general notation. Given a function $f$, we let $\mathrm{dom}(f)$ denote the domain of $f$. Given two sequences $\sigma$ and $\tau$, we denote by $\sigma \cdot \tau$ the concatenation of $\sigma$ and $\tau$. Given a set $S$, $|S|$ denotes the cardinality of $S$, whereas given a sequence $\sigma$, $|\sigma|$ denotes the length of $\sigma$.

Here we let the logical setting be purely propositional; a first-order setting would bring interesting challenges and rewards, but require substantially more space. By $\mathscr{A}$, we denote a finite set of propositional *atoms*. For convenience, we let the syntax that defines formulas have a couple of notable features. First, a negation normal form is imposed. Second, conjunction and disjunction are defined as unary operators over finite sets of formulas rather than binary operators between pairs of formulas. In particular, $\bigvee \varnothing$ and $\bigwedge \varnothing$ are formulas, that can play the role of False and True, respectively. So the set $\mathscr{F}$ of *formulas* (over $\mathscr{A}$) is the $\subseteq$-minimal set such that (i) for all $\varphi \in \mathscr{A}$, $\varphi$ and $\neg\varphi$ are in $\mathscr{F}$ and (ii) for all finite subsets $F$ of $\mathscr{F}$, $\bigvee F$ and $\bigwedge F$ are in $\mathscr{F}$. Having imposed a negation normal form, a unary operator is needed to negate an arbitrary formula, and the usual binary connectives are defined as abbreviations; all that could not be more standard. So given a formula $\varphi$, if $\varphi$ is an atom then $\sim\varphi$ denotes $\neg\varphi$, if $\varphi$ is of the form $\neg\psi$ then $\sim\varphi$ denotes $\psi$, if $\varphi$ is of the form $\bigvee F$ then $\sim\varphi$ denotes $\bigwedge\{\sim\psi \mid \psi \in F\}$, and if $\varphi$ is of the form $\bigwedge F$ then $\sim\varphi$ denotes $\bigvee\{\sim\psi \mid \psi \in F\}$. Also, given two formulas $\varphi$ and $\psi$, $\varphi \vee \psi$, $\varphi \wedge \psi$, $\varphi \to \psi$, $\varphi \leftrightarrow \psi$ and $\varphi \oplus \psi$ are alternative notations for $\bigvee\{\varphi, \psi\}$, $\bigwedge\{\varphi, \psi\}$, $\sim\varphi \vee \psi$, $(\varphi \to \psi) \wedge (\psi \to \varphi)$ and $\varphi \leftrightarrow \sim\psi$, respectively.

Each node of an RDR tree is associated with a condition, often required to be a formula of a particular form, with specific results obtained for some forms and not for others. It is convenient to have a versatile and concise notation to define the particular forms of interest. Here we will restrict the investigation to three forms

- $\mathscr{A}^{\neg}$, the set of *literals*, built from $\mathscr{A}$ using $\neg$;
- $\mathscr{A}^{\wedge}$, the set of *positive conjuncts*, built from $\mathscr{A}$ using conjunction;
- $\mathscr{A}^{\veebar}$, the set of *positive formulas*, built from $\mathscr{A}$ using conjunction and disjuntion.

We denote by $\mathscr{M}$ a nonempty set of (*propositional*) *interpretations* (over $\mathscr{A}$), that is, a nonempty set of subsets of $\mathscr{A}$ (the *possible models*, or *possible worlds*). And given a formula $\varphi$, we denote by $\mathrm{Mod}_{\mathscr{M}}(\varphi)$ the set of members of $\mathscr{M}$ that are models of $\varphi$, according to the usual interpretation of the truth of a formula in an interpretation; given a set $X$ of formulas, $\mathrm{Mod}_{\mathscr{M}}(X)$ obviously denotes $\bigcap_{\varphi \in X} \mathrm{Mod}_{\mathscr{M}}(\varphi)$. A formula $\varphi$ is said to be (i) *valid in $\mathscr{M}$* if $\mathrm{Mod}_{\mathscr{M}}(\varphi) = \mathscr{M}$, *invalid in $\mathscr{M}$* otherwise, (ii) *satisfiable in $\mathscr{M}$* if $\mathrm{Mod}_{\mathscr{M}}(\varphi) \neq \varnothing$, *unsatisfiable in $\mathscr{M}$* otherwise. Given two sets $X$ and $Y$ of formulas, we say that $Y$ *logically implies $X$ in $\mathscr{M}$*, and we write $X \models_{\mathscr{M}} Y$ if $\mathrm{Mod}_{\mathscr{M}}(\bigwedge X \to \bigwedge Y) = \mathscr{M}$, and we say that $X$ and $Y$ are *logically equivalent in $\mathscr{M}$* if $\mathrm{Mod}_{\mathscr{M}}(\bigwedge X \leftrightarrow \bigwedge Y) = \mathscr{M}$; when $X$ or $Y$ is a singleton $\{\varphi\}$, we can replace $X$ by $\varphi$ in all notions and notation, and when $\mathscr{M}$ is the set of all interpretations, we can omit "in $\mathscr{M}$" in the expressions and omit $\mathscr{M}$ as a subscript in the notation.

The notions of $\Sigma_{1,k}$, $\Pi_{1,k}$ and $\Delta_{1,k}$ formulas, for $k \in \mathbb{N}$ referring to a level in a so-called *difference hierarchy* [2, 3, 4], are relativised to $\mathscr{M}$, the models of the members of $\mathscr{A}$ making up the subbase of an underlying topology on $\mathscr{M}$.

**Definition 1.** Let a formula $\varphi$ be given.

If $\varphi$ is unsatisfiable in $\mathscr{M}$ or valid in $\mathscr{M}$ then $\varphi$ is said to be $\Sigma_{1,0}$ *in $\mathscr{M}$* or $\Pi_{1,0}$ *in $\mathscr{M}$*, respectively.

Let a strictly positive integer $k$ be given.

- $\varphi$ is said to be $\Sigma_{1,k}$ *in* $\mathcal{M}$ iff there exists positive formulas $\psi_1, \ldots, \psi_k$ such that:
  - for all $p \in \{1, \ldots, k-1\}$, $\psi_{p+1}$ logically implies $\psi_p$ in $\mathcal{M}$;
  - $\varphi$ is logically equivalent to $\bigvee_{1 \leq p \leq k, p \bmod 2 = 1} (\psi_p \wedge \bigwedge_{p < q \leq k} \sim \psi_q)$ in $\mathcal{M}$.
- $\varphi$ is said to be $\Pi_{1,k}$ *in* $\mathcal{M}$ iff $\sim\varphi$ is $\Sigma_{1,k}$ in $\mathcal{M}$.

Figure 7.2 illustrates the kind of picture that is associated with a formula that is $\Sigma_{1,8}$ in $\mathcal{M}$. We would have that $\psi_1$ is a positive formula that defines the outermost disk, $\psi_2$ a positive formula that defines the second outermost disk... and $\psi_8$ a positive formula that defines the innermost disk, the whole formula defining the union of all black rings: you are in the first and not in the second outermost disk, unless you are in the third and not in the fourth outermost disk, unless you are in the fifth and not in the sixth outmost disk, unless you are in the seventh and not in the eight outermost disk. More generally, as the value of $k$ increases in $\Sigma_{1,k}$, the number of disks in the associated picture increases, with the outermost ring being filled for any value of $k$, and with the innermost ring being filled for odd values of $k$, and not being filled for even values of $k$.

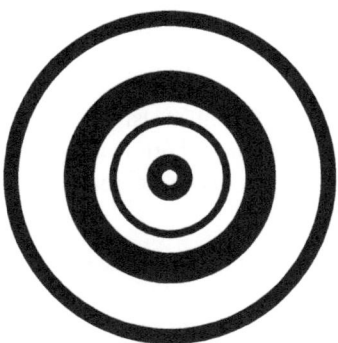

**Figure 7.2**

All formulas are $\Sigma_{1,k}$ (and $\Pi_{1,k}$) in $\mathcal{M}$ for some natural number $k$.

### 7.3.2  SPECIFIC BACKGROUND

Next comes the first notation which is specific to our topic, though not exclusively as it is appears in one form or another in a few areas, for instance, in the literature on preferential models of belief revision [9], in particular in the form of Grove's system of spheres [6].

**Notation 2.** We denote by $\mathscr{C}$ the set of finite sets $S$ of nonempty subsets of $\mathcal{M}$ such that $\mathcal{M} \in S$ and $S$ is totally ordered by inclusion (finite chains of nonempty subsets of $\mathcal{M}$ that contain $\mathcal{M}$).

**Example 3.** Suppose that $\mathscr{A}$ consists of three atoms $p$, $q$ and $r$ and $\mathscr{M}$ is the set of all interpretations over $\mathscr{A}$. Define nine (positive) formulas as follows.

- $\varphi_0 = p \wedge q \wedge r$
- $\varphi_1 = p \wedge q$
- $\varphi_2 = p \wedge (q \vee r)$
- $\varphi_3 = p$
- $\varphi_4 = p \vee (q \wedge r)$
- $\varphi_5 = p \vee q$
- $\varphi_6 = p \vee q \vee r$
- $\varphi_7 = \bigwedge \varnothing$
- $\varphi_8 = (p \wedge q) \vee (p \wedge r) \vee (q \wedge r)$.

For all $i \leq 8$, define $M_i$ as $\mathrm{Mod}\left(\varphi_i\right)$. Set $C_1 = \{M_i \mid i < 8\}$ and $C_2 = \{M_0, M_8, M_6, M_7\}$. Then $C_1$ and $C_2$ are both in $\mathscr{C}$.

Given a chain of models, the member of the chain that is most specific while being consistent with the information at hand is naturally of particular interest. In plain terms, this observation is captured by the notation that follows.

**Notation 4.** Let $C \in \mathscr{C}$ and $\mathfrak{M} \in \mathscr{M}$ be given. We denote by $\min_C(\mathfrak{M})$ the $\subseteq$-least member of $C$ that contains $\mathfrak{M}$.

Figure 7.3 illustrates Notation 4.

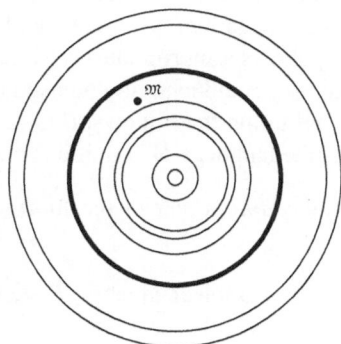

**Figure 7.3**

**Example 5.** Recall the convention and notation in Example 3. For all $\mathfrak{M} \in \mathscr{M}$, $\min_{C_1}(\mathfrak{M})$ and $\min_{C_2}(\mathfrak{M})$ are determined as shown in Figure 7.4.

| $\mathfrak{M}$ | $\min_{C_1}(\mathfrak{M})$ | $\min_{C_2}(\mathfrak{M})$ |
|:---:|:---:|:---:|
| $\{p,q,r\}$ | $M_0$ | $M_0$ |
| $\{p,q,\neg r\}$ | $M_1$ | $M_8$ |
| $\{p,\neg q,r\}$ | $M_2$ | $M_8$ |
| $\{p,\neg q,\neg r\}$ | $M_3$ | $M_6$ |
| $\{\neg p,q,r\}$ | $M_4$ | $M_8$ |
| $\{\neg p,q,\neg r\}$ | $M_5$ | $M_6$ |
| $\{\neg p,\neg q,r\}$ | $M_6$ | $M_6$ |
| $\{\neg p,\neg q,\neg r\}$ | $M_7$ | $M_7$ |

**Figure 7.4**

## 7.4   GRADATION TREES AND GRAPHS

The condition of an RDR tree can be considered semantically, as the set of possible worlds where it holds, or syntactically, as a description in some language meant to be appropriately interpreted. To account for both points of view and avoid formalising concepts twice, we define the notion of an $\mathscr{M}$-embedding, to trivially map an interpretation to itself or to map a syntactic representation to its interpretation. It is natural to abstract interpretations as Boolean algebras (for readers keen to extend the setting and make it first-order, a bounded distributive lattice would be the natural choice). There is also a need to distinguish between the language that lets us work with a whole RDR tree, and the language of conditions of an RDR tree. The former should be naturally closed under negation, disjunction and conjunction—that is the very reason why a Boolean algebra is a appropriate—, while the latter could be much more restricted—for instance, one could naturally demand that conditions be atoms, or positive conjuncts. In the definition that follows, $B$ targets the language of whole RDR trees, whereas $A$ targets the language of conditions of RDR trees.

**Definition 6.** We call $\mathscr{M}$-*embedding* a pair of the form $(h,A)$ with the following properties.

- $h$ is a homomorphism from a Boolean algebra $(B,\vee,\wedge,\bar{\phantom{x}},0,1)$ into $2^{\mathscr{M}}$;
- $A$ is a subset of $B$.

In contexts where there is no risk of confusion, we identify $A$ with $(h,A)$ and use $\vee$, $\wedge$, $\bar{\phantom{x}}$, 0 and 1 being tacitly understood that they denote the second to the last members of $(B,\vee,\wedge,\bar{\phantom{x}},0,1)$. We also use $\leq$, $<$, $>$ and $\geq$ in reference to the induced partial order on $\mathrm{dom}(h)$.

We identify $2^{\mathscr{M}}$ with the $\mathscr{M}$-embedding $(h,2^{\mathscr{M}})$ where $\mathrm{dom}(h)$ is identical to $(2^{\mathscr{M}},\cup,\cap,\bar{\phantom{x}},\varnothing,\mathscr{M})$ and $h$ is the identity function. Given a set $L$ of formulas, denoting by $\widehat{L}$ the closure of $L$ under $\bigvee$, $\bigwedge$ and $\sim$, we identify $L$ with the $\mathscr{M}$-embedding $(h,\widehat{L})$ where $\mathrm{dom}(h) = (\widehat{L},\vee,\wedge,\sim,\bigvee\varnothing,\bigwedge\varnothing)$ and $h$ maps each $\varphi \in \widehat{L}$ to the set of members of $\mathscr{M}$ in which $\varphi$ is true.

The notation that follows will be used to aggregate the conditions found along the branch of an RDR tree, an except-node introducing a conjunction, an elif-node introducing a disjunction, resulting in a condition for the branch itself. More precisely, a branch of what will be defined as an $\mathfrak{E}$-gradation tree, with $\mathfrak{E}$ an $\mathcal{M}$-embedding, will be a sequence $\sigma$ of the kind defined in Notation 7; with $\widehat{\sigma}$ as defined in that notation, the set of models $\mathfrak{E}(\widehat{\sigma})$ will be associated to that branch.

**Notation 7.** Given a Boolean algebra $(B, \vee, \wedge, \bar{\ }, 0, 1)$, we inductively map each finite sequence of members of $\{\vee, \wedge\} \times B$ to a member $\widehat{\sigma}$ of $B$, as follows.

- $\widehat{()} = 1$.
- For all $\mathbb{X} \in \{\vee, \wedge\}$ and $\mathfrak{v} \in B$, $\widehat{((\mathbb{X}, \mathfrak{v}))} = \mathfrak{v}$.
- Let $\mathbb{X}, \mathbb{X}' \in \{\vee, \wedge\}$, $\mathfrak{v}, \mathfrak{v}' \in B$, and a finite sequence $\sigma$ of members of $\{\vee, \wedge\} \times B$ be given. Set $\sigma' = ((\mathbb{X}, \mathfrak{v}), (\mathbb{X}', \mathfrak{v}')) \cdot \sigma$. Then $\widehat{\sigma'} = \mathfrak{v} \, \mathbb{X}' \, \widehat{((\mathbb{X}', \mathfrak{v}')) \cdot \sigma}$.

**Example 8.** Let a Boolean algebra $(B, \vee, \wedge, \bar{\ }, 0, 1)$ and members $b_1, \ldots, b_9$ of $B$ be given. Set

$$\sigma = ((\wedge, b_1), (\vee, b_2), (\vee, b_3), (\wedge, b_4), (\wedge, b_5), (\vee, b_6), (\wedge, b_7), (\wedge, b_8), (\vee, b_9)).$$

The ten initial segment $\tau$ of $\sigma$, considered from smallest to largest, are mapped to the following simplified members $\widehat{\tau}$ of $B$:

- $1$
- $b_1$
- $b_1 \vee b_2$
- $b_1 \vee b_2 \vee b_3$
- $b_1 \vee b_2 \vee (b_3 \wedge b_4)$
- $b_1 \vee b_2 \vee (b_3 \wedge b_4 \wedge b_5)$
- $b_1 \vee b_2 \vee (b_3 \wedge b_4 \wedge (b_5 \vee b_6))$
- $b_1 \vee b_2 \vee \left(b_3 \wedge b_4 \wedge (b_5 \vee (b_6 \wedge b_7))\right)$
- $b_1 \vee b_2 \vee \left(b_3 \wedge b_4 \wedge (b_5 \vee (b_6 \wedge b_7 \wedge b_8))\right)$
- $b_1 \vee b_2 \vee \left(b_3 \wedge b_4 \wedge \left(b_5 \vee (b_6 \wedge b_7 \wedge (b_8 \vee b_9))\right)\right)$

The notion of an $\mathcal{M}$-embedding, that remember, lets us work either purely semantically or syntactically and semantically, with possible restrictions on conditions, is all what is needed to define RDR trees in full generality. We expect an except-node, introducing a conjunction, to truly bring an exception and restrict the set of models, and an elif-node, introducing a disjunction, to truly bring an alternative and broaden the set of models. This justifies the introduction of the last item in the definition that follows.

**Definition 9.** Let an $\mathcal{M}$-embedding $\mathfrak{E} = (h, A)$ be given. An $\mathfrak{E}$-*gradation tree* is a nonempty finite set $T$ of sequences with the following properties.

- $T$ is closed under subsequences.
- For all $\sigma \in T$, every member of $\sigma$ is of the form $(\vee, \mathfrak{v})$ or $(\wedge, \mathfrak{v})$ for some $\mathfrak{v} \in A$.
- For all $\sigma \in T$, there is at most one $\mathfrak{v} \in A$ with $\sigma \cdot ((\vee, \mathfrak{v})) \in T$, and there is at most one $\mathfrak{v} \in A$ with $\sigma \cdot ((\wedge, \mathfrak{v})) \in T$.
- $\{\mathfrak{E}(\widehat{p}) \mid p \in T\} \setminus \{\varnothing\}$ has cardinality $|T|$.

A *gradation tree* (over $\mathcal{M}$) is an $\mathfrak{E}$-gradation tree for some $\mathcal{M}$-embedding $\mathfrak{E}$.

**Example 10.** Recall the convention and notation in Example 3. The closure of

$$\Big( \big((\wedge, p), (\wedge, q), (\wedge, r)\big), \big((\wedge, p), (\wedge, q), (\vee, r)\big),$$

$$\big((\wedge, p), (\vee, q), (\wedge, r)\big), \big((\wedge, p), (\vee, q), (\vee, r)\big) \Big)$$

under subsequences is an $\mathscr{A}$-gradation tree. It can be depicted as in Figure 7.5, with vertical links for pairs of the form $(\vee, \mathfrak{v})$ and horizontal links for pairs of the form $(\wedge, \mathfrak{v})$.

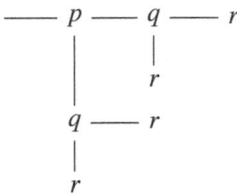

**Figure 7.5**

The evaluation of the conditions of the visited nodes of an RDR tree proceeds deterministically. Indeed, the nodes of a chain of elif nodes (a chain of possible alternatives) are to be evaluated in sequence. Evaluation stops at the first node in the chain, if any, whose condition evaluates to True. Usually, order matters; the order of alternatives cannot be changed, or at the very least it cannot be changed arbitrarily. It is interesting to consider the case where any chain of alternatives can be shuffled, in any way. This amounts to a non-deterministic RDR framework: it allows one to, at a given node, evaluate in parallel all possible alternatives and move to the node, if any, whose condition has first been found out to evaluate to True. This non-deterministic RDR framework starts with the definition that follows, that introduces the key concept of a *gradation graph*. We will then see how a gradation graph can be transformed into one or more gradation trees. Intuitively, the more gradation trees can be obtained from a gradation graph, the more nondeterminism the gradation graph encompasses. Some gradation graphs cannot be transformed in more than one gradation tree, so they are themselves deterministic. Still, they can prove valuable as gradation graphs allow us to get rid of the redundancy that is built into some gradation trees. The tree depicted in Figure 7.5 exhibits redundancy: the two subtrees rooted at $q$ are the same. We will see that this tree is the unique transformation of a gradation graph, the latter offering a more compact representation. There is actually more than one possible way to interpret "redundancy" in a gradation tree. To make sure that the interpretation is general enough and does not require more than finding identical subtrees in an RDR tree, ignoring the "contexts" where those identical subtrees appear, we resort to graphs over multisets rather than sets of vertices. Using formulas (or more generally, members of the lattice that subsumes the $\mathcal{M}$-embedding under consideration) as labels, we could instead consider a set of labelled vertices and possibly label distinct vertices with the same formula, but it is more direct and simpler to work with a multiset of formulas as vertices.

**Definition 11.** Let an $\mathcal{M}$-embedding $\mathfrak{E} = (h, A)$ be given. An $\mathfrak{E}$-*gradation graph* is a pair of the form $(V, E)$ where $V$ is a multisubset of $A \cup \{1\}$ and $E$ is finite nonempty binary relation over $V$ with the following properties.

- For all $\mathfrak{v} \in V$, $\mathfrak{v} = 1$ iff there is no $\mathfrak{v}' \in V$ with $(\mathfrak{v}', \mathfrak{v}) \in E$.
- $E$ is acyclic: there exists no $n \in \mathbb{N}$ and $\mathfrak{v}_0, \ldots \mathfrak{v}_n \in V$ such that $(\mathfrak{v}_n, \mathfrak{v}_0) \in E$ and for all $i < n$, $(\mathfrak{v}_i, \mathfrak{v}_{i+1}) \in E$.

A *gradation graph* (over $\mathcal{M}$) is an $\mathfrak{E}$-gradation graph for some $\mathcal{M}$-embedding $\mathfrak{E}$.

**Example 12.** Recall the convention and notation in Example 3. Let $V$ denote $\{\bigwedge \varnothing, p, q, r\}$ and set:

$$E = \{(\bigwedge \varnothing, p), (\bigwedge \varnothing, q), (\bigwedge \varnothing, r), (p, q), (p, r), (q, r)\}.$$

Then $(V, E)$ is an $\mathscr{A}$-gradation graph. It can be depicted as in Figure 7.6.

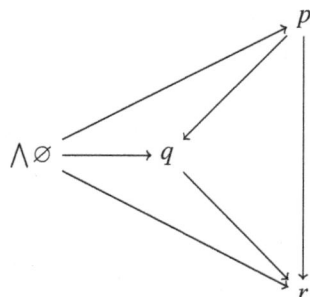

**Figure 7.6**

**Definition 13.** Let a gradation graph $G = (V,E)$ be given. We call *path of $G$* any sequence of the form $(\mathfrak{v}_0, \ldots, \mathfrak{v}_n)$, $n \in \mathbb{N}$, $\mathfrak{v}_0, \ldots, \mathfrak{v}_n \in V$, such that there exists no $\mathfrak{v} \in V$ with $(\mathfrak{v}, \mathfrak{v}_0) \in E$ and for all $i < n$, $(\mathfrak{v}_i, \mathfrak{v}_{i+1}) \in E$. We denote by Paths$(G)$ the set of paths of $G$.

**Property 14.** *Let a gradation graph $G = (V,E)$ be given.*

- *The multiplicity of 1 in $V$ is equal to 1.*
- *Every member of* Paths$(G)$ *starts with 1.*
- *Every member of $V$ occurs in some member of* Paths$(G)$.

A gradation graph can be "unfolded" and turned into at least one gradation tree, with Figures 7.6 and 7.5 as an example (for this specific example, the "unfolding" is unique). This is what is expressed in the proposition and definition that follow.

**Definition 15.** Let a gradation graph $G = (V,E)$ be given. Set $|E| = n$. We call *presentation of $G$* any enumeration of $E$ such that for all $\mathfrak{v}, \mathfrak{w}, \mathfrak{w}' \in V$ with $(\mathfrak{v}, \mathfrak{w}) \in E$ and $(\mathfrak{v}, \mathfrak{w}') \in E$, if there exists a member of Paths$(G)$ that ends in $(\mathfrak{w}, \mathfrak{w}')$ then $(\mathfrak{v}, \mathfrak{w})$ occurs before $(\mathfrak{v}, \mathfrak{w}')$ in the enumeration.

**Proposition 16.** *Let an $\mathcal{M}$-embedding $\mathfrak{E}$, an $\mathfrak{E}$-gradation graph $G = (V,E)$, and a presentation of $G$ be given. Map each $\sigma \in$ Paths$(G)$ to a finite sequence $[\sigma]$ of members of $\{\vee, \wedge\} \times V$, as follows. Set $[(\wedge \varnothing)] = ()$. Given $\sigma \in$ Paths$(G)$ of the form $(\mathfrak{v}_0, \ldots, \mathfrak{v}_n)$, $n > 0$, define $[\sigma]$ as*

$$\left( (\wedge, \mathfrak{w}_1^0), (\vee, \mathfrak{w}_1^1), \ldots, (\vee, \mathfrak{w}_1^{k_1}), \ldots, (\wedge, \mathfrak{w}_n^0), (\vee, \mathfrak{w}_n^1), \ldots, (\vee, \mathfrak{w}_n^{k_n}) \right),$$

*$k_1, \ldots, k_n \in \mathbb{N}$, where for all nonzero $i \le n$, $(\mathfrak{w}_i^0, \ldots, \mathfrak{w}_i^{k_i})$ is the longest sequence of members of $V$ such that $\mathfrak{w}_i^{k_i} = \mathfrak{v}_i$ and $(\mathfrak{v}_{i-1}, \mathfrak{w}_i^0), \ldots, (\mathfrak{v}_{i-1}, \mathfrak{w}_i^{k_i})$ all occur in $E$, in this order in the given presentation of $G$. Then $\{[\sigma] \mid \sigma \in$ Paths$(G)\}$ is an $\mathfrak{E}$-gradation tree.*

*Proof.* This is easily verified using the left-child, right-sibling representation of the tree defined by the closure of Paths$(G)$ under subsequences. $\qquad\square$

**Definition 17.** Let a gradation graph $G$ be given.

Given a presentation $\mathscr{R}$ of $G$, we say of the gradation tree defined in Proposition 16 from $G$ and $\mathscr{R}$ that it is *determined by $G$ and $\mathscr{R}$*.

We say of a gradation tree that it is *determined by $G$* if it is determined by $G$ and one of $G$'s presentations.

**Example 18.** Recall the convention and notation in Examples 10 and 12. The gradation graph $G$ defined in the latter determines a unique gradation tree $T$, which is the one defined in the former. Based on the unique presentation of $G$, Proposition 16 maps each $\sigma \in$ Paths$(G)$ to a member $[\sigma]$ of $T$. Figure 7.7 shows $\sigma$ and $\widehat{[\sigma]}$ for all $\sigma \in$ Paths$(G)$.

| $\sigma$ | $\widehat{[\sigma]}$ |
|---|---|
| $(\bigwedge\varnothing)$ | $\bigwedge\varnothing$ |
| $(\bigwedge\varnothing,r)$ | $p\vee q\vee r$ |
| $(\bigwedge\varnothing,q)$ | $p\vee q$ |
| $(\bigwedge\varnothing,q,r)$ | $p\vee(q\wedge r)$ |
| $(\bigwedge\varnothing,p)$ | $p$ |
| $(\bigwedge\varnothing,p,r)$ | $p\wedge(q\vee r)$ |
| $(\bigwedge\varnothing,p,q)$ | $p\wedge q$ |
| $(\bigwedge\varnothing,p,q,r)$ | $p\wedge q\wedge r$ |

**Figure 7.7**

**Definition 19.** Given a gradation tree $T$, the *depth* of $T$ is defined as the largest integer $n$ such that there exists a member $\sigma$ of $T$ that has $n+1$ elements of the form $(\wedge,\mathfrak{v})$.

Given a gradation graph $G$, the *depth* of $G$ is defined as $\max_{\sigma\in\mathrm{Paths}(G)}|\sigma|$.

**Property 20.** *Given a gradation graph $G$ and a gradation tree $T$ that is determined by $G$, the depth of $G$ equals the depth of $T$.*

Except-nodes shrink a set of models, elif-nodes expand it. It turns out that the branches of an RDR tree are associated with sets of models that make up a chain under inclusion (that is, the sets $\mathfrak{E}(\widehat{\sigma})$ with $\sigma$ ranging over an $\mathfrak{E}$-gradation tree form a chain under inclusion). The strict order relation defined in Lemma 21 is designed to order the branches of a gradation tree accordingly, from the branch associated with the smallest set of models, to the branch associated with the largest set of models. Such is the contents of Proposition 29—a consequence of Lemma 27.

**Lemma 21.** *Let a gradation tree $T$ be given. Let $\prec$ be the binary relation on $T$ such that for all $\sigma,\tau\in T$, $\sigma\prec\tau$ iff $\sigma\neq\tau$ and*

- *either $\tau$ is the empty sequence, or*
- *$\sigma$ is of the form $\tau\cdot((\wedge,\mathfrak{v}))\cdot\tau'$, or*
- *$\tau$ is of the form $((\mathbb{X}_0,\mathfrak{v}_0),\ldots,(\mathbb{X}_n,\mathfrak{v}_n))$, $n\in\mathbb{N}$, and there exists $m<n$ with $\mathbb{X}_{m+1}=\vee$ such that $\sigma$ is of the form $((\mathbb{X}_0,\mathfrak{v}_0),\ldots,(\mathbb{X}_m,\mathfrak{v}_m))\cdot\sigma'$ with $\sigma'$ being either empty or of the form $((\wedge,\mathfrak{v}))\cdot\sigma''$.*

*Then $\prec$ is a total strict order on $T$.*

*Proof.* Let nonempty $\sigma_1,\sigma_2,\sigma_3\in T$ be such that $\sigma_1\prec\sigma_2\prec\sigma_3$. Write $\sigma_3$ as $((\mathbb{X}_0,\mathfrak{v}_0),\ldots,(\mathbb{X}_n,\mathfrak{v}_n))$, $n\in\mathbb{N}$.

- Suppose that $\sigma_2$ is of the form $\sigma_3\cdot((\wedge,\mathfrak{v}))\cdot\sigma$.
  - If $\sigma_1$ is of the form $\sigma_2\cdot((\wedge,\mathfrak{w}))\cdot\sigma'$ then there exists a sequence $\sigma''$ such that $\sigma_1$ is $\sigma_3\cdot((\wedge,\mathfrak{v}))\cdot\sigma''$, hence $\sigma_1\prec\sigma_3$.

- Write $\sigma_2$ as $\big((\mathbb{X}_0', \mathfrak{v}_0'), \ldots, (\mathbb{X}_p', \mathfrak{v}_p')\big)$, $p > n$. If there exists $m < p$ with $\mathbb{X}_{m+1}' = \vee$ and a sequence $\sigma'$ such that $\sigma_1$ is $\big((\mathbb{X}_0', \mathfrak{v}_0'), \ldots, (\mathbb{X}_m', \mathfrak{v}_m')\big) \cdot \sigma'$ with $\sigma'$ being either empty or of the form $\big((\wedge, \mathfrak{v}')\big) \cdot \sigma''$, then either $m > n$, in which case there exists a sequence $\tau$ such that $\sigma_1$ is $\sigma_3 \cdot \big((\wedge, \mathfrak{v})\big) \cdot \tau$, hence $\sigma_1 \prec \sigma_3$, or $m < n$, in which case $\sigma_1$ is $\big((\mathbb{X}_0, \mathfrak{v}_0), \ldots, (\mathbb{X}_m, \mathfrak{v}_m)\big) \cdot \sigma'$, hence $\sigma_1 \prec \sigma_3$ again.
- Suppose that there exists $m < n$ with $\mathbb{X}_{m+1} = \vee$ and there exists a sequence $\sigma$ being either empty or of the form $\big((\wedge, \mathfrak{v})\big) \cdot \sigma'$ such that $\sigma_2$ is $\big((\mathbb{X}_0, \mathfrak{v}_0), \ldots, (\mathbb{X}_m, \mathfrak{v}_m)\big) \cdot \sigma$.
  - If $\sigma_1$ is of the form $\sigma_2 \cdot \big((\wedge, \mathfrak{w})\big) \cdot \tau$ then there exists a sequence $\tau'$ of the form $\big((\wedge, \mathfrak{v}')\big) \cdot \tau''$ such that $\sigma_1$ is $\big((\mathbb{X}_0, \mathfrak{v}_0), \ldots, (\mathbb{X}_m, \mathfrak{v}_m)\big) \cdot \tau'$, hence $\sigma_1 \prec \sigma_3$.
  - Write $\sigma_2$ as $\big((\mathbb{X}_0', \mathfrak{v}_0'), \ldots, (\mathbb{X}_p', \mathfrak{v}_p')\big)$, $p \geq m$. If there exists $k < p$ with $\mathbb{X}_{k+1}' = \vee$ and a sequence $\tau$ such that $\sigma_1$ is $\big((\mathbb{X}_0', \mathfrak{v}_0'), \ldots, (\mathbb{X}_k', \mathfrak{v}_k')\big) \cdot \tau$ with $\tau$ being either empty or of the form $\big((\wedge, \mathfrak{v}')\big) \cdot \tau'$, then either $k \geq m$, in which case there exists a sequence $\gamma$ being either empty or of the form $\big((\wedge, \mathfrak{w})\big) \cdot \gamma'$ such that $\sigma_1$ is $\big((\mathbb{X}_0, \mathfrak{v}_0), \ldots, (\mathbb{X}_m, \mathfrak{v}_m)\big) \cdot \gamma$, hence $\sigma_1 \prec \sigma_3$, or $k < m$, in which case $\sigma_1$ is $\big((\mathbb{X}_0, \mathfrak{v}_0), \ldots, (\mathbb{X}_k, \mathfrak{v}_k)\big) \cdot \tau$, hence $\sigma_1 \prec \sigma_3$, again.

We conclude that in all cases, $\sigma_1 \prec \sigma_3$, hence $\prec$ is transitive.

Let distinct $\sigma, \tau \in T$ be given.

- If $\sigma$ is of the form $\tau \cdot \big((\wedge, \mathfrak{v})\big) \cdot \tau'$ then $\sigma \prec \tau$.
- If $\tau$ is of the form $\sigma \cdot \big((\vee, \mathfrak{v})\big) \cdot \sigma'$ then $\sigma \prec \tau$.
- If there exists a sequence $\gamma$ such that $\sigma$ and $\tau$ are of the form $\gamma \cdot \big((\wedge, \mathfrak{v})\big) \cdot \sigma'$ and $\gamma \cdot \big((\vee, \mathfrak{w})\big) \cdot \tau'$, respectively, then $\sigma \prec \tau$.

We conclude that for all distinct $\sigma, \tau \in T$, either $\sigma \prec \tau$ or $\tau \prec \sigma$, thereby completing the proof of the lemma. $\qquad \square$

The notation that follows won't be used before Section 7.5 but Example 23, first meant to illustrate the strict order relation defined in Lemma 21, illustrates that notation as well.

**Notation 22.** Let a gradation tree $T$ and $\sigma \in T$ be given. Let $X$ be the set of all elements $\mathfrak{v}$ such that some initial segment $\tau$ of $\sigma$ ends in $(\vee, \mathfrak{v})$ or $(\wedge, \mathfrak{v})$ and $\tau \not\prec \sigma$ with $\prec$ as defined in Lemma 21. We let $\mathring{\sigma}$ denote $\bigwedge X$.

**Example 23.** Figure 7.8 represents a member $\tau$ of a gradation tree $T$, as the path that ends at the blue dot.

- With $\prec$ defined as in Lemma 21, the members $\sigma$ of $T$ such that $\sigma \prec \tau$ correspond to the paths that end at a green dot as well as the strict extensions to the right, if any, of the paths that end at a green or blue dot.

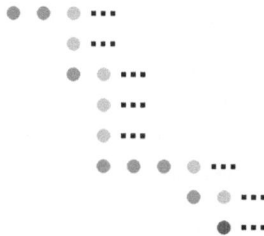

**Figure 7.8**

- $\mathring{\sigma}$, defined in Notation 22, is a conjunction over a set whose members correspond to the red and blue dots.

**Notation 24.** Given a gradation tree $T$, we denote by $\rho_T$ the mapping of domain $\{1, \ldots, |T|\}$ that maps each $i \in \mathrm{dom}(\rho_T)$ to the $i$-th member of $T$ w.r.t. the total strict order on $T$ defined in Lemma 21. We sometimes tacitly assume that $\mathrm{dom}(\rho_T)$ is rather $\{0, \ldots, |T|\}$, in which case $\rho_T(0) = 0$.

**Definition 25.** Given a gradation tree $T$, we refer to $(\rho_T(i))_{1 \le i \le |T|}$ as $T$'s *standard enumeration*.

**Example 26.** Figure 7.9 represents the standard enumeration of a gradation tree $T$ of size 16. Each number refers to $\rho_T^{-1}(\sigma)$, as defined in Notation 24, for the corresponding member $\sigma$ of $T$.

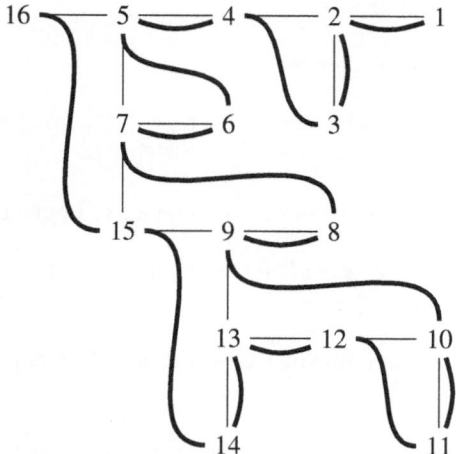

**Figure 7.9**

**Lemma 27.** *Let a gradation tree and distinct members $\sigma$ and $\tau$ of $T$ be given.*

- *If $\sigma$ is of the form $\tau \cdot \big((\wedge, \mathfrak{v})\big) \cdot \tau'$ then $\sigma \leq \tau$.*
- *If $\tau$ is of the form $\sigma \cdot \big((\vee, \mathfrak{v})\big) \cdot \sigma'$ then $\sigma \leq \tau$.*
- *If there exists a sequence $\gamma$ such that $\sigma$ and $\tau$ are of the form $\gamma \cdot \big((\wedge, \mathfrak{v})\big) \cdot \sigma'$ and $\gamma \cdot \big((\vee, \mathfrak{w})\big) \cdot \tau'$, respectively, then $\sigma \leq \tau$.*

*Proof.* In the first case, if $\tau$ is the empty sequence then obviously, $\widehat{\sigma} \leq \widehat{\tau}$. We examine the rest of the first case and the last two cases.

- Suppose that $\sigma$ is of the form $\tau \cdot \big((\wedge, \mathfrak{v})\big) \cdot \tau'$ and $\tau \neq ()$. Write $\sigma$ as $\big((\mathbb{X}_0, \mathfrak{v}_0), \ldots, (\mathbb{X}_n, \mathfrak{v}_n)\big)$, $n > 0$, and let $i < n$ be such that $\tau$ is $\big((\mathbb{X}_0, \mathfrak{v}_0), \ldots, (\mathbb{X}_i, \mathfrak{v}_i)\big)$. For all $j \leq i$, let $\tau_j$ denote $\big((\mathbb{X}_j, \mathfrak{v}_j), \ldots, (\mathbb{X}_i, \mathfrak{v}_i)\big)$ and let $\sigma_j$ denote $\big((\mathbb{X}_j, \mathfrak{v}_j), \ldots, (\mathbb{X}_n, \mathfrak{v}_n)\big)$. Note that $\widehat{\sigma_i} \leq \mathfrak{v}_i$. It is immediately verified by induction, letting $j$ decrease from $i$ down to 0, that for all $j \leq i$, $\widehat{\sigma_j} \leq \widehat{\tau_j}$. In particular, $\widehat{\sigma} \leq \widehat{\tau}$.
- Suppose that $\tau$ is of the form $\sigma \cdot \big((\vee, \mathfrak{v})\big) \cdot \sigma'$. So $\sigma \neq ()$. Write $\tau$ as $\big((\mathbb{X}_0, \mathfrak{v}_0), \ldots, (\mathbb{X}_n, \mathfrak{v}_n)\big)$, $n > 0$, and let $i < n$ be such that $\sigma$ is $\big((\mathbb{X}_0, \mathfrak{v}_0), \ldots, (\mathbb{X}_i, \mathfrak{v}_i)\big)$. For all $j \leq i$, let $\sigma_j$ denote $\big((\mathbb{X}_j, \mathfrak{v}_j), \ldots, (\mathbb{X}_i, \mathfrak{v}_i)\big)$ and let $\tau_j$ denote $\big((\mathbb{X}_j, \mathfrak{v}_j), \ldots, (\mathbb{X}_n, \mathfrak{v}_n)\big)$. Note that $\mathfrak{v}_i \leq \widehat{\tau_i}$. It is immediately verified by induction, letting $j$ decrease from $i$ down to 0, that for all $j \leq i$, $\widehat{\sigma_j} \leq \widehat{\tau_j}$. In particular, $\widehat{\sigma} \leq \widehat{\tau}$.
- Suppose that there exists a sequence $\gamma$ such that $\sigma$ and $\tau$ are of the form $\gamma \cdot \big((\wedge, \mathfrak{v})\big) \cdot \sigma'$ and $\gamma \cdot \big((\vee, \mathfrak{w})\big) \cdot \tau'$, respectively. So $\gamma \neq ()$. Write $\gamma$ as $\big((\mathbb{X}_0, \mathfrak{v}_0), \ldots, (\mathbb{X}_n, \mathfrak{v}_n)\big)$, $n \in \mathbb{N}$. For all $j \leq n$, set $\sigma_j = \big((\mathbb{X}_j, \mathfrak{v}_j), \ldots, (\mathbb{X}_n, \mathfrak{v}_n)\big) \cdot \big((\wedge, \mathfrak{v})\big) \cdot \sigma'$ and $\tau_j = \big((\mathbb{X}_j, \mathfrak{v}_j), \ldots, (\mathbb{X}_n, \mathfrak{v}_n)\big) \cdot \big((\vee, \mathfrak{w})\big) \cdot \tau'$. It is immediately verified by induction that for all $j \leq n$, $\widehat{\sigma_j} \leq \widehat{\tau_j}$. In particular, $\widehat{\sigma} \leq \widehat{\tau}$.

This completes the proof of the lemma. $\qquad\qquad\qquad\qquad\qquad\qquad\qquad\quad\square$

**Proposition 28.** *For all gradation trees $T$ and $i, j \in \{1, \ldots, |T|\}$, if $i \leq j$ then $\rho_T(i) \leq \rho_T(j)$.*

*Proof.* The proposition is an immediate consequence of Lemma 27. $\qquad\qquad\quad\square$

**Proposition 29.** *Given an $\mathscr{M}$-embedding $\mathfrak{E}$ and an $\mathfrak{E}$-gradation tree $T$, $\big\{\mathfrak{E}(\widehat{\sigma}) \mid \sigma \in T\big\}$ is a chain for inclusion.*

*Proof.* The proposition is an immediate consequence of Lemma 27 and the fact that $\mathfrak{E}$ is monotone. $\qquad\qquad\qquad\qquad\qquad\qquad\qquad\qquad\qquad\qquad\qquad\quad\square$

**Corollary 30.** *For all $\mathscr{M}$-embeddings $\mathfrak{E}$ and $\mathfrak{E}$-gradation trees $T$, $\big\{\mathfrak{E}(\widehat{\sigma}) \mid \sigma \in T\big\}$ is a member of $\mathscr{C}$ of cardinality $|T|$.*

A chain of models can of course be organised a gradation tree, and more particularly as a gradation graph, in many ways, with two limiting cases for organisation.

**Property 31.** *Let $n \in \mathbb{N}$ and $C \in \mathscr{C}$ with $|C| = n+1$ be given. Write $C$ as $\{S_0, \ldots, S_n\}$ where for all $i < n$, $S_i \subset S_{i+1}$.*

- *Set $E_1 = \big((S_0, S_1), \ldots, (S_0, S_n)\big)$ and $G_1 = (C, E_1)$.*
- *Set $E_2 = \big((S_n, S_{n-1}), \ldots, (S_1, S_0)\big)$ and $G_2 = (C, E_2)$.*

*Both $G_1$ and $G_2$ are $2^{\mathscr{M}}$-gradation graphs that determine unique gradation trees $T_1$ and $T_2$, respectively. Moreover, $C$ is equal to both $\{\widehat{\sigma} \mid \sigma \in T_1\}$ and $\{\widehat{\sigma} \mid \sigma \in T_2\}$.*

Figure 7.9 illustrates how to, from a given node of an RDR tree, access the previous node and access the following one, if they exist, for the strict order defined in Lemma 21. Proposition 32 and Corollary 34 express it in full generality.

**Proposition 32.** *Let a gradation tree $T$ with $|T| > 1$ and let $\sigma \in T$ be given.*

- *If $\sigma$ is the longest sequence of the form $\big((\wedge, \mathfrak{v}_0), \ldots, (\wedge, \mathfrak{v}_n)\big)$, $n \in \mathbb{N}$, then $\rho_T^{-1}(\sigma)$ equals 1.*
- *Assume that $T$ contains a sequence of the form $\sigma \cdot \big((\wedge, \mathfrak{v})\big)$, and let $\tau$ be the (unique) longest sequence of the form $\big((\wedge, \mathfrak{v}_0), (\vee, \mathfrak{v}_1), \ldots, (\vee, \mathfrak{v}_n)\big)$, $n \in \mathbb{N}$, such that $\sigma \cdot \tau$ is in $T$. Then $\rho_T^{-1}(\tau)$ equals $\rho_T^{-1}(\sigma) - 1$.*
- *Suppose that none of the previous conditions applies. We can write $\sigma$ as $\big((\mathbb{X}_0, \mathfrak{v}_0), \ldots, (\mathbb{X}_n, \mathfrak{v}_n)\big)$, $n > 1$, and there exists a (unique) nonzero $m \leq n$ such that $\big((\mathbb{X}_m, \mathfrak{v}_m), \ldots, (\mathbb{X}_n, \mathfrak{v}_n)\big)$ is of the form $\big((\vee, \mathfrak{v}_m)\big) \cdot \big((\wedge, \mathfrak{v}_{m+1}), \ldots, (\wedge, \mathfrak{v}_n)\big)$. Then denoting $\big((\mathbb{X}_0, \mathfrak{v}_0), \ldots, (\mathbb{X}_{m-1}, \mathfrak{v}_{m-1})\big)$ by $\tau$, $\rho_T^{-1}(\tau)$ equals $\rho_T^{-1}(\sigma) - 1$.*

*Proof.* The proof is by induction on the size of gradation trees. The result is straightforward for gradation trees of size 2. Let $k \geq 2$ be given, and assume that the result holds for all gradation trees of size between 2 and $k$. Let $T$ be a gradation tree of size $k+1$. Let $\sigma \in T$ and gradation tree $T'$ be such that $T = T' \cup \{\sigma\}$. Let $\sigma' \in T'$ be such that $\sigma$ is of the form $\sigma' \cdot \big((\wedge, \mathfrak{v})\big)$ or $\sigma' \cdot \big((\vee, \mathfrak{v})\big)$. We consider both cases in turn. Set $i = \rho_{T'}^{-1}(\sigma')$. Note that $\sigma'$ is not empty, so we can write $\sigma'$ as $\big((\mathbb{X}_0, \mathfrak{v}_0), \ldots, (\mathbb{X}_n, \mathfrak{v}_n)\big)$, $n \in \mathbb{N}$, and $i < |T'|$.

**Case 1** $\sigma = \sigma' \cdot \big((\wedge, \mathfrak{v})\big)$.
- Assume that $\mathbb{X}_0, \ldots, \mathbb{X}_n$ are all $\wedge$. Then $i = 1$, and as the result holds for $T'$, we infer that $T$'s standard enumeration is $(\sigma_j)_{1 \leq j \leq |T|}$ where $\sigma_1 = \sigma$ and for all $j \in \{2, \ldots, |T|\}$, $\sigma_i = \rho_{T'}(j-1)$.
- Otherwise, $i > 0$ and there exists $m \leq n$ such that $\big((\mathbb{X}_m, \mathfrak{v}_m), \ldots, (\mathbb{X}_n, \mathfrak{v}_n)\big)$ is of the form $\big((\vee, \mathfrak{v}_m)\big) \cdot \big((\wedge, \mathfrak{v}_{m+1}), \ldots, (\wedge, \mathfrak{v}_n)\big)$. Let $\tau$ denote $\big((\mathbb{X}_0, \mathfrak{v}_0), \ldots, (\mathbb{X}_{m-1}, \mathfrak{v}_{m-1})\big)$. By inductive hypothesis, $\rho_{T'}^{-1}(\tau) = \rho_{T'}^{-1}(\sigma') - 1$. From this and the fact that the result holds for $T'$, we infer that $T$'s standard enumeration is $(\sigma_j)_{1 \leq j \leq |T|}$ where $\sigma_i = \sigma$, $\sigma_j = \rho_{T'}(i)$ for all $j \in \{1, \ldots, i-1\}$, and $\sigma_j = \rho_{T'}(j-1)$ for all $j \in \{i+1, \ldots, |T|\}$.

**Case 2** $\sigma = \sigma' \cdot ((\vee, \mathfrak{v}))$. There exists $m \le n$ such that $((\mathbb{X}_m, \mathfrak{v}_m), \ldots, (\mathbb{X}_n, \mathfrak{v}_n))$ is of the form $((\wedge, \mathfrak{v}_m)) \cdot ((\vee, \mathfrak{v}_{m+1}), \ldots, (\vee, \mathfrak{v}_n))$. Let $((\mathbb{X}_0, \mathfrak{v}_0), \ldots (\mathbb{X}_m, \mathfrak{v}_{m-1}))$ be denoted by $\tau$. By inductive hypothesis, $\rho_{T'}^{-1}(\tau) = \rho_{T'}^{-1}(\sigma') + 1$. From this and the fact that the result holds for $T'$, we infer that $T$'s standard enumeration is $(\sigma_j)_{1 \le j \le |T|}$ where $\sigma_{i+1} = \sigma$, $\sigma_j = \rho_{T'}(i)$ for all $j \in \{1, \ldots, i\}$, and $\sigma_j = \rho_{T'}(j-1)$ for all $j \in \{i+2, \ldots, |T|\}$.

This completes the proof of the proposition. $\qquad\qquad\qquad\qquad\square$

**Example 33.** Figure 7.10 illustrates the second and third cases of Proposition 32.

**Figure 7.10**

**Corollary 34.** *Let a gradation tree $T$ with $|T| > 1$ and let $\sigma \in T$ be given.*

- *If $\sigma$ is the empty sequence then $\rho_T^{-1}(\sigma)$ equals $|T|$.*
- *Assume that $T$ contains a sequence of the form $\sigma \cdot ((\vee, \mathfrak{v}))$, and let $\tau$ be the (unique) longest sequence of the form $((\vee, \mathfrak{v}_0), (\wedge, \mathfrak{v}_1), \ldots, (\wedge, \mathfrak{v}_n))$, $n \in \mathbb{N}$, such that $\sigma \cdot \tau$ is in $T$. Then $\rho_T^{-1}(\tau)$ equals $\rho_T^{-1}(\sigma) + 1$.*
- *Suppose that none of the previous conditions applies. We can write $\sigma$ as $((\mathbb{X}_0, \mathfrak{v}_0), \ldots, (\mathbb{X}_n, \mathfrak{v}_n))$, $n \in \mathbb{N}$, and there exists a (unique) $m \le n$ such that $((\mathbb{X}_m, \mathfrak{v}_m), \ldots, (\mathbb{X}_n, \mathfrak{v}_n))$ is of the form $((\wedge, \mathfrak{v}_m)) \cdot ((\vee, \mathfrak{v}_{m+1}), \ldots, (\vee, \mathfrak{v}_n))$. Then denoting $((\mathbb{X}_0, \mathfrak{v}_0), \ldots, (\mathbb{X}_{m-1}, \mathfrak{v}_{m-1}))$ by $\tau$, $\rho_T^{-1}(\tau)$ equals $\rho_T^{-1}(\sigma) + 1$.*

**Example 35.** Figure 7.11 illustrates the second and third cases of Corollary 34.

**Figure 7.11**

Let an interpretation $\mathfrak{M}$, an $\mathscr{M}$-embedding $\mathfrak{E}$ and an $\mathfrak{E}$-gradation tree $T$ be given. Let $i$ in $\{1, \ldots, |T|\}$ be least with the following property: if $\sigma$ is the (unique) member of $T$ such that $\rho_T(i) = \sigma$, then $\mathfrak{M} \in \mathfrak{E}(\widehat{\sigma})$. Let $C$ denotes $\{\mathfrak{E}(\widehat{\tau}) \mid \tau \in T\}$. Then $\mathfrak{E}(\widehat{\sigma})$ is $\min_C(\mathfrak{M})$, as defined in Notation 4.

Let an $\mathscr{M}$-embedding $\mathfrak{E}$ and an $\mathfrak{E}$-gradation tree $T$ be given. In order to use $T$ and label a case, one needs to evaluate $\widehat{\sigma}$ for various $\sigma \in T$ and identify the unique $\sigma \in T$ such that $\widehat{\sigma}$ evaluates to True and $\rho_T^{-1}(\sigma)$ is minimal for the case under consideration. This can be done by first evaluating the member $\sigma$ of $T$ for which $\rho_T^{-1}(\sigma) = 1$, then possibly the member $\sigma$ of $T$ for which $\rho_T^{-1}(\sigma) = 2\dots$ Or it could be done using binary search by first evaluating the member $\sigma$ of $T$ for which $\rho_T^{-1}(\sigma) = \lfloor \frac{|T|}{2} \rfloor$. As $\mathfrak{E}$ is Boolean, we can work with $T$'s individual conditions, starting at $T$'s root and making our way along some initial segment of some branch. Indeed, we can work with negations of conditions, and the evaluation of a case can proceed in the way it is standardly done in RDR: being at a node $N$ whose condition evaluates to True, consider in turn the nodes $N_1, \dots, N_k$ such that $N_1$ is $N$'s exception and for all $i \in \{1,\dots,k-1\}$, $N_{i+1}$ is $N_i$'s alternative, move to $N_1$ if the condition at $N_1$ evaluates to True, move to $N_2$ if the condition at $N_1$ evaluates to False but the condition at $N_2$ evaluates to True, ..., and stay at $N$ if the conditions at all of $N_1, \dots, N_k$ all evaluate to False. We next turn our attention to Boolean gradation trees, with Notation 36 mapping each $\sigma \in T$ to an element of the underlying Boolean algebra, $\sigma\|_T$, meant to capture the standard RDR evaluation of a case. The notation is then illustrated and exemplified, before we establish a lemma thanks to which we can prove Proposition 40, thereby verifying that $\sigma\|_T$ indeed serves its intended purpose.

**Notation 36.** Let a Boolean $\mathscr{M}$-embedding $\mathfrak{E}$ and an $\mathfrak{E}$-gradation tree $T$ be given. Map each $\sigma \in T$ to $\sigma\|_T$, defined as follows. Let $\tau$ be the longest sequence of the form $((\wedge, \mathfrak{w}_0), (\vee, \mathfrak{w}_1), \dots, (\vee, \mathfrak{w}_m))$, $m \in \mathbb{N}$, with $\sigma \cdot \tau \in T$. If $\sigma$ is empty then define $\sigma\|_T$ as $\bigwedge_{i \leq m} \overline{\mathfrak{w}}_i$. Otherwise, write $\sigma$ as $((s_0, \mathfrak{v}_0), \dots, (s_n, \mathfrak{v}_n))$, $n \in \mathbb{N}$, and define $\sigma\|_T$ as

$$\mathfrak{v}_n \wedge \bigwedge_{i<n,\,s_{i+1}=\wedge} \mathfrak{v}_i \wedge \bigwedge_{i<n,\,s_{i+1}=\vee} \overline{\mathfrak{v}}_i \wedge \bigwedge_{i \leq m} \overline{\mathfrak{w}}_i.$$

**Example 37.** Figure 7.12 represents a member of a gradation tree $T$, of the form $\sigma \cdot \tau$, assuming that $\tau$ is the longest sequence of the form $((\wedge, \mathfrak{w}_0), (\vee, \mathfrak{w}_1), \dots, (\vee, \mathfrak{w}_m))$,

**Figure 7.12**

$m \in \mathbb{N}$, with $\sigma \cdot \tau \in T$ ($\tau$ could be empty). Here, $\sigma$ ends at the blue dot, which corresponds to $\mathfrak{v}_n$ in Notation 36. The green dots before the blue dot correspond to the conjuncts in $\bigwedge_{i<n,\, s_{i+1}=\wedge} \mathfrak{v}_i$. The red dots before the blue dot correspond to the conjuncts in $\bigwedge_{i<n,\, s_{i+1}=\vee} \overline{\mathfrak{v}_i}$. The red dots after the blue dot correspond to the conjuncts in $\bigwedge_{i\leq m} \overline{\mathfrak{w}_i}$.

**Example 38.** Recall the convention and notation in Example 10. The simplified values of $\sigma\|_T$ for all $\sigma \in T$ as defined in Notation 36 can be depicted as in Figure 7.13.

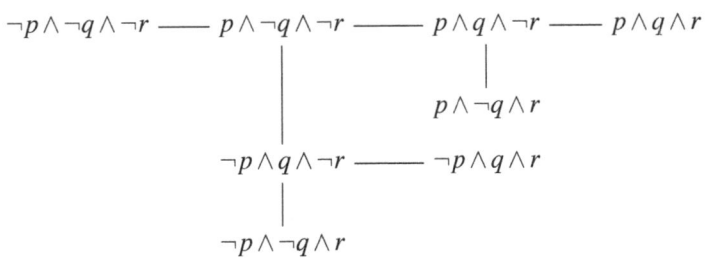

**Figure 7.13**

**Lemma 39.** *Let a Boolean $\mathcal{M}$-embedding $\mathfrak{E}$, an $\mathfrak{E}$-gradation tree $T$ with $T| > 1$, and a nonempty member $\sigma$ of $T$ be given. Set $i = \rho_T^{-1}(\sigma)$. Let $\mathfrak{v}$ be such that $\sigma$ ends in $(\vee, \mathfrak{v})$ or $(\wedge, \mathfrak{v})$. For all $\mathfrak{M} \in \mathfrak{E}(\rho_T(i+1)) \setminus \mathfrak{E}(\rho_T(i-1))$, $\mathfrak{M} \in \mathfrak{E}(\rho_T(i))$ iff $\mathfrak{M} \in \mathfrak{E}(\mathfrak{v})$.*

*Proof.* The result is straightforward if $\mathfrak{E}(\rho_T(i+1)) = \mathfrak{E}(\rho_T(i-1))$, so suppose otherwise. The proof is by induction on the size of $\mathfrak{E}$-gradation trees. The result is straightforward for $\mathfrak{E}$-gradation trees of size 2. Let $k \geq 2$ be given, and assume that the result holds for all $\mathfrak{E}$-gradation trees of size between 2 and $k$. Let $T$ be an $\mathfrak{E}$-gradation tree of size $k+1$. Let $\sigma \in T$ and $\mathfrak{E}$-gradation tree $T'$ be such that $T = T' \cup \{\sigma\}$. Let $\sigma' \in T'$ be such that $\sigma$ is of the form $\sigma' \cdot ((\wedge, \mathfrak{v}))$ or $\sigma' \cdot ((\vee, \mathfrak{v}))$. We consider both cases in turn. Set $i = \rho_{T'}^{-1}(\sigma')$. Note that $\sigma'$ is not empty, so we can write $\sigma'$ as $((\mathbb{X}_0, \mathfrak{v}_0), \ldots, (\mathbb{X}_n, \mathfrak{v}_n))$, $n \in \mathbb{N}$, and $i < |T'|$.

**Case 1** $\sigma = \sigma' \cdot ((\wedge, \mathfrak{v}))$.

- Assume that $\mathbb{X}_0, \ldots, \mathbb{X}_n$ are all $\wedge$, so $i = 1$. Obviously, for all $\mathfrak{M} \in \mathfrak{E}(\widehat{\sigma'})$, $\mathfrak{M} \in \mathfrak{E}(\widehat{\sigma})$ iff $\mathfrak{M} \in \mathfrak{E}(\mathfrak{v})$.
- Otherwise, $i > 1$ and there exists a nonzero $m \leq n$ such that $((\mathbb{X}_m, \mathfrak{v}_m), \ldots, (\mathbb{X}_n, \mathfrak{v}_n))$ is of the form $((\vee, \mathfrak{v}_m)) \cdot ((\wedge, \mathfrak{v}_{m+1}), \ldots, (\wedge, \mathfrak{v}_n))$. Let $\tau$ denote $((\mathbb{X}_0, \mathfrak{v}_0), \ldots, (\mathbb{X}_{m-1}, \mathfrak{v}_{m-1}))$. By Proposition 32, $\rho_{T'}^{-1}(\tau) = i - 1$. Note that

$$\mathfrak{E}(\mathfrak{v}_m \wedge \mathfrak{v}_{m+1} \wedge \cdots \wedge \mathfrak{v}_n \wedge \mathfrak{v}) = \mathfrak{E}(\mathfrak{v}_m \wedge \mathfrak{v}_{m+1} \wedge \cdots \wedge \mathfrak{v}_n) \cap \mathfrak{E}(\mathfrak{v}).$$

Let $\mathfrak{M} \in \mathfrak{E}\big(\rho_{T'}(i+1)\big) \setminus \mathfrak{E}\big(\rho_{T'}(i-1)\big)$ be given.
- If $\mathfrak{M} \in \mathfrak{E}(\mathfrak{v})$ then since $\mathfrak{M} \in \mathfrak{E}(\widehat{\sigma'})$, $\mathfrak{M} \in \mathfrak{E}(\widehat{\sigma})$.
- If $\mathfrak{M} \notin \mathfrak{E}(\mathfrak{v})$ then since $\mathfrak{M} \notin \mathfrak{E}(\widehat{\tau})$, $\mathfrak{M} \notin \mathfrak{E}(\widehat{\sigma})$.

**Case 2** $\sigma = \sigma' \cdot \big((\vee, \mathfrak{v})\big)$. There exists $m \leq n$ such that $\big((\mathbb{X}_m, \mathfrak{v}_m), \ldots, (\mathbb{X}_n, \mathfrak{v}_n)\big)$ is of the form $\big((\wedge, \mathfrak{v}_m)\big) \cdot \big((\vee, \mathfrak{v}_{m+1}), \ldots, (\vee, \mathfrak{v}_n)\big)$. Let $\tau$ denote $\big((\mathbb{X}_0, \mathfrak{v}_0), \ldots, (\mathbb{X}_m, \mathfrak{v}_{m-1})\big)$. By Corollary 34, $\rho_{T'}^{-1}(\tau) = i + 1$. Note that

$$\mathfrak{E}(\mathfrak{v}_m \vee \mathfrak{v}_{m+1} \vee \cdots \vee \mathfrak{v}_n \vee \mathfrak{v}) = \mathfrak{E}(\mathfrak{v}_m \vee \mathfrak{v}_{m+1} \vee \cdots \vee \mathfrak{v}_n) \cup \mathfrak{E}(\mathfrak{v}).$$

Let $\mathfrak{M} \in \mathfrak{E}\big(\rho_{T'}(i+1)\big) \setminus \mathfrak{E}\big(\rho_{T'}(i-1)\big)$ be given.
- If $\mathfrak{M} \in \mathfrak{E}(\mathfrak{v})$ then since $\mathfrak{M} \in \mathfrak{E}(\widehat{\tau})$, $\mathfrak{M} \in \mathfrak{E}(\widehat{\sigma})$.
- If $\mathfrak{M} \notin \mathfrak{E}(\mathfrak{v})$ then since and $\mathfrak{M} \notin \mathfrak{E}(\widehat{\sigma'})$, $\mathfrak{M} \notin \mathfrak{E}(\widehat{\sigma})$.

From all this and the fact that the result holds for $T'$, we infer easily with the help of Proposition 32 and Corollary 34 that the result holds for $T$. $\qquad\square$

**Proposition 40.** *For all Boolean $\mathcal{M}$-embeddings $\mathfrak{E}$, $\mathfrak{E}$-gradation trees $T$ and $\sigma \in T$,*

$$\mathfrak{E}(\sigma\|_T) = \mathfrak{E}(\widehat{\sigma}) \setminus \mathfrak{E}\Big(\rho_T\big(\rho_T^{-1}(\sigma) - 1\big)\Big).$$

*Proof.* The proof is by induction on the size of $\mathfrak{E}$-gradation trees. The result is straightforward for $\mathfrak{E}$-gradation trees of size 2. Let $k \geq 2$ be given, and assume that the result holds for all $\mathfrak{E}$-gradation trees of size between 2 and $k$. Let $T$ be an $\mathfrak{E}$-gradation tree of size $k + 1$. Let $\sigma \in T$ and $\mathfrak{E}$-gradation tree $T'$ be such that $T = T' \cup \{\sigma\}$. Let $\sigma' \in T'$ be such that $\sigma$ is of the form $\sigma' \cdot \big((\wedge, \mathfrak{v})\big)$ or $\sigma' \cdot \big((\vee, \mathfrak{v})\big)$. We consider both cases in turn. Set $i = \rho_{T'}^{-1}(\sigma')$.

**Case 1** $\sigma = \sigma' \cdot \big((\wedge, \mathfrak{v})\big)$.
- Writing $\sigma'$ as $\big((\mathbb{X}_0, \mathfrak{v}_0), \ldots, (\mathbb{X}_n, \mathfrak{v}_n)\big)$, $n \in \mathbb{N}$, assume that $\mathbb{X}_0, \ldots, \mathbb{X}_n$ are all $\wedge$, so $i = 1$. Clearly,
  - $\mathfrak{E}\big(\sigma'\|_{T'} \wedge \mathfrak{v}\big) = \mathfrak{E}(\widehat{\sigma})$;
  - $\mathfrak{E}\big(\sigma'\|_{T'} \wedge \overline{\mathfrak{v}}\big) = \mathfrak{E}(\widehat{\sigma'}) \setminus \mathfrak{E}(\widehat{\sigma})$.
- Otherwise, $n > 1$. Set $\tau = \rho_{T'}(i - 1)$. By inductive hypothesis, $\mathfrak{E}\big(\sigma'\|_{T'}\big) = \mathfrak{E}(\widehat{\sigma'}) \setminus \mathfrak{E}(\widehat{\tau})$. Together with Proposition 32 and Lemma 39, this implies that:
  - $\mathfrak{E}\big(\sigma'\|_{T'} \wedge \mathfrak{v}\big) = \big(\mathfrak{E}(\widehat{\sigma'}) \setminus \mathfrak{E}(\widehat{\tau})\big) \cap \mathfrak{E}(\widehat{\sigma}) = \mathfrak{E}(\widehat{\sigma}) \setminus \mathfrak{E}(\widehat{\tau})$;
  - $\mathfrak{E}\big(\sigma'\|_{T'} \wedge \overline{\mathfrak{v}}\big) = \big(\mathfrak{E}(\widehat{\sigma'}) \setminus \mathfrak{E}(\widehat{\tau})\big) \cap \overline{\mathfrak{E}(\widehat{\sigma})} = \mathfrak{E}(\widehat{\sigma'}) \setminus \mathfrak{E}(\widehat{\sigma})$.

Also, note that in both cases,
- $\sigma\|_T$ is defined as $\sigma'\|_{T'} \wedge \mathfrak{v}$;
- $\sigma'\|_T$ is defined as $\sigma'\|_{T'} \wedge \overline{\mathfrak{v}}$.

**Case 2** $\sigma = \sigma' \cdot \big((\vee, \mathfrak{v})\big)$. Set $\tau = \rho_{T'}(i + 1)$. By inductive hypothesis, $\mathfrak{E}\big(\tau\|_{T'}\big) = \mathfrak{E}(\widehat{\tau}) \setminus \mathfrak{E}(\widehat{\sigma'})$. Together with Corollary 34 and Lemma 39, this implies that:
- $\mathfrak{E}\big(\tau\|_{T'} \wedge \mathfrak{v}\big) = \big(\mathfrak{E}(\widehat{\tau}) \setminus \mathfrak{E}(\widehat{\sigma'})\big) \cap \mathfrak{E}(\widehat{\sigma}) = \mathfrak{E}(\widehat{\sigma}) \setminus \mathfrak{E}(\widehat{\sigma'})$;
- $\mathfrak{E}\big(\tau\|_{T'} \wedge \overline{\mathfrak{v}}\big) = \big(\mathfrak{E}(\widehat{\tau}) \setminus \mathfrak{E}(\widehat{\sigma'})\big) \cap \overline{\mathfrak{E}(\widehat{\sigma})} = \mathfrak{E}(\widehat{\tau}) \setminus \mathfrak{E}(\widehat{\sigma})$.

Also, note that
- $\sigma\|_T$ is defined as $\tau\|_{T'} \wedge \mathfrak{v}$;
- $\tau\|_T$ is defined as $\tau\|_{T'} \wedge \bar{\mathfrak{v}}$.

From all this and the fact that the result holds for $T'$, we infer easily with the help of Proposition 32 and Corollary 34 that the result holds for $T$. $\qquad\square$


## 7.5 NORMAL FORMS

Let a gradation tree $T$ and a member $\sigma$ of $T$ be given. Defined as it is, $\hat{\sigma}$ can have $\vee$s within $\wedge$s within $\vee$s within $\wedge$s... all the more so that $\sigma$ is longer and has more "direction changes". This is in contrast to the flat structure of disjunctive or conjunctive normal forms, that limit embedding depth to 2 (disjunctions within conjunctions, or conjunctions within conjunctions). Notation 41 captures the natural way to convert $\hat{\sigma}$ to disjunctive and conjunctive normal forms. Corollary 44 characterises the disjunctive and conjunctive normal forms that can be expressed as formulas of the form $\hat{\sigma}$.

**Notation 41.** Let a gradation tree $T$ be given. Let both $\mathrm{DNF}(\sigma)$ and $\mathrm{CNF}(\sigma)$ denote $\bigwedge\varnothing$. Associate each nonempty member $\sigma$ of $T$ with two collections of sets as follows.

- Write $\sigma$ as

$$((\wedge, \mathfrak{v}_0^0), \ldots (\wedge, \mathfrak{v}_0^{p_0}), (\vee, \mathfrak{v}_1), \ldots (\vee, \mathfrak{v}_{n_0}), (\wedge, \mathfrak{v}_1^0), \ldots (\wedge, \mathfrak{v}_1^{p_1}),$$
$$(\vee, \mathfrak{v}_{n_0+1}), \cdots \vee, \mathfrak{v}_{n_0+n_1}), \ldots,$$
$$\ldots, (\wedge, \mathfrak{v}_k^0), \ldots, (\wedge, \mathfrak{v}_k^{p_k}), (\vee, \mathfrak{v}_{\Sigma_{j<k}n_j+1}), \ldots, (\vee, \mathfrak{v}_{\Sigma_{j\leq k}n_j}))$$

with $k, p_0, \ldots, p_k, n_k \in \mathbb{N}$ and $n_0, \ldots, n_{k-1} \in \mathbb{N}\setminus\{0\}$. Given $i \leq \Sigma_{j\leq k}n_j$, set $C_i = \{\mathfrak{v}_0^0\}$ and do the following.
  - For all $j \leq k$, if $n_0 + \cdots + n_{j-1} \leq i$ then add $\mathfrak{v}_j^0, \ldots, \mathfrak{v}_j^{p_j-1}$ to $C_i$.
  - If there exists a (unique) nonzero $j < k$ with $n_0 + \cdots + n_{j-1} = i$ then add $\mathfrak{v}_j^{p_j}$ to $C_i$.
  - If $j \leq k$ is largest with $n_0 + \cdots + n_j \leq i$, and either if $j < k$ or if $j = k$ and $n_k \neq 0$, then add $\mathfrak{v}_{n_0}, \ldots, \mathfrak{v}_{n_j}$ to $C_i$.
- Write $\sigma$ as

$$((\wedge, \mathfrak{v}_1), \ldots (\wedge, \mathfrak{v}_{p_0}), (\vee, \mathfrak{v}_0^1), \ldots (\vee, \mathfrak{v}_0^{n_0}),$$
$$(\wedge, \mathfrak{v}_{p_0+1}), \ldots (\wedge, \mathfrak{v}_{p_0+p_1}), (\vee, \mathfrak{v}_1^1), \ldots (\vee, \mathfrak{v}_1^{n_1}), \ldots,$$
$$\ldots, (\wedge, \mathfrak{v}_{\Sigma_{j<k}p_j+1}), \ldots, (\wedge, \mathfrak{v}_{\Sigma_{j\leq k}p_j}), (\vee, \mathfrak{v}_k^1), \ldots, (\vee, \mathfrak{v}_k^{n_k}))$$

with $k, n_k \in \mathbb{N}$ and $p_0, \ldots, p_k, n_0, \ldots, n_{k-1} \in \mathbb{N}\setminus\{0\}$. Given $0 < i \leq \Sigma_{j\leq k}p_j$, set $D_i = \{\mathfrak{v}_1\}$ and do the following.
  - For all $j \leq k$, if $p_0 + \cdots + p_j \leq i$ then add $\mathfrak{v}_j^0, \ldots, \mathfrak{v}_j^{n_j-1}$ to $D_i$.

- If there exists a (unique) $j \leq k$ with $p_0 + \cdots + p_j = i$ then add $\mathfrak{v}_j^{n_j}$ to $D_i$.
- If $j \leq k$ is largest with $p_0 + \cdots + p_j \leq i$, then add $\mathfrak{v}_{p_0}, \ldots, \mathfrak{v}_{p_j}$ to $D_i$.

We let $\mathrm{DNF}(\sigma)$ denote $\bigvee_{i \leq \Sigma_{j \leq k} n_j} \bigwedge C_i$, and $\mathrm{CNF}(\sigma)$ denote $\bigvee_{1 \leq i \leq \Sigma_{j \leq k} P_j} \bigwedge D_i$.

**Proposition 42.** *For all gradation trees $T$ and members $\sigma$ of $T$, $\hat{\sigma}$ is equal to both* $\mathrm{DNF}(\sigma)$ *and* $\mathrm{CNF}(\sigma)$.

*Proof.* This is easily verified by induction on the length of the members of $T$, using the fact that a Boolean algebra is distributive. $\qquad\square$

**Example 43.** Figures 7.14 and 7.15 represent a nonempty member $\sigma$ of a gradation tree and illustrate $\mathrm{DNF}(\sigma)$ and $\mathrm{CNF}(\sigma)$ defined in Proposition 42.

- Figure 7.14 illustrates the value of $\mathrm{DNF}(\sigma)$, that is, $\bigvee_{i \leq \Sigma_{j \leq k} n_j} \bigwedge C_i$, as defined in Notation 41. It is the particular case where $k = 3$, $p_0 = 2$, $n_0 = 3$, $p_1 = 0$, $n_1 = 1$, $p_2 = 2$, $n_2 = 2$, $p_3 = 0$, and $n_3 = 0$. So $\Sigma_{j \leq k} n_j = 6$. The sets $C_0$ to $C_6$ are represented with $C_0$ in the middle of the top row, and $C_6$ in the bottom right corner, reading row by row, and on a given row from left to right. For all $i \leq 6$, the members of $C_i$ are shown as black dots.

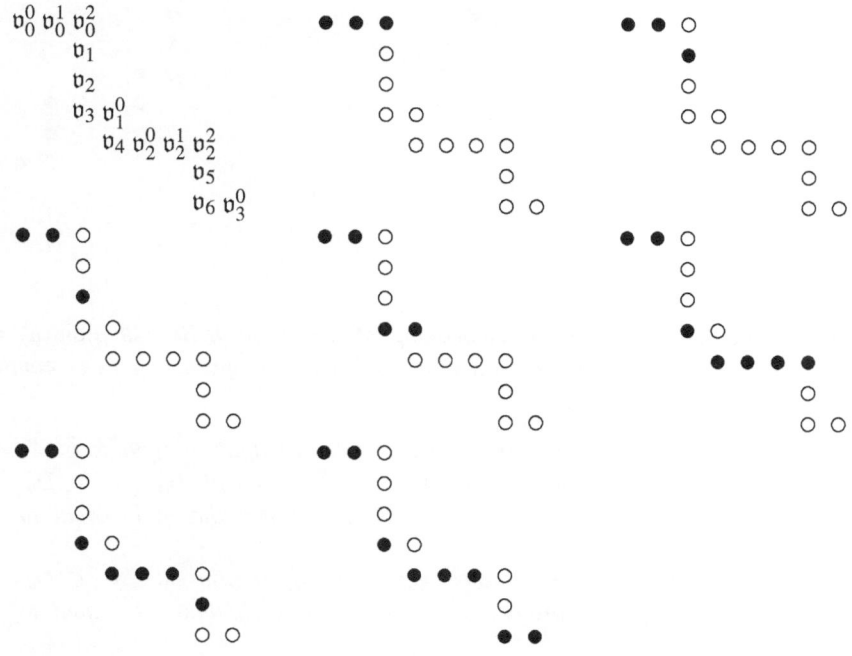

**Figure 7.14**

- Figure 7.15 illustrates the value of $\mathrm{CNF}(\sigma)$, that is, $\bigvee_{1\le i\le\Sigma_{j\le k}p_j}\bigwedge D_i$, as defined in Notation 41. It is the particular case where $k=3$, $p_0=3$, $n_0=3$, $p_1=1$, $n_1=1$, $p_2=3$, $n_2=2$, $p_3=1$, and $n_3=0$. So $\Sigma_{j\le k}p_j=8$. The sets $D_1$ to $D_8$ are represented with $D_1$ in the middle of the top row, and $D_8$ in the bottom right corner, reading row by row, and on a given row from left to right. For all $i\in\{1,\dots,8\}$, the members of $D_i$ are shown as black dots.

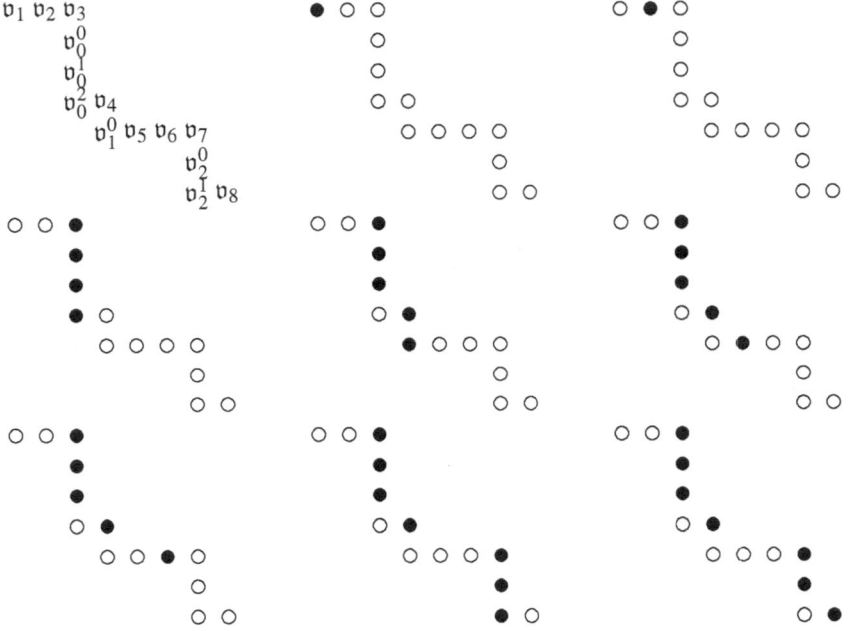

**Figure 7.15**

**Corollary 44.** *Let $\mathfrak{E}$ be an $\mathscr{M}$-embedding of the form $(h,B)$ with $\mathrm{dom}(h)=(B,\vee,\wedge,0,1)$. Let a member $\mathfrak{v}$ of $B$ distinct to 0 and 1 be given. The three conditions that follow are equivalent.*

- *There exists an $\mathfrak{E}$-gradation tree $T$ and $\sigma\in T$ such that $\mathfrak{v}$ is equal to $\widehat{\sigma}$.*
- *There exists $n\in\mathbb{N}$, finite subsets $D_0,\dots,D_n$ of $B$ with $D_0\subset\dots\subset D_n$, and nonempty finite subsets $E_0,\dots,E_n$ of $B$ such that $\mathfrak{v}$ is equal to $\bigvee_{i\le n}\bigwedge_{\mathfrak{v}\in E_i}(D_i\cup\{\mathfrak{v}\})$.*
- *There exists $n\in\mathbb{N}$, finite subsets $D_0,\dots,D_n$ of $B$ with $D_0\subset\dots\subset D_n$, and nonempty finite subsets $E_0,\dots,E_n$ of $B$ such that $\mathfrak{v}$ is equal to $\bigwedge_{i\le n}\bigvee_{\mathfrak{v}\in E_i}(D_i\cup\{\mathfrak{v}\})$.*

**Example 45.** Continuing Example 43, let Figures 7.14 and 7.15 further illustrate Corollary 44.

- In Corollary 44, $\mathrm{DNF}(\sigma)$ is written as $\bigvee_{i\leq 3} \bigwedge_{\mathfrak{v}\in E_i} (D_i \cup \{\mathfrak{v}\})$ where:
  - $D_0 = \{\mathfrak{v}_0^0, \mathfrak{v}_0^1\}$ and $E_0 = \{\mathfrak{v}_0^2, \mathfrak{v}_1, \mathfrak{v}_2\}$;
  - $D_1 = D_0 \cup \{\mathfrak{v}_3\}$ and $E_1 = \{\mathfrak{v}_1^0\}$;
  - $D_2 = D_1 \cup \{\mathfrak{v}_4, \mathfrak{v}_2^0, \mathfrak{v}_2^1\}$ and $E_2 = \{\mathfrak{v}_2^2, \mathfrak{v}_5\}$;
  - $D_3 = D_2 \cup \{\mathfrak{v}_6\}$ and $E_1 = \{\mathfrak{v}_3^0\}$.
- In Corollary 44, $\mathrm{CNF}(\sigma)$ is written as $\bigwedge_{i\leq 3} \bigvee_{\mathfrak{v}\in E_i} (D_i \cup \{\mathfrak{v}\})$ where:
  - $D_0 = \varnothing$ and $E_0 = \{\mathfrak{v}_1, \mathfrak{v}_2\}$;
  - $D_1 = D_0 \cup \{\mathfrak{v}_3, \mathfrak{v}_0^0, \mathfrak{v}_0^1\}$ and $E_1 = \{\mathfrak{v}_0^2\}$;
  - $D_2 = D_1 \cup \{\mathfrak{v}_4\}$ and $E_2 = \{\mathfrak{v}_1^0, \mathfrak{v}_5, \mathfrak{v}_6\}$;
  - $D_3 = D_2 \cup \{\mathfrak{v}_7, \mathfrak{v}_2^0\}$ and $E_3 = \{\mathfrak{v}_2^1, \mathfrak{v}_8\}$.

**Property 46.** *For all gradation trees $T$ and nonempty $\sigma \in T$, $\mathring{\sigma} \in \mathrm{DNF}(\sigma)$.*

## 7.6 LABELLED GRADATION TREES AND GRAPHS

Given an RDR tree and a case, evaluation of the conditions of some of the nodes of the tree, using a rich enough description of the case, eventually points to a specific node in the tree. That node is meant to be associated with a useful piece of information about the case and reveal something interesting and not known about it. The information can be 1 or 0 as a way to classify the case and let the user know whether it has a particular property. It can be the name of a class the case belongs to. Here we focus on the former, so on binary classification, and leave it to the reader to generalise the setting to multiclass classification.

**Definition 47.** Given a gradation tree $T$ or a gradation graph $G$, a *classifier for $T$* or $G$ is a mapping whose domain is $T$ or $\mathrm{Paths}(G)$, respectively, and whose codomain is $\{0,1\}$.

**Definition 48.** A *classifying gradation tree* or *graph* is a pair of the form $(S, \ell)$ where $S$ is a gradation tree or graph, respectively, and $\ell$ is a classifier for $S$.

**Notation 49.** Given an $\mathscr{M}$-embedding $\mathfrak{E}$, a classifying $\mathfrak{E}$-gradation tree $(T, \ell)$ and $\mathfrak{M} \in \mathscr{M}$, we let $\ell\langle\mathfrak{M}\rangle$ denote $\ell(\rho_T(i))$ for the least $i \in \{1,\ldots,|T|\}$ such that $\mathfrak{M} \in \widehat{\mathfrak{E}(\rho_T(i))}$.

We now formalise how a classifying gradation tree or graph $S$ yields a classification.

**Definition 50.** A classifying gradation tree $(T, \ell)$ is said to *recognise* a formula $\varphi$ iff for all $\mathfrak{M} \in \mathscr{M}$, $\ell\langle\mathfrak{M}\rangle = 1$ iff $\mathfrak{M} \models \varphi$.

**Definition 51.** A classifying gradation graphs $\mathscr{F}$ is said to *recognise* a formula $\varphi$ iff the classifying gradation tree associated with $\mathscr{F}$ recognise $\varphi$.

We will more closely study two special kinds of classifiers. The first kind of classifier corresponds to switching classification between "in the class" and "not in the class" at every exception, starting with one or the other, e.g.: by default, the case is in the class, except if this condition, the first one from this sequence of alternatives, holds, in which case the case is not in the class, except if this condition, the first one from this sequence of alternatives, holds, in which case the case is in the class... This is related to the notion of mind change bound [8], developed in the paradigm of formal learning theory [7], even though in the simpler framework developed here, there is no need for infinite ordinals...

**Definition 52.** Let a classifying gradation tree $(T, \ell)$ be given. If $\ell^{-1}(1)$ is the set of all $\sigma \in T$ that contain an even number of pairs of the form $(\wedge, \mathfrak{v})$ or the set of all $\sigma \in T$ that contain an odd number of pairs of the form $(\wedge, \mathfrak{v})$, then we say that $(T, \ell)$ is *parity-based*, *positive by default* in the first case, *negative by default* in the second case.

Let a classifying gradation graph $(G, \ell)$ be given. If $\ell^{-1}(1)$ is the set of all $\sigma \in$ Paths$(G)$ of odd length the set of all $\sigma \in$ Paths$(G)$ of even length, then we say that $(T, \ell)$ is *parity-based*, *positive by default* in the first case, *negative by default* in the second case.

**Property 53.** *Let a classifying gradation graph $\mathcal{G}$ be given. Then $\mathcal{F}$ is parity-based iff the classifying gradation tree $\mathcal{F}$ that is determined by $\mathcal{G}$ is parity-based. Moreover, if $\mathcal{G}$ is parity based then $\mathcal{G}$ is positive by default or negative by default iff $\mathcal{F}$ is positive by default or negative by default, respectively.*

The second kind of classifier corresponds to classifying a case as being in the class if and only if evaluation stops at a node that has no exception, that is, at a node where evaluation cannot possibly proceed any further.

**Definition 54.** A classifying gradation tree $(T, \ell)$ is said to be *end-based* iff $\ell^{-1}(1)$ is the set of all $\sigma \in T$ such that $T$ contains no element of the form $\sigma \cdot ((\wedge, \mathfrak{v}))$.

A classifying gradation graph $(G, \ell)$ is said to be *end-based* iff $\ell^{-1}(1)$ is the set of members of Paths$(G)$ that have no proper extension in Paths$(G)$.

**Example 55.** Recall the convention and notation in Example 10. The tree $T$ uniquely defines a negative by default, parity-based classifying $\mathscr{A}$-gradation tree. Figure 7.5 implicitly depicts it; it could be explicitly depicted in Figure 7.16. It recognises $p \oplus q \oplus r$.

**Example 56.** Recall the convention and notation in Example 10. Some classifying $\mathscr{A}$-gradation trees recognises $p \wedge q$, but none of them is parity-based.

*Proof.* In Figure 7.17 are two classifying $\mathscr{A}$-gradation trees that recognise $p \wedge q$: It is easy to verify that if $T$ is a classifying $\mathscr{A}$-gradation tree that recognises $p \wedge q$, then $T$ is one of those two, possibly (uselessly) extended, hence $T$ is not parity-based. $\square$

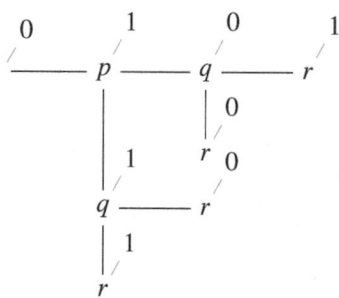

**Figure 7.16**

**Figure 7.17**

The following result demonstrates how a single $\mathscr{A}$-gradation tree suffices to classify all formulas.

**Proposition 57.** *There exists an $\mathscr{A}$-gradation tree $T$ such that for all formulas $\varphi$, there exits a classifier $\ell$ for $T$ such that $(T, \ell)$ recognises $\varphi$.*

*Proof.* Set $|\mathscr{A}| = k$. Let $(\xi_i)_{i<k}$ be an enumeration of $\mathscr{A}$. Inductively define for all $i < k$ a finite set $S_i$ of literals as follows. Let $i < k$ be given, and assume that $S_j$ has been defined for all $j < i$. Define $S_i$ as the set of all sets of the form $X \cup \{\xi_i\}$ and all sets of the form $X \cup \{\neg \xi_i\}$ such that:

- $X$ is a $\subseteq$-maximal member of $\bigcup_{j<i} S_i$;
- $\varnothing \subset \mathrm{Mod}_{\mathscr{M}}(X \cup \{\xi_i\}) \subset \mathrm{Mod}_{\mathscr{M}}(X)$.

Let $S$ be the set of all $\subseteq$-maximal members of $\bigcup_{i<k} S_i$. Let $U$ be the set of finite sequences of the form $(i_1, \ldots, i_p)$ with $0 \le p < k$ and $0 \le i_1 < \cdots < i_p < k$ for which there exists a (necessarily unique) member $X$ of $S$ such that for all $i < k$, $i \in \{i_1, \ldots, i_p\}$ iff $\xi_i \in X$. Now define an $\mathscr{A}$-gradation tree $T$ as the $\subseteq$ smallest set of finite sequences of atoms such that $T$ contains the empty sequence and for all $\sigma \in T$, the following holds. By construction, $\sigma$ can be written as $((\mathbb{X}_1, \xi_{i_1}), \ldots, (\mathbb{X}_p, \xi_{i_p}))$ with $0 \le p \le k$, $\mathbb{X}_i \in \{\vee, \wedge\}$ for all nonzero $i \le p$, and $(i_1, \ldots, i_p) \in U$.

- Suppose that there exists $m < k$ either with $p$ being equal to 0 or with $p \neq 0$ and $m > i_p$, such that $(i_1, \ldots, i_p, m) \in U$. Then choose the smallest such integer $m$ and add $\sigma \cdot ((\wedge, \xi_m))$ to $T$.

- Suppose that $p \neq 0$ and there exists $m < k$ such that $m > i_p$ and $(i_1, \ldots, i_{p-1}, m) \in U$. Then choose the smallest such integer $m$ and add $((\maltese_1, \xi_{i_1}), \ldots, (\maltese_{p-1}, \xi_{i_{p-1}}), (\vee, \xi_m))$ to $T$.

Note that there exists a one-to-one mapping $F$ from $S$ into $T$ (as well as a one-to-one mapping from $U$ into $T$). Clearly, $\{ \mathrm{Mod}_{\mathscr{M}}(X) \mid X \in S \}$ is a partition of $\mathscr{M}$. Also, it is easily verified that for all $\sigma \in T$, $\sigma \|_T = \bigwedge F^{-1}(\sigma)$. Let $\varphi$ be a formula. Let $\ell$ be the classifier for $T$ such that for all $\sigma \in T$, $\ell(\sigma) = 1$ iff there exists $\mathfrak{M} \in \mathscr{M}$ with $\mathfrak{M} \models \varphi$ and $\mathfrak{M} \in F^{-1}(\sigma)$. We immediately conclude from Proposition 40 together with the previous observations that $(T, \ell)$ recognises $\varphi$, thereby completing the proof of the proposition. □

**Example 58.** Suppose that $\mathscr{A}$ consists of 5 atoms, $p_i$, $0 \leq i \leq 4$, and $\mathscr{M}$ is the set of models of:

- $p_0 \rightarrow p_2$
- $p_1 \wedge p_2 \rightarrow p_3$
- $\neg p_1 \vee \neg p_3 \rightarrow \neg p_4$
- $\neg p_2 \rightarrow p_4$

Assume that $(p_i)_{i<5}$ corresponds to the enumeration $(\xi_i)_{i<k}$ of $\mathscr{A}$ in the proof. The sets $S_0$, $S_1$, $S_2$ and $S_3$ in the proof are shown in Figure 58, the set $S_4$ being empty. Each member of $S_2 \cup S_3$ logically implies either $p_i$ or $\neg p_i$ in $\mathscr{M}$ for all $i < 5$; they are the sets that make up the set $S$ in the proof.

| $S_0$ | $S_1$ | $S_2$ | $S_3$ | ... which implies... in $\mathscr{M}$ |
|---|---|---|---|---|
| $\{p_0\}$ | $\{p_0, p_1\}$ | $\{p_0, p_1, p_4\}$ | | $p_0 \wedge p_1 \wedge p_2 \wedge p_3 \wedge p_4$ |
| | | $\{p_0, p_1, \neg p_4\}$ | | $p_0 \wedge p_1 \wedge p_2 \wedge p_3 \wedge \neg p_4$ |
| | $\{p_0, \neg p_1\}$ | $\{p_0, \neg p_1, p_3\}$ | | $p_0 \wedge \neg p_1 \wedge p_2 \wedge p_3 \wedge \neg p_4$ |
| | | $\{p_0, \neg p_1, \neg p_3\}$ | | $p_0 \wedge \neg p_1 \wedge p_2 \wedge \neg p_3 \wedge \neg p_4$ |
| $\{\neg p_0\}$ | $\{\neg p_0, p_1\}$ | $\{\neg p_0, p_1, p_2\}$ | $\{\neg p_0, p_1, p_2, p_4\}$ | $\neg p_0 \wedge p_1 \wedge p_2 \wedge p_3 \wedge p_4$ |
| | | | $\{\neg p_0, p_1, p_2, \neg p_4\}$ | $\neg p_0 \wedge p_1 \wedge p_2 \wedge p_3 \wedge \neg p_4$ |
| | | $\{\neg p_0, p_1, \neg p_2\}$ | | $\neg p_0 \wedge p_1 \wedge \neg p_2 \wedge p_3 \wedge p_4$ |
| | $\{\neg p_0, \neg p_1\}$ | $\{\neg p_0, \neg p_1, p_3\}$ | | $\neg p_0 \wedge \neg p_1 \wedge p_2 \wedge p_3 \wedge \neg p_4$ |
| | | $\{\neg p_0, \neg p_1, \neg p_3\}$ | | $\neg p_0 \wedge \neg p_1 \wedge p_2 \wedge \neg p_3 \wedge \neg p_4$ |

The tree $T$ in the proof can be depicted as on the left of Figure 7.18. The one-to-one mapping, defined in the proof, between $U$ and $T$ can be depicted as on the right of the figure.

The one-to-one mapping $F$, defined in the proof, between the (conjunctions over the members of) $S$ and $T$ can be depicted as in the upper part of Figure 7.18.

For an illustration of the proposition that follows, besides Example 60, also refer to Figure 7.6 and view it as a parity-based, negative by default gradation graph. It is the gradation graph constructed in the proof of the proposition for the case where

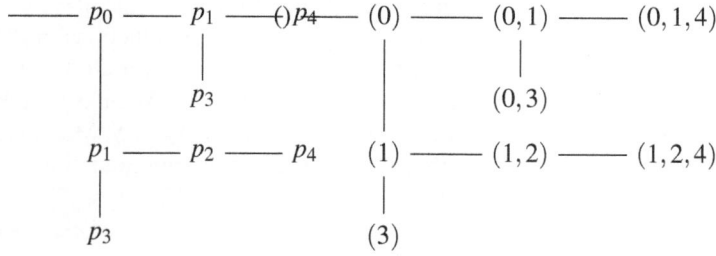

**Figure 7.18**

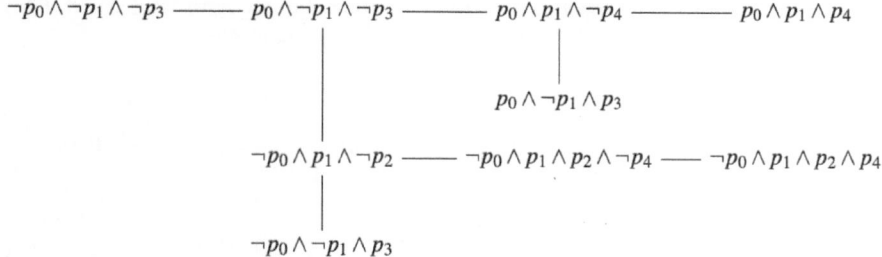

$n = 3$. The graph lets us randomly choose which of $p_1, \ldots, p_n$ to evaluate in sequence. It also avoids the redundancy that has to be built in any $\mathscr{A}$-gradation tree, and even in each $\mathscr{A}^{\wedge}$-gradation tree, thanks to which $\bigoplus_{1 \leq i \leq n} p_i$ can be correctly classified, bringing the complexity of the structure from exponential down to quadratic.

**Proposition 59.** *Suppose that $\mathscr{A}$ consists of $n$ atoms $p_1, \ldots, p_n$, $n \in \mathbb{N} \setminus \{0\}$, and $\mathscr{M}$ is the set of all interpretations.*

- *Some classifying $\mathscr{A}$-gradation graph with $n + 1$ nodes and $\frac{n(n+1)}{2}$ edges recognises $\bigoplus_{1 \leq i \leq n} p_i$.*
- *For all classifying $\mathscr{A}^{\wedge}$-gradation trees $T$ that recognise $\bigoplus_{1 \leq i \leq n} p_i$, $|T| \geq 2^n$.*

*Proof.* Set $\varphi_0 = \bigwedge \varnothing$ and $V = \{p_i \mid i < n\}$. Let $E$ be the set of all pairs of the form $(p_i, p_j)$, $0 \leq i < j \leq n$. Obviously, if $\mathscr{R}$ is a presentation of $(V, E)$ then for all $i, j, k \leq n$ with $i < j < k$, $(i, j)$ occurs before $(i, k)$ in $\mathscr{R}$. Using that observation, it is easy to verify that $(V, E)$, which has $n + 1$ nodes and $\frac{n(n+1)}{2}$ edges, is a parity-based, negative by default classifying $\mathscr{A}$-gradation graph that recognises $\bigoplus_{1 \leq i \leq n} p_i$.

Let $(T, \ell)$ be a classifying $\mathscr{A}^{\wedge}$-gradation tree that recognises $\bigoplus_{1 \leq i \leq n} p_i$. Recall from Notation 36 the definition of $\sigma \|_T$ for all $\sigma \in T$. In a related way, map each $\sigma \in T$ to $S_\sigma$, defined as follows. Set $S_{()} = \varnothing$. Let a nonempty $\sigma \in T$ be given, and write $\sigma$ as $((\mathbb{X}_0, \mathfrak{v}_0), \ldots, (\mathbb{X}_n, \mathfrak{v}_n))$, $n \in \mathbb{N}$. Set $X = \{\mathfrak{v}_n\} \cup \{\mathfrak{v}_i \mid i < n, \mathbb{X}_{i+1} = \wedge\}$.

Let $X'$ be the set of atoms in $X$. Define $S_\sigma$ as the set of members of $\mathscr{A}$ that either belong to $X'$, or that are conjuncts in some of the conjunctions in $X \setminus X'$. Suppose for a contradiction that there exists $S \subseteq \mathscr{A}$ with $S \neq S_\sigma$ for all $\sigma \in T$. Let $\mathfrak{M}$ be the interpretation such that for all $p \in \mathscr{A}$, $\mathfrak{M} \models p$ iff $p \in S$. We infer from Proposition 40 that there exists $\sigma \in T$ with $\mathfrak{M} \models \sigma\|_T$. Obviously, $S_\sigma \subset S$. Moreover, it is easy to verify that for all $S' \subseteq S$ with $S_\sigma \subseteq S'$, if $\mathfrak{M}'$ is the interpretation such that for all $p \in \mathscr{A}$, $\mathfrak{M}' \models p$ iff $p \in S'$, then $\mathfrak{M}' \models \sigma\|_T$, hence $\ell\langle\mathfrak{M}'\rangle = \ell\langle\mathfrak{M}\rangle$, in contradiction with the assumption that $(T, \ell)$ recognises $\bigoplus_{1 \leq i \leq n} p_i$. Therefore, since there are $2^n$ many subsets of $\mathscr{A}$, $T$ must have at least $2^n$ many elements. $\qquad\square$

**Example 60.** Recall the convention and notation in Example 55. Figure 7.16 displays one of the classifying $\mathscr{A}$-gradation trees that recognise $p \oplus q \oplus r$. More generally, there are many classifying $\mathscr{A}^\wedge$-gradation trees that recognise $p \oplus q \oplus r$. They are no smaller than the former. Figure 7.19 shows three examples.

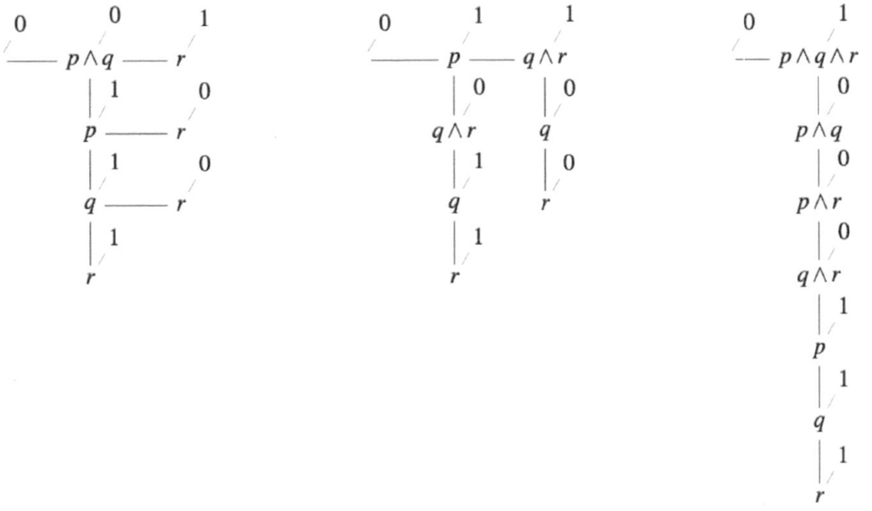

**Figure 7.19**

The proposition that follows demonstrates that when dealing with positive formulas, constrained by using the simplest possible conditions, end-based classification is always possible.

**Proposition 61.** *For all positive formulas $\varphi$ that are satisfiable in $\mathscr{M}$, there exists an end-based classifying $\mathscr{A}$-gradation tree that recognises $\varphi$.*

*Proof.* Let a positive formula $\varphi$ be satisfiable in $\mathscr{M}$. Let (necessarily nonzero) $n \in \mathbb{N}$ be least and let $D_0, \ldots, D_{n-1}$ be $\subseteq$-minimal sets of atoms such that $\varphi$ is logically equivalent in $\mathscr{M}$ to $\bigvee_{m<n} \bigwedge D_m$. Without loss of generality, suppose that

$\mathscr{A} = \bigcup_{m<n} D_m$. Set $|\mathscr{A}| = k$. Let $(\xi_i)_{i<k}$ be an enumeration of $\mathscr{A}$. Inductively define for all $i < k$ a finite set $S_i$ of literals as follows. Let $i < k$ be given, and assume that $S_j$ has been defined for all $j < i$. Define $S_i$ as the $\subseteq$-minimal set that satisfies the following condition. Let $X$ be a $\subseteq$-maximal member of $\bigcup_{j<i} X_j$.

Suppose that there exists $m < n$ such that:
- for all $j < i$, if $\xi_j \in D_m$ then $\xi_j \in X$;
- $\xi_i \in D_m$.

Then $S_i$ contains $X \cup \{\xi_i\}$. If that is the case, suppose that there exists $m' < n$ such that:
- for all $j < i$, if $\xi_j \in D_{m'}$ then $\xi_j \in X$;
- $D_{m'} \cap \{\xi_{i+1}, \ldots, \xi_{k-1}\} \neq \varnothing$;
- $\xi_i \notin D_{m'}$.

Then $S_i$ also contains $X \cup \{\neg \xi_i\}$.

Let $U$ be the set of finite sequences of the form $(i_0, \ldots, i_p)$ with $0 \leq p < k$ and $0 \leq i_0 < \cdots < i_p < k$ for which there exists a (necessarily unique) member $X$ of $\bigcup_{i<k} S_i$ such that for all $i < k$, $i \in \{i_0, \ldots, i_p\}$ iff $\xi_i \in X$. Now define an $\mathscr{A}$-gradation tree $T$ as the $\subseteq$ smallest set of finite sequences of atoms such that $T$ contains the empty sequence and for all $\sigma \in T$, the following holds. By construction, $\sigma$ can be written as $((\mathbb{X}_1, \xi_{i_1}), \ldots, (\mathbb{X}_p, \xi_{i_p}))$ with $0 \leq p \leq k$, $\mathbb{X}_i \in \{\vee, \wedge\}$ for all $0 < i \leq p$, and $(i_1, \ldots, i_p) \in U$.

- Suppose that there exists $m < k$ either with $p$ being equal to 0 or with $p \neq 0$ and $m > i_p$, such that $(i_1, \ldots, i_p, m) \in U$. Then choose the smallest such integer $m$ and add $\sigma \cdot ((\wedge, \xi_m))$ to $T$.
- Suppose that $p \neq 0$ and there exists $m < k$ such that $m > i_p$ and $(i_1, \ldots, i_{p-1}, m) \in U$. Then choose the smallest such integer $m$ and add $((\mathbb{X}_1, \xi_{i_1}), \ldots, (\mathbb{X}_{p-1}, \xi_{i_{p-1}}), (\vee, \xi_m))$ to $T$.

Note that there exists a one-to-one mapping $F$ from $\bigcup_{i<k} S_i$ into $T$ (as well as a one-to-one mapping from $U$ into $T$). Let $S$ be the set of all $\subseteq$-maximal members of $\bigcup_{i<k} S_i$.

Let us prove that $\mathrm{Mod}_{\mathscr{M}}(\varphi) = \bigcup_{X \in S} \mathrm{Mod}_{\mathscr{M}}(X)$. First note that the following holds.

1. For all $i < k$ and $X \in S_i$, there exists $m < n$ such that for all $j \leq i$, $\xi_j \in X$ iff $\xi_j \in D_m$.
2. For all $i < k$ and $m < n$, there exists $X \in S_i$ such that for all $j \leq i$, $\xi_j \in X$ iff $\xi_j \in D_m$.
3. For all $i < k$, $m < n$ and members of $S_i$ of the form $X \cup \{\xi_i\}$ such that
   - for all $j < i$, $\xi_j \in X$ iff $\xi_j \in D_m$, and
   - $X \cup \{\neg \xi_i\}$ is not in $S_i$,
   $\mathrm{Mod}_{\mathscr{M}}(X \cup \{\xi_i\}) \cap \mathrm{Mod}_{\mathscr{M}}(D_m) = \mathrm{Mod}_{\mathscr{M}}(X) \cap \mathrm{Mod}_{\mathscr{M}}(D_m)$.

Applying (2) to $i = k - 1$, we infer that $\bigcup_{X \in S} \text{Mod}_{\mathscr{M}}(X) \subseteq \text{Mod}_{\mathscr{M}}(\varphi)$. It is easy to derive from (1) and (3) that $\text{Mod}_{\mathscr{M}}(\varphi) \subseteq \bigcup_{X \in S} \text{Mod}_{\mathscr{M}}(X)$. Hence $\text{Mod}_{\mathscr{M}}(\varphi) = \bigcup_{X \in S} \text{Mod}_{\mathscr{M}}(X)$ as claimed. Observe that $\{F(X) \mid X \in S\}$ is the set of all $\sigma \in T$ such that $T$ contains no element of the form $\sigma \cdot ((\wedge, \mathfrak{v}))$. So in order to complete the proof of the proposition, it suffices to check that for all $X \in \bigcup_{i<k} S_i$. $\text{Mod}_{\mathscr{M}}(X) \setminus \text{Mod}_{\mathscr{M}}(\varphi) \neq \varnothing$. But that follows easily from (1) together with the minimality assumptions on $n$ and $D_0, \ldots, D_{n-1}$. $\hfill\square$

**Example 62.** Suppose that $\mathscr{A}$ consists of 9 atoms $p_i$, $0 \leq i \leq 8$. Suppose that $\mathscr{M}$ is the set of all interpretations. Let $\varphi$ be the formula

$$p_0 \vee (p_1 \wedge p_2) \vee (p_3 \wedge p_4 \wedge p_5) \vee (p_3 \wedge p_4 \wedge p_6) \vee (p_4 \wedge p_7 \wedge p_8).$$

Note that defining $D_0$ as $\{p_0\}$, $D_1$ as $\{p_1, p_2\}$, $D_2$ as $\{p_3, p_4, p_5\}$, $D_3$ as $\{p_3, p_4, p_6\}$ and $D_4$ as $\{p_4\, p_7\, p_8\}$, $\varphi$ is logically equivalent to $\bigvee_{m<5} \bigwedge D_m$ and the assumption made in Proposition 61, namely that 4 is minimal and $D_m$, $m < 5$, are all $\subseteq$-minimal, holds. Assume that $(p_i)_{i<9}$ corresponds to the enumeration $(\xi_i)_{i<k}$ of $\mathscr{A}$ in the proof. The sets $S_0$ to $S_8$ in the proof are shown in Figure 7.20. More precisely, for all $i < 9$, the set $S_i$ contains for atom in its column, all atoms that occur last in one of the previous columns either on the same line line or above. The set $S$ consists of 1 member of $S_0$, one member of $S_2$, two members of $S_5$, 2 members of $S_6$, and the 4 members of $S_8$. Each of these sets is associated with one of the conjuncts $\bigwedge D_m$, $m < 4$, of $\bigvee_{m<5} \bigwedge D_m$, represented in the last column of the picture.

| $S_0$ | $S_1$ | $S_2$ | $S_3$ | $S_4$ | $S_5$ | $S_6$ | $S_7$ | $S_8$ | Conjunct |
|---|---|---|---|---|---|---|---|---|---|
| $p_0$ | | | | | | | | | $p_0$ |
| $\neg p_0$ | $p_1$ | $p_2$ | | | | | | | $p_1 \wedge p_2$ |
| | | $\neg p_2$ | $p_3$ | $p_4$ | $p_5$ | | | | $p_3 \wedge p_4 \wedge p_5$ |
| | | | | | $\neg p_5$ | $p_6$ | | | $p_3 \wedge p_4 \wedge p_6$ |
| | | | | | | $\neg p_6$ | $p_7$ | $p_8$ | $p_4 \wedge p_7 \wedge p_8$ |
| | | | $\neg p_3$ | $p_4$ | | | $p_7$ | $p_8$ | $p_4 \wedge p_7 \wedge p_8$ |
| | $\neg p_1$ | | $p_3$ | $p_4$ | $p_5$ | | | | $p_3 \wedge p_4 \wedge p_5$ |
| | | | | | $\neg p_5$ | $p_6$ | | | $p_3 \wedge p_4 \wedge p_6$ |
| | | | | | | $\neg p_6$ | $p_7$ | $p_8$ | $p_4 \wedge p_7 \wedge p_8$ |
| | | | $\neg p_3$ | $p_4$ | | | $p_7$ | $p_8$ | $p_4 \wedge p_7 \wedge p_8$ |

**Figure 7.20**

The tree $T$ in the proof can be depicted as in Figure 7.21.

We next turn our attention to parity-based classification. The proposition that follows expresses that only one level of exception is needed, and conjuncts are expressive enough for this.

**Proposition 63.** *Given a formula $\varphi$, some parity-based classifying $\mathscr{A}^{\wedge}$-gradation tree of depth at most 2 recognises $\varphi$.*

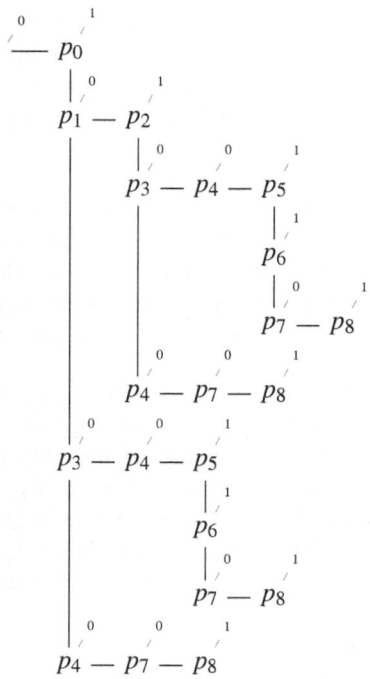

**Figure 7.21**

*Proof.* Without loss of generality, assume that all atoms occur in $\varphi$. Let $\varphi^*$ denote $\varphi$ if for every $\subseteq$-maximal set $D$ of literals such that $\text{Mod}_{\mathscr{M}}(D \cup \{\varphi\}) \neq \varnothing$, $D$ contains at least one atom; otherwise, let $\varphi^*$ denote $\sim\varphi$. Let $X$ be the set of all $\subseteq$-maximal sets $D$ of literals such that $\text{Mod}_{\mathscr{M}}(D \cup \{\varphi^*\}) \neq \varnothing$. For all $D \in X$, let $D^+$ be the set of atoms in $D$. Set $|\mathscr{A}| = k$. Let $(\xi_i)_{i<k}$ be an enumeration of $\mathscr{A}$. Set $|X| = n$. Let $(D_m)_{m<n}$ be an enumeration of $X$ such that for all $m, m' < n$, if $D_m^+ \supset D_{m'}^+$ then $m < m'$. Inductively define for all $m < n$ a set $X_m$ of sets of atoms. Let $m < n$ be given, and assume that $X_{m'}$ has been defined for all $m' < m$. Let $X_m$ consist of:

- $D_m^+$;
- every set of the form $D_m^+ \cup \{\xi_i\}$, $i < k$, that does not include any member of $\bigcup_{m' < m} X_{m'}$.

Now define an $\mathscr{A}^\wedge$-gradation tree $T$ as the $\subseteq$-smallest set of finite sequences of members of $\mathscr{A}^\wedge$ closed under sequences such that for all $m < n$, the following holds. Let $p$ denote $|X_m| - 1$. In case $p > 0$, let $i_1, \ldots, i_p \in \mathbb{N}$ be such that $i_1 < \cdots < i_p < k$ and for all $i < k$, $\xi_i \notin D_m^+$ and $D_m^+ \cup \{\xi_i\} \in X_m$ iff $i \in \{i_1, \ldots, i_p\}$. Then $T$ contains

- $\big((\wedge, \bigwedge D_0^+)\big)$ if $m = 0$ and $p = 0$;
- $\big((\wedge, \bigwedge D_0^+), (\wedge, \xi_{i_1})\big)$ if $m = 0$ and $p = 1$;

- $((\wedge, \wedge D_0^+), (\wedge, \xi_{i_1}), (\vee, \xi_{i_2}), \ldots, (\vee, \xi_{i_p}))$ if $m = 0$ and $p > 1$;
- $((\wedge, \wedge D_0^+), (\vee, \wedge D_1^+), \ldots, (\vee, \wedge D_m^+))$ if $m > 0$ and $p = 0$.
- $((\wedge, \wedge D_0^+), (\vee, \wedge D_1^+), \ldots, (\vee, \wedge D_m^+), (\wedge, \xi_{i_1}))$ if $m > 0$ and $p = 1$.
- $((\wedge, \wedge D_0^+), (\vee, \wedge D_1^+), \ldots, (\vee, \wedge D_m^+), (\wedge, \xi_{i_1}), (\vee, \xi_{i_2}), \ldots, (\vee, \xi_{i_p}))$ if $m > 0$ and $p > 1$.

Using the condition imposed on $(D_m)_{m<n}$ and the definition of $(X_m)_{m<n}$, it is immediately established that if $\varphi^*$ is $\varphi$ then $T$ is a negative by default, parity-based classifying tree that recognises $\varphi$ (this includes the case where $\varphi$ is unsatisfiable in $\mathcal{M}$), whereas if $\varphi^*$ is $\sim\varphi$ then $T$ is a positive by default, parity-based classifying tree that recognises $\varphi$. Obviously, the depth of $T$ is at most equal to 2. $\qquad\square$

**Example 64.** Suppose that $\mathcal{A}$ consists of 3 atoms $p_0$, $p_1$ and $p_2$. Suppose that $\mathcal{M}$ is the set of all interpretations. Let $\varphi$ be the formula $(p_0 \wedge \neg p_1) \vee (p_1 \wedge \neg p_2)$. On the left hand side of Figure 7.22, the 4 lines of the truth table where $\varphi$ evaluates to True, read from top to bottom, determine the sets $X_m$, $m < 4$, in the proof of Proposition 63, the 1s on the line making up the set $D_m^+$, and each red 0 on the line, if any, being associated with a larger set of the form $D_m^+ \cup \{\xi_i\}$. The negative by default, classifying tree that recognises $\varphi$, constructed in the proof of the proposition, is depicted on the right hand side of the figure.

| $p_0$ | $p_1$ | $p_2$ | $\varphi$ |
|---|---|---|---|
| 1 | 1 | 1 | 0 |
| 1 | 1 | 0 | 1 |
| 1 | 0 | 1 | 1 |
| 1 | 0 | 0 | 1 |
| 0 | 1 | 1 | 0 |
| 0 | 1 | 0 | 1 |
| 0 | 0 | 1 | 0 |
| 0 | 0 | 0 | 0 |

**Figure 7.22**

**Example 65.** Suppose that $\mathcal{A}$ consists of 3 atoms $p_0$, $p_1$ and $p_2$. Suppose that $\mathcal{M}$ is the set of all interpretations and $\{p_0, p_1, p_2\}$ corresponds to the set $B$ in the proof of Proposition 63. Let $\varphi$ be the formula $\sim(p_0 \oplus p_1 \oplus p_2)$. On the left of Figure 7.23, the 4 lines of the truth table where $\varphi$ evaluates to False, read from top to bottom, determine the sets $X_m$, $m < 4$, in the proof of Proposition 63, the 1s on the line making up the set $D_m^+$, and each red 0 on the line, if any, being associated with a larger set of the form $D_m^+ \cup \{\xi_i\}$. The positive by default, classifying tree that recognises $\varphi$, constructed in the proof of the proposition, is depicted on the right of the figure.

The proof of Proposition 63 shows that determinism is essential to enforce parity-based classification with only one level of exceptions. If nondeterminism is allowed,

| $p_0$ | $p_1$ | $p_2$ | $\varphi$ |
|---|---|---|---|
| 1 | 1 | 1 | 0 |
| 1 | 1 | 0 | 1 |
| 1 | 0 | 1 | 1 |
| 1 | 0 | 0 | 0 |
| 0 | 1 | 1 | 1 |
| 0 | 1 | 0 | 0 |
| 0 | 0 | 1 | 0 |
| 0 | 0 | 0 | 1 |

**Figure 7.23**

then the complexity of the formula to classify as it is measured in the difference hierarchy gives an upper bound on the maximum number of exceptions to go through when classifying a case.

**Proposition 66.** *Let a formula $\varphi$ be $\Sigma_{1,k}$ but not $\Pi_{1,k}$ in $\mathcal{M}$, or $\Pi_{1,k}$ but not $\Sigma_{1,k}$ in $\mathcal{M}$. Then some parity-based classifying $\mathscr{A}^\wedge$-gradation graph of depth $k+1$ recognises $\varphi$, that is negative by default or positive by default, respectively.*

*Proof.* Without loss of generality, assume that all atoms occur in $\varphi$. Given a finite set $D$ of atoms, let $\widetilde{D}$ denote $D \cup \{\neg\psi \mid \psi \in \mathscr{A} \setminus D\}$. Inductively define sets $X_0$, ..., $X_k$ of finite subsets of $A$ and a binary relation $E$ on $\bigcup_{i \leq k} X_i$, setting $X_0$ to $\{\varnothing\}$ and $E$ to $\varnothing$ to start with. Let $i < k$ be given, and assume that $X_i$ has been defined and $E$ has been appropriately extended. For all $D \in X_i$, put in $X_{i+1}$ all $\subseteq$-minimal subsets $D'$ of $A$ such that $\widetilde{D'} \models_{\mathcal{M}} \varphi$ iff $\widetilde{D} \models_{\mathcal{M}} \sim\varphi$, and extend $E$ with $(\bigwedge D, \bigwedge D')$. Set $V = \{\bigwedge D \mid D \in \bigcup_{i \leq k} X_i\}$. It is immediately verified that $(V,E)$ is an $\mathscr{A}^\wedge$-gradation graph that satisfies the claim of the proposition. $\square$

**Example 67.** Suppose that $\mathscr{A}$ consists of 4 nullary atoms $p_0$, $p_1$, $p_2$ and $p_3$. Suppose that $\mathcal{M}$ is the set of all interpretations and $\{p_0, p_1, p_2, p_3\}$ corresponds to the set $B$ in the proof of Proposition 66. Let $\varphi$ be the formula

$$\Big( p_0 \wedge \big( (p_1 \vee p_2 \vee p_3) \wedge \sim (p_1 \oplus p_2 \oplus p_3) \big) \Big) \vee$$
$$\Big( \neg p_0 \wedge \big( (\neg p_1 \wedge \neg p_2) \vee (p_1 \wedge (p_2 \vee p_3)) \big) \Big).$$

The left hand side of Figure 7.23 displays the truth table for $\varphi$. When $p_0, \ldots, p_3$ are all False, $\varphi$ is true, hence there exists a positive integer $k$ such that $\varphi$ is $\Pi_{1,k}$ and not $\Sigma_{1,k}$.

- $\{p_0\}$, $\{p_1\}$ and $\{p_2\}$ are the $\subseteq$-minimal supersets $D$ of $\varnothing$ such that making the member of $D$ and the member of $D$ only True switches the truth of $\varphi$ from True to False.

- (i) $\{p_0, p_1, p_2\}$, $\{p_0, p_1, p_3\}$ and $\{p_0, p_2, p_3\}$ are the $\subseteq$-minimal supersets $D$ of $\{p_0\}$, (ii) $\{p_1, p_2\}$ and $\{p_1, p_3\}$ are the $\subseteq$-minimal supersets $D$ of $\{p_1\}$, and (iii) $\{p_1, p_2\}$ and $\{p_0, p_2, p_3\}$ are the $\subseteq$-minimal supersets $D$ of $\{p_2\}$ such that making the members of $D$ and the members of $D$ only True switches the truth of $\varphi$ from False to True.
- $\{p_0, p_1, p_2\}$, $\{p_0, p_1, p_3\}$, $\{p_0, p_2, p_3\}$, $\{p_1, p_2\}$ and $\{p_1, p_3\}$ all have $\{p_0, p_1, p_2, p_3, p_4\}$ as unique $\subseteq$-minimal superset $D$ such that making all members of $D$ and the members of $D$ only True switches the truth of $\varphi$ from True to False.

Hence $\varphi$ is $\Pi_{1,3}$. The right hand side of Figure 7.23 displays the gradation graph constructed in the proof of Proposition 66, with three simplifications (the proof could have formalised those simplifications in full generality, but that was not necessary to establish the result):

- the vertex $p_0 \wedge p_1 \wedge p_2$ is simplified to $p_1 \wedge p_2$;
- the vertex $p_0 \wedge p_1 \wedge p_3$ is simplified to $p_1 \wedge p_3$;
- the vertex $p_1 \wedge p_3$ is simplified to $p_3$.

| $p_0$ | $p_1$ | $p_2$ | $p_3$ | $\varphi$ |
|---|---|---|---|---|
| 1 | 1 | 1 | 1 | 0 |
| 1 | 1 | 1 | 0 | 1 |
| 1 | 1 | 0 | 1 | 1 |
| 1 | 1 | 0 | 0 | 0 |
| 1 | 0 | 1 | 1 | 1 |
| 1 | 0 | 1 | 0 | 0 |
| 1 | 0 | 0 | 1 | 0 |
| 1 | 0 | 0 | 0 | 0 |
| 0 | 1 | 1 | 1 | 1 |
| 0 | 1 | 1 | 0 | 1 |
| 0 | 1 | 0 | 1 | 1 |
| 0 | 1 | 0 | 0 | 0 |
| 0 | 0 | 1 | 1 | 0 |
| 0 | 0 | 1 | 0 | 0 |
| 0 | 0 | 0 | 1 | 1 |
| 0 | 0 | 0 | 0 | 1 |

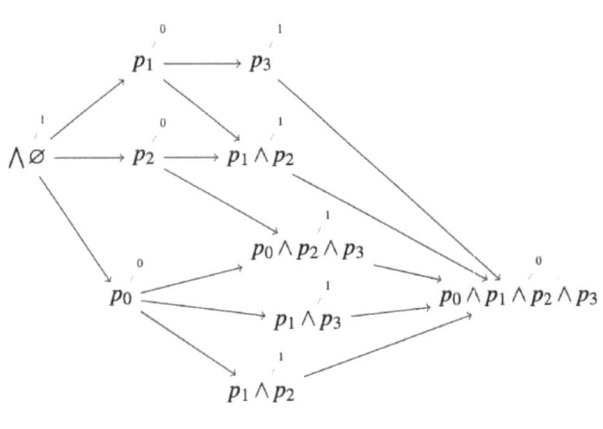

## REFERENCES

1. Paul Compton and Byeong Ho Kang. *Ripple-Down Rules*.
2. Yu L. Ershov. A certain hierarchy of sets. i. *Algebra i Logika*, 7(1):47–74.
3. Yu L. Ershov. A certain hierarchy of sets. ii. *Algebra i Logika*, 7(4):15–47.
4. Yu L. Ershov. A certain hierarchy of sets. iii. *Algebra i Logika*, 9(1):34–51.
5. Brian R. Gaines and Paul Compton. Induction of ripple-down rules applied to modeling large databases. *Journal of Intelligent Information Systems*, 5(3):211–228.

6. Adam Grove. Two modellings for theory change. *Journal of Philosophical Logic*, 17(2):157–170.

7. Sanjay Jain, Daniel N. Osherson, James R. Royer, and Arun Sharma. *Systems That Learn: An Introduction to Learning Theory*.

8. Sanjay Jain and Arun Sharma. On a generalized notion of mistake bounds. *Information and Computation*, 166(2):156–166.

9. Sarit Kraus, Daniel Lehmann, and Menachem Magidor. Nonmonotonic reasoning, preferential models and cumulative logics. *Artificial Intelligence*, 44(1):167–207.

# 8 Counterfeits and Kill Switches
## *How Hardware Security can Impact You*

*Hammond Pearce*
School of Computer Science and Engineering, UNSW Sydney
Kensington, Australia

## 8.1 COUNTERFEITS AND KILL SWITCHES: HOW HARDWARE SECURITY CAN IMPACT YOU

As the digital world expands, privacy and operational threats against computer systems are becoming ever more pervasive. Personal information is frequently stolen in breaches, and essential services face shutdowns due to cyberattacks. Recent high-profile incidents, such as the 2022 Medibank data breach of over 9 million Australian's medical data, and the 2023 disruption of Sydney's port systems, highlight the growing danger. While most focus remains on software vulnerabilities, hardware-based attacks present even graver, often invisible threats. Here, a compromised circuit could shut down essential infrastructure or result in the failure of aircraft controls. This chapter introduces readers to the emerging field of hardware security, exploring how counterfeit electronics and hardware Trojans can infiltrate and compromise critical systems. It also discusses the countermeasures being developed to combat these insidious risks, making the case for why hardware security deserves broader attention in today's world.

## 8.2 INTRODUCTION: WHAT IS HARDWARE SECURITY?

Consider this scenario. You have a large number of photos, videos, documents, and other files on your computer. You need to get these files to another computer. What's the easiest way to move a large number of files? Why, an external USB hard drive, of course.

So, you go to your local shop, or even an e-shop online. You take a look at external hard drives. Wow! There are so many options. Walmart in the USA lists 282

DOI: 10.1201/9781032702797-8

results when searching 'USB hard drive'. Some of them are made by Samsung, some by Seagate, some by Western Digital, and so many other brands besides. Target Australia has over 100 of these, too. When you ask Amazon, it refuses to list a count, but suffice to say there are so many results for this search it would take weeks to traverse them.

So, what should you do? I guess you could just buy any of them – they're all as good as one another, right?

Well, unfortunately – probably not.

Never mind their listed specifications, never mind their purported brand names: unfortunately, computer electronics, like many other commodity products such as shoes and children's products, have been overwhelmed with fake listings selling counterfeit products. These inferior goods can be both frustrating (when they underperform) or dangerous (when considering items meant for human use or consumption). Despite attention, such issues have come up again and again (e.g. [14, 25, 5]).

So why is this? Why is it so difficult to ensure that our products match their design? Well, part of the challenge – beyond simply the presence of unscrupulous actors in this world who are endlessly motivated to obtain money at minimum cost – is that it is fundamentally difficult to ensure that a given piece of the real-world is exactly what it claims to be. How can you, a consumer at home, validate that a bottle of shampoo is actually made by the company written on the bottle? How can you be sure that a shoe with Nike's logo came from a Nike factory? So too, how could you be sure if the hard drive you want to purchase is actually genuine?

Counterfeits have always been a problem, but it's only recently been that those same circumstances which allow us to buy a fake hard drive also might allow for even more harmful happenstances to occur. For a recent example, consider the story of the "pager attacks" as reported by the BBC [20]. Here, after the Hezbollah paramilitary group found they were unable to prevent the Israeli intelligence and military services from hacking and tracking their cellphones, in February 2024 their secretary-general Hassan Nasrallah issued instructions for the group's members to use old-fashioned and low-tech pagers instead. These pagers were then nominally purchased from the global marketplace. Except – instead of receiving the intended Gold Apollo models, Hezbollah received shipments of devices secretly compromised by the Israeli Mossad to contain small explosive charges. Mossad then repeated this supply chain attack on a series of walkie-talkies also destined for the paramilitary group.

Putting aside the politics of the situation, this is a situation beyond mere counterfeiting. This is an escalation, a supply chain compromise taking the device from having fake branding and cost-saving cutouts to one where the device has been maliciously compromised to have the ability to perform an attack on the owner. These are called Hardware Trojans [6], so named for the apocryphal Trojan Horse. In the story, the Trojan Horse was a sculpture left as a gift for the defending city of Troy, which brought it inside their city only to later discover it was full of Greek soldiers (who then proceeded to attack the city from the inside, and opened the gates for the main army to enter). Hardware Trojans can be similarly destructive, as these compromised pagers and walkie-talkies cruelly demonstrated. In September 2024, Mossad activated both sets of explosives. They ultimately killed dozens of people including civilians and children, and injured thousands more.

Such physical tampering need not be so extreme as to physically include hidden explosives in order to have the desired effect, though. One of the scariest concepts for the modern world, powered as it is by a veritable sea of interconnected devices and computers, is that these devices might have hidden "Kill Switches" which would render them inoperable at the very moment of an attacker's choosing. You could imagine such an ability to be considerably attractive to cyber-criminals: imagine a blackmailer who rings you while you are in a self-driving car, and threatens to disable the brakes on a highway unless you transfer them thousands of dollars!

Such a capability is also interesting to nation-states. Imagine how strategically beneficial it would be if your country could sneak a 'Kill Switch' into a foreign adversary's military equipment. Here, though, we do not have to imagine hard – this is exactly what was reported by IEEE Spectrum [1] to have happened in September 2007, when Israeli fighter jets were able to stealthily enter Syrian airspace as part of Operation Outside the Box. At the time, it was a mystery to how exactly the jets had hidden themselves from state-of-the-art defensive radar installations. But, it was soon reported that a supply chain attack against commercial off-the-shelf microprocessor integrated circuits had been secretly completed, allowing the Israeli military to disrupt radar functions – having them report clear skies even as jets flew overhead.

So, what is hardware security?

Hardware security tries to protect the real-world chips, circuits, and devices that build up our real-world computing and communications infrastructure. It tries to prevent counterfeiting attacks, where low-cost poor-quality imitations impact both our bottom lines as producers but also our strength as a brand. So too it tries to prevent the possibility of hardware Trojan attacks, where adversaries aim to sneak malicious changes into our designs that might compromise their functionality or cause real-world harms.

The security of our computer systems impacts all of us. When our private data is stolen, attackers can impersonate us by opening credit cards in our names, attempt to swindle money from our personal relations, and can attempt to drain our savings accounts. These attacks can occur in many different ways, from leaked passwords to faulty websites. Sometimes they happen due to malicious employees – and sometimes they can be engineered to occur socially, from cold-emailing unsuspecting victims to strategic placement of scam advertisements.

Most people are familiar with the concept of software vulnerabilities – flaws or bugs in code that cybercriminals can exploit to gain unauthorized access, disrupt operations, or extract sensitive data. Unfortunately, as we have now introduced, the hardware that makes up our digital devices, from smartphones to critical infrastructure systems, is just as susceptible to being compromised. Worse, unlike software issues, which can often be patched remotely, hardware vulnerabilities – like the aforementioned 'kill switches' – can be embedded in the physical components. This can make them significantly harder to detect and mitigate, particularly if a fix requires changes to the underlying hardware.

While hardware security is (a lot!) bigger than just the two topics of counterfeits and kill switches, these are what we'll focus on in this chapter. Most hardware security concepts start from the same place as these: that is, the risk of misplaced trust in the manufacturers and suppliers of our devices. This foundation can provide you with a launch-point into other areas of hardware security as you find interest!

So, in this chapter, we'll cover how a little of how counterfeits and hardware Trojan attacks are possible in the first place, and what the possible consequences of such attacks are. We'll talk a little bit about defence – in particular, what manufacturers of devices can be doing to try and protect their products. Finally, we'll reflect on the future of hardware security, and how it might continue to impact you, the general reader, in future.

## 8.3 THE FOUNDATIONS OF HARDWARE: CHIP & CIRCUIT MANUFACTURING

Inside almost every modern device is a vast cornucopia of electronic components. Our cars, our televisions, our smart toothbrushes and our cellphones, our bluetooth speakers and our wireless headphones, our keyboards and electric guitars, and more – these are empowered by thousands of tiny microchips, also known as Integrated Circuits (ICs), each of which has been soldered onto larger Printed Circuit Boards (PCBs). For an example, see Figure 8.1.

**Figure 8.1** A close-up photo of several microchip integrated circuits (ICs) soldered to a printed circuit board (PCB)

Electronics such as these actually underpin more than just our households and personal items. They actually enable the entire modern world. They are in our infrastructure, with interconnected traffic lights and algorithmically controlled smart grids and municipal water supplies. They look after our communications and financial markets, with wireless communication towers and satellites in space. They are in our factories and our supermarkets, and they are in every vehicle of a modern military's fleet. It is this reach which makes the concept that they could be tampered with so troubling.

Historically, electronics and integrated circuit development could happen in-house. Many of the early electronics device companies around the world, such as Commodore, were good examples of vertically-integrated powerhouses capable of producing everything from the chip to the computer. But, during the late 20th and early 21st century, manufacturing trends shifted globally, with outsourcing becoming more feasible, profitable, and popular. Nowadays, few countries have the sovereign capabilities to perform mass in-house manufacturing of electronic devices and components, and though the design of electronics continues in-house, most electronic devices and components in the modern era are now currently produced in vast factories in Asia, particularly in Taiwan and China.

This separation of design and manufacturing has led to extremely long and complex supply chains for electronic devices. Devices can have components from dozens-to-hundreds of companies based out of an array of different countries. The supply chains include dependencies on both integrated circuits and the printed circuit boards they will be soldered to. Each IC and PCB also has to be specified, designed, and then tested. The magnitude of the complexity of this network is attempted to be illustrated in Figure 8.2.

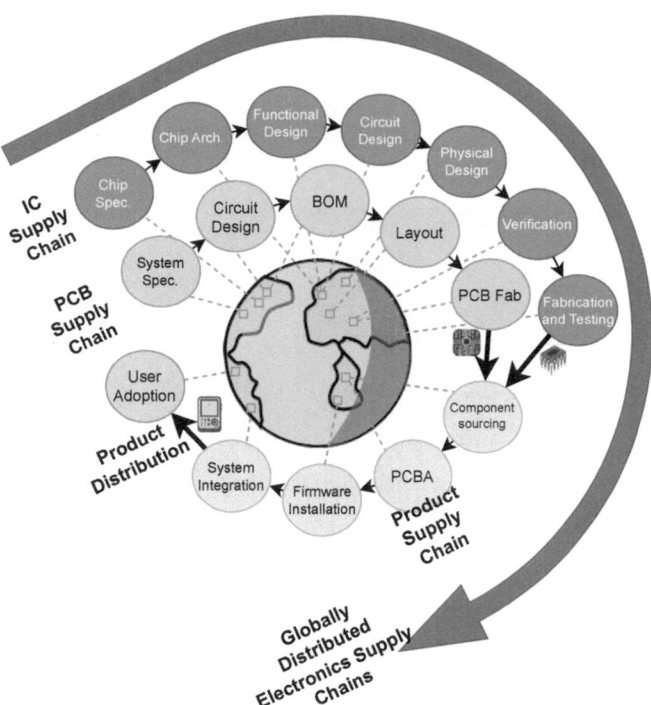

**Figure 8.2** Electronic product supply chains depend upon the creation of both Integrated Circuits and Printed Circuit Boards, which can happen in design houses and factories all over the world

Of course, it is this complex globalized supply chain which enables the majority of the risks involved in electronics manufacturing. With so many different companies and employees involved in the design of a single product, there are many more opportunities for a malicious actor to take part. These devices are not built in the same way that a bottle or a pot might be.

Printed circuit boards are first designed in software, using computer-aided design tools like Altium, EasyEDA, or KiCAD. They are designed against specifications, i.e. a list of everything the final customer needs the system to do. PCBs can have a mix of analog and digital components, like resistors, transistors, and integrated circuits, which will interact with one another according to electrical rules like Ohms and Kirchhoff's Laws. During this phase, the circuit designers will need to choose from a list of components which are available to them. They can peruse endless inventories from suppliers like Digikey, element14, and LSCC. You can think of this as finding the perfect piece of Lego to make a large set, or the exact size of screw you might need for securing the drawers in your kitchen at home.

During the design phase, the circuit can be simulated using software like LT-SPICE and Proteus. This can be done in part or in whole, to ensure it meets the needed device specifications. Once satisfied, the designers now have a confirmed Bill of Materials (BOM) which lists all the parts and their quantities. They also have a schematic, which describes how each of the components are connected. The job will now pass to layout designers who will use this information to architect the actual physical circuit layout, where each component will actually be placed on the final printed circuit board, and the wires and copper tracks which actually join each component will be drawn. Another round of simulation can follow this step, and when satisfied, the layout and component position files can be passed with the BOM to the actual manufacturing company.

To actually produce the printed circuit board itself, manufacturing processes proceed in layers, much like a cake. A base layer (often fiberglass) will get a thin layer of copper added, before a design is painted on using a special resistive material. This protects those areas when the board is then dipped into a chemical acid bath to etch away the unprotected copper, leaving only the desired circuit traces. This process might be repeated after an internal insulating layer if the board has additional copper layers – four and six layer boards are very popular. Then, holes can be drilled for components, and the board will get cleaned and plated, with a solder mask added to protect the board. Now it's ready for the components to be added!

Of course, someone also has to design the components which the PCB is going to rely on. This would usually have happened well before the design, but in rare cases could happen in parallel with the board design. For integrated circuits, this job actually looks remarkably similar to that already described, just on a smaller, more microscopic scale! Once again, designers will work to a specification, and design a circuit, although here the tools are likely to look quite different. Digital logic devices like computer processors will more often be designed using hardware description languages such as Verilog and VHDL. Chips with analogue components, meanwhile, may be designed via schematics and layout similar to the larger printed circuit boards. Simulation at this phase is possible for both digital and analogue chips.

Once the design phase is completed, the chips can be synthesized to production files using Electronic Design Automation (EDA) software such as that provided by Synopsys and Cadence. Another way of testing them here is known as *emulation*, where special-purpose chips known as Field Programmable Gate Arrays (FPGAs) can be reprogrammed to mimic the chip being designed. All this testing is vitally important for integrated circuits, as there is usually quite an expensive cost associated with producing the final products, so one wants to make sure it will work after it comes out of the factory. Finally, once all the pre-silicon verification is finished, the designer will hand off to a fabrication company to physically produce (and usually package) the integrated circuits. The manufacturing of these chips is themselves a mind-bogglingly complex process worthy of a dozen books, but suffice to say it is usually completed with expensive photolithography machines which use light waves to transfer patterns onto silicon wafer substrates. Those machines are highly specialised, and the world leader in producing them is a company called ASML, which is based out of Europe.

So, once the integrated circuits (and supporting components like resistors and capacitors) are all found on the global market, they will be purchased for assembly with the printed circuit board. This might happen in the same factory that produced the physical printed circuit board, or it can happen later at a different facility. A lot of things might need to be shipped around the world to make this happen. Once the components are obtained alongside the PCB, they can be hand- or machine-placed in the correct positions, with solder being used as the joining material. A soldering iron can be used to slowly melt the solder joint by joint, or a hot oven or plate could do it in a single pass.

Once all this is completed, testing will usually need to happen again! If the board requires any on-board software or firmware, it could be installed as part of this process. Finally, the printed circuit board can be integrated with the rest of the product it is destined for.

## 8.4   HARDWARE TROJAN COMPROMISES IN MANUFACTURING

There are many, many ways in which the aforementioned process could be tampered with by a malicious actor. They might not even need to change very much of a circuit to achieve their nefarious goals. So what might a circuit's compromise look like? Let's consider what a malicious actor in the Integrated Circuit supply chain could do. This could be from a designer, who inserts a Hardware Trojan circuit at the early stages of the chip's architecture, or it could be from a malicious foundry, which modifies the IC as it is being built. It could involve the addition of whole new circuits, or it could be as small as the modification of single gates.

Let's explore the theory behind a generalized IC's Hardware Trojan here. Consider the circuit fragment depicted in Figure 8.3. Here, we have four inputs, 'Alert1', 'Alert2', 'Alert3', 'Alert4' which are joined with 'OR' gates such that if any one of the Alert signals is raised, an output 'Alarm' signal will also be raised.

You could imagine how this circuit might be similar to something like a burglar alarm which could be triggered if any one of four windows was opened. Sounds

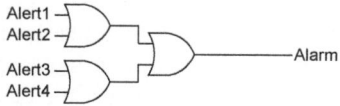

**Figure 8.3**   A digital circuit fragment. Any of four 'Alert' signals can raise an 'Alarm' signal

useful, right? Now, let's imagine what might happen if an additional gate is added to the circuit. We'll make this gate have an additional input, which we'll call the 'Trojan' input. We show this in Figure 8.4.

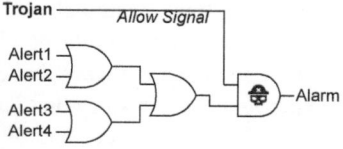

**Figure 8.4**   The digital circuit fragment now has a Trojan input which controls if the Alarm is 'allowed' to be raised

This circuit has had an 'AND' gate added on the output, which combines the Trojan's signal. While the Trojan outputs a logical '1', the circuit will behave as before, and Alerts will propagate to Alarms. But, if the Trojan was ever to output a logical '0' instead, no Alerts would ever propagate, and the circuit has been "killed"!

We can actually make this attack even more powerful. By changing the Trojan 'AND' gate to an 'XOR' gate, we can give the Trojan the ability to not only suppress the alarm, but create spurious, fictional ones as well. We show this in Figure 8.5.

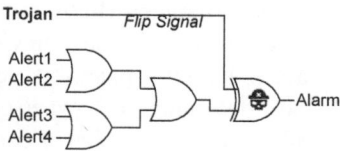

**Figure 8.5**   The digital circuit fragment Trojan can now 'flip' the Alarm output, to either suppress it if it should be active, or activate it if it should not be present

Given that real circuits contain many millions and billions of such logic gates, it's easy to imagine how such a tiny compromise could be sneaked into the design. Hardware Trojans such as these are therefore such a concern that manufacturers and research expend considerable expertise trying to avoid them! We'll discuss such defences later, in Section 8.6.

For now, let us move on to the kinds of attacks that might also be done in the Printed Circuit Board supply chain. Once again, these could be done via the addition, or removal, of circuit components, but remember – PCBs are a lot less small than ICs, meaning that it's much easier to visually scan a board for any unexpected changes! Indeed, taking photos of printed circuit boards during construction is already a fairly standard procedure, and comparing them against the design files sent to the build house is a relatively straightforward thing to do. As a result, we might have to get more creative with our Trojans. We could instead base them on the properties of the material being worked with. One could imagine how the board manufacturing process could use lower-quality chemical baths or thinner copper layers than advertised, meaning that a board might work, but it might work with reduced quality or shorter device lifespans.

A more controllable compromise could happen at the assembly stage of the manufacturing process. As we discussed earlier, this is when all the board components are arranged and then soldered to the final printed circuit boards. Now we might be able to imagine how an intended component might be able to be substituted for a different device. Indeed, this was an attack pathway that actually happened, at least according to Bloomberg's controversial 2018 story on 'The Big Hack' [23]. Here, it was alleged that the Chinese intelligence services had designed and inserted a tiny microchip inside components destined for installation in SuperMicro server motherboards which would be activated after installation in their customer's data centres, including those of Apple and Amazon.

This chip, smaller than a grain of rice, had access to the signals passing through a data line. It would then alter those signals – and in this case, the signals related to the program memory being loaded for the so-called "Baseband Management Controller", an extremely powerful server computer subsystem which has the ability to control many other aspects of the server. In this case, the Trojan would actually insert a vulnerability allowing the server to be remotely logged in to by the attackers.

It is worth noting that every company involved strenuously denied these allegations, and it is still an open question as to whether or not the attack happened. This is somewhat ancillary to the theory of the attack, though, and such an attack was eventually proven to be possible by one Trammell Hudson with his presentation 'Modchips of the State' at the 2018 Chaos Communication Congress in Germany [15]. This means that even if the attack did not happen, it at least could have happened, something that should be deeply concerning to all cybersecurity professionals.

Finally, one need not actually modify the design or compromise the manufacturing at all to introduce the Hardware Trojan. The secretive 'Tailored Access Operations' (TAO) unit by the US National Security Agency (NSA) sought to do exactly this kind of compromise, among others. Here, the program would perform supply-chain interdiction to modify hardware in transit [10] – i.e., after it had left the factory, but before it reached the final customer, as shown in Figure 8.6 from a leaked report [22] hosted by the Electronic Frontier Foundation (EFF).

These modifications could be targeted at software or firmware, but as later disclosed by the ANT catalogue [3] a variety of Hardware Trojans was also available for embedding. These included COTTONMOUTH-I, a Trojan which embedded a fake keyboard in the design so that sequences of compromising commands could be

(TS//SI//NF) Such operations involving **supply-chain interdiction** are some of the most productive operations in TAO, because they pre-position access points into hard target networks around the world.

(TS//SI//NF) Left: Intercepted packages are opened carefully; Right: A "load station" implants a beacon

**Figure 8.6** Except from [22] showing an example of how the NSA TAO could intercept and alter hardware

issued surreptitiously; and FIREWALK, a device identical to a standard RJ45 socket but allows for remote monitoring of the data being transmitted. Such compromises also further validate the premise of the 'Big Hack' as discussed earlier, and so it appears that actually a litany of possible attack strategies exist for meddling with computer hardware.

To summarise the key takeaways for this section: Computer hardware cannot simply spring into existence. Both Integrated Circuits (ICs) and Printed Circuit Boards must be designed, produced, and shipped to their eventual customers, and this occurs over a globalised supply chain featuring multiple companies and countries. We must be wary of compromise that could occur at any stage of this process, from malicious insiders who change the original design files, to manufacturers who might tamper with what is being built, and finally to actors who can intercept and modify the physical artifacts as they are being shipped from place to place.

## 8.5 COUNTERFEIT ELECTRONICS: RISKS AND OCCURRENCES

Of course, the risks of these complex electronics supply chains is not limited just to tampering, and indeed, the chances that the average person will be subject to tampering seems quite low given the relative cost and perceived benefits for the given attacker. Certain high-value individuals and organisations might be targeted, but overall, given the relatively low rate of reporting of these kinds of attacks, it seems like society is getting off relatively unscathed.

Indeed a far more likely form of attack – and one we as a society do see, and do have to interact with – comes from product counterfeiting. The typical threat actor here is a malicious manufacturer, but not one that is interested in modifying your designs. Instead, they are motivated in stealing them. The simplest method for doing this is via 'Overbuilding', where a factory contracted to make a certain number of units of a product instead makes more than that. For instance, assume that you are an inventor of a brand new computer gadget – let's say a neat new keyboard.

Congratulations! You think that you could sell 10,000 of your new keyboard, so you contact a factory and draw up a contract to have 10,000 keyboards produced and shipped. Unbeknownst to you, however, that factory has done its own market analysis and they think that 20,000 of your keyboard could be sold. So, they instead build 20,000 units, and then ship the last 10,000 themselves – and keep the margin, your profit, for themselves!

This is only one type of counterfeiting, a black-market industry sector worth up to US$1 trillion annually [12]. In other cases, devices can be reverse engineered and copied, or they might simply be imitated by creating similar products illicitly bearing another company's logo. This introduces risks, particularly where corners are cut on the counterfeit products – something that is often the case when a malicious manufacturer is pretending to be someone else! After all, if a product fails early, it will hardly harm your own reputation when nothing can be traced back to your factory. As such, counterfeit products are often of poor quality.

This can be a real risk when they end up in safety-critical systems. A years-long investigation by the U.S. Senate discovered over 1,800 cases of counterfeit parts in U.S. military vehicles, including cargo aircraft, special operations helicopters, and surveillance planes [2]. They found that Chinese suppliers were producing tens of thousands of counterfeit, low-quality components which end up in military equipment, risking mission successes such as missile firing and helicopter night vision. In some cases, these were discovered after installation, such as when counterfeit memory chips were found in failing L-3 Display Systems in fielded aircraft. Similar counterfeits were identified in parts available in online catalogues (see Figure 8.7).

**Figure 8.7** Example counterfeit electronic components (transistors and integrated circuits) identified in a study by the U.S. GAO [11] for the U.S. Senate

Counterfeit parts also impact consumers as well. As an early example, 50,000 LG-branded cell-phones had to be recalled in 2004 after counterfeit batteries entered the supply chain [9]. These batteries were dangerous: they lacked overcharge protection circuits, meaning that they could overheat or catch fire if left on a charger too long. Since then, the numbers of counterfeit consumer electronics have only continued to grow. In a single seizure US CBP agents in Philadelphia were able to seize hundreds of fake cellphone screen components [8] in 2023, and likewise US HSI and CBP agents seized US$14.7 million in counterfeit electronics devices, toys, and furniture on the World Trade Bridge in 2021 [16].

Another type of counterfeiting comes from the re-use or re-packaging of old, re-cycled components. Here, you could imagine how a product might have reached the end of its usable life, and so it is sent to a disposal facility, which might disassemble it into its parts. Some of these could be legitimately re-used, which is a good thing! Unnecessary wastage of products is undesirable. However, when second-hand parts are sold, they should be clearly marked as such, and this is not always the case. Second hand parts will have shorter lifespans than newer products, which means they must usually be sold at a discount – financially motivating malicious sellers to lie. In severe cases, they may even clean, re-number, or re-package devices so that they appear to be newly produced. This was what occurred in several of the aforementioned US military counterfeit cases, including one instance where used Xilinx FPGAs were re-sold as new before being installed in U.S. Navy P-8A Poseidon aircraft [28].

Like hardware Trojans, counterfeits are therefore a risk and a threat to the security of our electronic devices. Although perhaps not as deliberate as introducing designed-to-be-malicious circuits, defective components which under-perform and fail early can just as easily cause real-world harm.

Unfortunately, it is not easy to detect if a given component is counterfeit, particularly if they were original parts that have been illicitly recycled. Given the complexity of the electronics supply chain, components need only to function well enough to pass basic tests they might be subjected to – tests which are designed to weed out defective parts, not fakes. Some counterfeit parts are visually suspect, or can be identified with scans such as by X-rays or electron microscopes to show that the internals of a chip are not lining up with what's expected. If re-labelling has been done with low quality materials (e.g. paint) this can be identified with simple chemical tests (e.g. using acetone to show the original markings). Other, more comprehensive counterfeits, might require more complex testing – for instance, the age and grade of a chip can alter transistor performance, meaning that electrical testing can show that a chip is suspiciously under-performing.

It is much more difficult to address overbuilding, the first challenge posed in this section. Here, components will be performing exactly to their specification, as they may be being built by the original factory and production line. As noted, the illicit manufacturer can still make financial gains here, by simply avoiding license payments to the original designer.

This overbuilding issue underscores a fundamental challenge in modern manufacturing: trust. When intellectual property (IP) is shared with a manufacturer, especially one overseas, it becomes incredibly difficult to enforce boundaries on how that IP is used. Factories with the expertise and equipment to produce high-quality, genuine components can just as easily produce unauthorized extras or share proprietary designs with competitors. This creates an ecosystem where counterfeit and overbuilt parts can be nearly indistinguishable from legitimate ones, yet they enter the market through unauthorized channels, eroding consumer confidence and undercutting legitimate businesses.

The issue of counterfeiting extends beyond the direct risks to systems or users – it also has profound economic implications. The presence of counterfeit goods undermines the market for genuine products, and can discourage innovation by harming legitimate manufacturers who invest heavily in research and development. Furthermore, the financial impact of counterfeit components often goes beyond replacing defective parts. It includes the costs of investigating failures, recalling products, and potentially dealing with lawsuits or regulatory penalties.

## 8.6   HARDWARE SECURITY: DEFENDING ICS AND PCBS

It seems that the obvious method to protect against both Hardware Trojans and low-performing Counterfeits would be to **test**, i.e., simply take the suspect IC or PCB, and see how it performs. However, although commercial electronics makers can and do test chips and circuits to see how they perform, they can't usually afford to test anything, as there is a nearly infinite universe of possible things that are not specified for a given design. Instead, they will focus on testing known functionalities. A component destined for a cellphone, for instance, might be subject to energy emission tests and hardware in the loop functional tests. But, extraneous circuits that don't interfere with the normal functionality, or circuits that might fail early due to age, likely won't show up in these tests [1].

Other tests, such as 'decapping' an integrated circuit and examining it under a scanning electronic microscope could reveal if there are unexpected changes to the design of the silicon. But, this process involves grinding away the chip, layer by layer – destroying it in the process. This means that you might verify the chip you tested, but not necessarily any other that you have from the batch. This can be a tough assumption when an attack strategy might be to compromise a small number of random parts to minimize the chances of detection. Further, this strategy also assumes you can cope with mapping the real chip to your design files – for an IC with potentially hundreds of millions of internal transistors this might be a very difficult ask. It also implies you can trust the design files itself! Remember, your chip might be passing through multiple stages as you pass from design to implementation, and at each phase the design is in a different form, such as in hardware description language (code), a netlist, or in the layout form.

On the other hand, printed circuit boards can be more straightforward to verify against their design files. This is because everything is happening on a physically larger scale. Still, like integrated circuits, PCBs can have multiple layers, and if a change happens to an internal layer, one will need to rely on scans such as X-rays to see through the material. Alternatively, electrical tests can verify which traces are connected to which other traces, and might also be able to identify if an individual circuit has been tampered with in some way (e.g. changing a track width to alter a characteristic impedance of a circuit). However, these only work to a point, and once again destructive testing might be the only avenue to be certain if a given PCB is trustworthy.

However, there is a solution. Let's assume that a given product – either an IC, or a PCB, is potentially untrustworthy. We have several of these products, and we know that we can conclusively prove that they are or are not trustworthy, but this must happen destructively, e.g. via decapping. What we can do is take a large number of so-called *side-channel* measurements of all the samples. This is depicted in Figure 8.8.

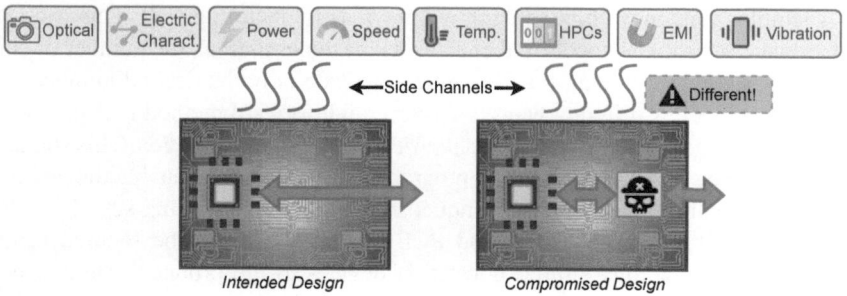

**Figure 8.8** Side channel analysis examines the non-functional emissions from electrical devices. It can be used to non-destructively identify suspicious differences

Side channels are any property of the device which is not directly associated with its function, so side-channel tests can include optical (e.g. take a photo), electrical characteristics (e.g. resistance, impedance, capacitance, slew rates, etc.), emissions (e.g. electro-magnetic interference waves which are produced during operation), heat (change in temperature as components warm up), vibration and acoustic (if there are moving parts), reaction times and clock frequency (how quickly does the device operate), power consumption (how much energy is it using), and so on. Some designs might even include 'Hardware Performance Counters' (HPCs), a type of internal circuit which can record instances of events occurring – more often used for functional testing, they provide yet another way we can characterise our circuits. Assuming all products have similar measurements, we can now perform destructive testing on just one of the samples. Then, if we prove that sample safe, each of the other samples should likewise be safe. Otherwise, if a sample does deviate, it is suspicious and it should also be more thoroughly tested. As an example, timing measurements were used to detect Trojan-introduced deviations in PCBs based on industrial controllers [21].

Another method for defence, which can be used in conjunction with side-channel analysis, is to perform *split manufacturing* of a given product [13]. More typically used for integrated circuits, split manufacturing prevents overbuilding as well as greatly complicates the process for adding complex Hardware Trojans. Here, the process for building a given IC is split over two processes which will be done at two different foundries, ideally owned by two different companies. This prevents any one manufacturer from having the complete design files to compromise or plagiarize. Of course, split manufacturing is not a panacea, and certain attacks can still overcome this complication [29].

Another defence for ICs is known as logic obfuscation or *logic locking*. This is a technique to manipulate a given circuit to add a *key* input. This input is designed to make sure that the overall circuit will only function correctly when provided the correct key value. Simultaneously, it should be difficult to figure out that key value! Logic locking is an enormous topic, and interested readers should explore Kamali's recent survey [17].

A simpler version of logic locking is known as IC metering [18]. This is a class of hardware security protocols that enables the designer to track the number of chips produced from the same mask and remotely activate only the desired number. This can be done in a few different ways, but one straightforward method is to have chips generate a unique signature based on a *physically unclonable function*. This signature needs to then be combined with a cryptographic key in order to enable the circuit to function – because the signature is unique; so too will the unlocking key.

Related to this idea, both ICs and PCBs might be able to be secured against counterfeiting by adding similar attestation devices to the products. Here, special encrypted components are added to a given design. One example of these is found in modern Windows-based computers, known as trusted platform modules (TPMs) [4]. This can provide a variety of security benefits, from storing passwords safely to ensuring that the electronic components in the computer motherboard are authentic. Of course, no implementation is perfectly correct, and a variety of attacks exist, including leveraging side-channels for a timing-based analysis attack [19] (unfortunately, side channel analysis can work both ways!).

A simpler defence technique, though not one that provides much protection, is to embed covert watermarks as design attributes inside hardware. These can be like icons and logos, or might be more subtle, such as an unusual and inefficient circuit trace. Watermarking is performed to provide evidence of ownership of a given circuit or IC layout.

Each of these solutions come with their own complexities and costs. Anything based on cryptographic tags or keys can be overcome if the key management is weak or compromised. Most defences still rely at least in part on the trustworthiness, honesty, and vigilance of individual actors in the supply chain.

Sometimes, the globalised and complex nature of the supply chain can itself be its own enemy. Any local or wide-scale shut-down of any of the geographic areas or companies which electronics manufacturing relies on can have disproportionate impact. The major example of this, of course, comes from the 2019-2020 Coronavirus pandemic COVID-19. Here, like many other sectors, the electronics supply chain was catastrophically disrupted, causing production lines to shut down and air and sea freight to dramatically cut capacity [31]. This resulted in shut downs and delays across the entire electronics sector, including Apple having to postpone deliveries of its new products, and Samsung and LG shutting down production. Overall, the Covid Chip Shortage had a huge impact on the automotive sector in particular, with Tesla, Volkswagen, Toyota, Fiat Chrysler, Nissan and Daimler all shutting factories or reducing production [30]. Access to in-demand chips and electronics became restricted via brokers, and manufacturers could pay more than eight times the pre-COVID value when items were eventually sourced. The consequences of these shortages were, naturally, a further explosion of counterfeits and illicit second-hand components.

This highlighting of the fragile nature of the supply chain, and increasing attention on possible hardware hacks, is now encouraging a return to sovereign electronics manufacturing worldwide, particularly considering the production of Integrated

Circuits. In the U.S., the CHIPS act included billions of dollars for companies to build new Integrated Circuit manufacturing plants within the country [26]. This aims to boost both national security as well as spur national R&D. Similar legislation was also passed in the European Union [24] and United Kingdom. Even non-powerhouses such as Australia are also considering on-shoring some microchip manufacturing capability [7]. Combined with design defences such as those outlined in this chapter, such on-shoring may boost the trust within IC manufacturing.

## 8.7 CONCLUDING REMARKS

When considering the cybersecurity of a given computer system, much attention is placed on the software involved in that system. However, the security of the hardware that builds up each computer should be considered of equal importance. In general, we need to trust that our hardware will be designed and implemented according to our specifications, and will not include components and circuits we don't desire! However, in this chapter we discussed how such hardware can in fact be compromised, either deliberately through the insertion of hardware Trojans or as a side effect of underperforming counterfeit parts.

In general, the global nature of electronics manufacturing means that it is difficult to ensure trust in the supply chain. Individual actors can compromise systems passing through their hands, from malicious manufacturers to governments with the power to intercept shipments in progress.

There are defences to these kinds of breaches. Traditional enforcement of intellectual property rights often depends on cooperation between countries with vastly different regulatory and legal frameworks, which can make legal recourse both slow and uncertain. Technical defences therefore include making our circuits difficult to compromise or copy by using techniques such as logic obfuscation, IC metering, and watermarking; and we can insert components like trusted platform modules to provide attestation that a given circuit is trustworthy. We can also use side-channel analysis, including power and timing measurements as well as visual checks to monitor our designs to make sure they appear to be operating with normal characteristics. This allows us to detect if a given circuit is suspiciously misbehaving.

Of course, this chapter only provided the smallest introduction to Hardware Security. Though we briefly introduced how side channels can be used for defence, we did not present the universe of side channel *attacks*, whereby those same emissions are leveraged to steal data and secrets. Likewise, we did not present much detail on IP piracy, where malicious manufacturers might only steal part of a design, rather than a whole chip. We did not present many techniques on testing, including hardware fuzzing, as well as test-oriented attacks such as those based on JTAG and scan chains. Finally, we also didn't in any detail cover the materials security side of things: hardware depends on physical inputs such as rare earth elements and chemicals, and these can likewise be tampered with to cause downstream effects.

Interested readers can find many of these details in other resources, such as the recent book 'Hardware Security' [27] and its predecessor [6].

# REFERENCES

1. Sally Adee. The Hunt for the Kill Switch. *IEEE Spectrum*, May 2008.
2. Tara Andringa and Brian Rogers. Senate Armed Services Committee Releases Report on Counterfeit Electronic Parts. Technical report, U.S. Senate Committee on Armed Services, May 2012.
3. Jacob Appelbaum, Judith Horchert, and Christian Stöcker. Catalog Reveals NSA Has Back Doors for Numerous Devices. *Der Spiegel*, December 2013.
4. Will Arthur, David Challener, and Kenneth Goldman. *A practical guide to TPM 2.0: Using the new trusted platform module in the new age of security*. Springer Nature, 2015.
5. Jason Aten. Walmart's Website Is Selling Fake Products. Even Worse, It's Advertising Them on Instagram, October 2023.
6. Swarup Bhunia and M Tehranipoor. *The Hardware Trojan War*. Springer, 2018. Publisher: Springer.
7. Alex Capri and Robert Clark. Australia's semiconductor national moonshot. Technical Report 63/2022, Australian Strategic Policy Institute, September 2022.
8. USA CBP. Philadelphia CBP Officers Seize 648 Counterfeit Samsung Smartphone Digitizers | U.S. Customs and Border Protection, March 2023.
9. USA CPSC. CPSC, Verizon Wireless Announce Recall of Counterfeit Cell Phone Batteries. Technical Report Recall 04-559, June 2004.
10. Sean Gallagher. Photos of an NSA "upgrade" factory show Cisco router getting implant, May 2014.
11. US GAO. DoD Supply Chain | Suspect Counterfeit Electronic Parts Can Be Found on Internet Purchasing Platforms. Technical Report GAO-12-375, February 2012.
12. Gilberto Garcia-Vazquez. The Electronics Industry's Counterfeit Parts Problem | MacroFab, January 2023.
13. Siddharth Garg and Jeyavijayan (JV) Rajendran. Split Manufacturing. In Domenic Forte, Swarup Bhunia, and Mark M. Tehranipoor, editors, *Hardware Protection through Obfuscation*, pages 243–262. Springer International Publishing, Cham, 2017.
14. Eli Greenblat. Target sued by US giant for selling fake cosmetics. *The Sydney Morning Herald*, September 2012.
15. Trammell Hudson. Modchips of the State, December 2018.
16. USA ICE. HSI, CBP seize $14.7 million in counterfeit electronics at South Texas' World Trade Bridge | ICE, March 2021.
17. Hadi Mardani Kamali, Kimia Zamiri Azar, Farimah Farahmandi, and Mark Tehranipoor. Advances in Logic Locking: Past, Present, and Prospects, 2022. Publication info: Preprint. MINOR revision.
18. Farinaz Koushanfar. Hardware metering: A survey. In *Introduction to Hardware Security and Trust*, pages 103–122. Springer, 2011.
19. Daniel Moghimi, Berk Sunar, Thomas Eisenbarth, and Nadia Heninger. TPM-FAIL: TPM meets Timing and Lattice Attacks. In *29th USENIX Security Symposium (USENIX Security 20)*, pages 2057–2073. USENIX Association, August 2020.
20. Matt Murphy and Joe Tidy. Hezbollah pagers and walkie-talkies: How did they explode and who did it? *BBC News*, September 2024.
21. Hammond Pearce, Virinchi Roy Surabhi, Prashanth Krishnamurthy, Joshua Trujillo, Ramesh Karri, and Farshad Khorrami. Detecting Hardware Trojans in PCBs Using Side Channel Loopbacks. *IEEE Transactions on Very Large Scale Integration (VLSI) Systems*, 30(7):926–937, July 2022. Conference Name: IEEE Transactions on Very Large Scale Integration (VLSI) Systems.

22. Redacted. (U) Stealthy Techniques Can Crack Some of SIGINT's Hardest Targets. Technical report, Hosted by Electronic Frontier Foundation (EFF), June 2010.

23. Jordan Robertson and Michael Riley. The Big Hack: How China Used a Tiny Chip to Infiltrate U.S. Companies. *Bloomberg.com*, October 2018.

24. Toby Sterling. EU Chips Act 2.0 should include legacy chips, says industry group chief. *Reuters*, November 2024.

25. Ganda Suthivarakom. Welcome to the Era of Fake Products. *The New York Times | Wirecutter*, February 2020.

26. Ana Swanson. The CHIPS Act Is About More Than Chips: Here's What's in It. *The New York Times*, February 2023.

27. Mark Tehranipoor, Kimia Zamiri Azar, Navid Asadizanjani, Fahim Rahman, Hadi Mardani Kamali, and Farimah Farahmandi. *Hardware Security: A Look into the Future*. Springer Nature Switzerland, Cham, 2024.

28. John Villasenor and Mohammad Tehranipoor. The Hidden Dangers of Chop-Shop Electronics. *EEE Spectrum*, September 2013.

29. Yujie Wang, Pu Chen, Jiang Hu, and Jeyavijayan (JV) Rajendran. The cat and mouse in split manufacturing. In *Proceedings of the 53rd Annual Design Automation Conference*, DAC '16, pages 1–6, New York, NY, USA, June 2016. Association for Computing Machinery.

30. Xiling Wu, Caihua Zhang, and Wei Du. An Analysis on the Crisis of "Chips shortage" in Automobile Industry—Based on the Double Influence of COVID-19 and Trade Friction. *Journal of Physics: Conference Series*, 1971(1):012100, July 2021. Publisher: IOP Publishing.

31. Zhitao Xu, Adel Elomri, Laoucine Kerbache, and Abdelfatteh El Omri. Impacts of COVID-19 on Global Supply Chains: Facts and Perspectives. *IEEE Engineering Management Review*, 48(3):153–166, 2020. Conference Name: IEEE Engineering Management Review.

# Index